DEPRESSION:

THEORY AND RESEARCH

THE SERIES IN CLINICAL PSYCHOLOGY

Charles D. Spielberger · Consulting Editor

JOSEPH BECKER · *Depression: Theory and Research*

DEPRESSION:
THEORY AND RESEARCH

JOSEPH BECKER

UNIVERSITY OF WASHINGTON
SEATTLE, WASHINGTON

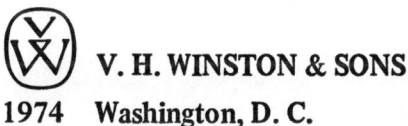
V. H. WINSTON & SONS

1974   Washington, D. C.

A HALSTED PRESS BOOK

JOHN WILEY & SONS
New York   Toronto   London   Sydney

V. H. Winston & Sons, Inc., Publishers
1511 K St. N.W., Washington, D.C. 20005

Distributed solely by Halsted Press Division, John Wiley & Sons, Inc., New York.

Library of Congress Cataloging in Publication Data:

Becker, Joseph, 1927–
  Depression: theory and research.

  (The series in clinical psychology)
  Includes bibliographical references.
  1. Depression, Mental. I. Title.
  RC537.B43   616.8′95   73-21595
  ISBN 0-470-06147-2

Printed in the United States of America

CONTENTS

To my esteemed parents:
Bessie and Rudolph Becker

PREFACE

Although depression has the highest mortality rate of any personality disturbance and possibly the highest incidence as well, it has been relatively neglected by most social science disciplines. In the writer's opinion, social scientists are overlooking an intensely interesting burgeoning of bio-social-psychological findings on depression that are as yet tentative, fragmentary, unreplicated and unsynthesized yet intriguing and richly promising of alleviation for one of humankind's severest afflictions. This volume reviews contemporary efforts to understand the nature and genesis of depressive disorders.

Until quite recently most of the literature on depression was provided by psychodynamically or biologically oriented investigators. The psychodynamic studies have yielded a rich crop of clinical observations and generated abundant theoretical speculation. But these speculations have stimulated few systematic investigations. The paucity of alternative psychosocial formulations is somewhat dismaying.

The relative lack of interest by social scientists in depression is not shared by their colleagues in psychiatry. Provocative hypotheses about the relations of depression to such traditional psychological concerns as aggression and cognition have been spearheaded by psychiatrists not psychologists. Only among Lewinsohn's social learning oriented group at Oregon do we see innovative theory and research on depression flourishing in a non-psychiatric social science setting.

The writer's hope is that some readers will be motivated to pursue investigations on depression. Even if this wish is unrealized, but some readers grasp the breadth of training increasingly needed for sophisticated scholarship in psychopathology, a prime objective will have been achieved. The "innards" of the "black box" and its socio-cultural surround contain much of vital interest to the prospective investigator. A working grasp of genetics, biochemistry and neurophysiology at one end of the spectrum, and of epidemiology, sociology and anthropology at the other are invaluable. To many gifted students nowadays, such pursuits seem antihumanistic as contrasted with skilled practice of the behavioral or experiential therapies. But major human maladies have usually been ameliorated by prevention, not by remediation. The data base for rational preventive measures are most likely to proceed from the disciplined labors of multifaceted clinically sophisticated investigative teams than from the brilliant insights of isolated clinicians. As long as the writer is on his soap box anyway, let him voice a brief diatribe for sustaining a limited number of centers of excellence for research in psychopathology. The diminished funding for such operations is alarming. Much of the finest current work on the functional disorders has come from the clinical-research facilities of the National Institute of Mental Health. Their integrated clinical and research facilities are well nigh unique. Few settings other than the Federal Government can or will fund such facilities. Their preservation and growth deserve the highest priority.

Returning to more mundane matters, a volume of this scope inevitably and regrettably slights many topics meriting attention such as research on suicide, and treatment effects; existential theories and related psychological areas like self-esteem, level of aspiration, aggression, and conscience development.

This monograph will probably be of most interest to advanced students, residents, and professionals in any discipline concerned with psychopathology. The volume does not deal directly with treatment methods or the evaluation of treatment effectiveness. Rather, it discusses the evolution of current thinking about depression, its empirical basis, evolving trends, areas in acute need of further study, and some of the methodological problems in pursuing such studies.

Special thanks are due to Professors C. D. Spielberger and J. B. Parker who activated my interest in depression, and to Professor Garmezy, who initiated my writing of this monograph. Professor M. B. Shapiro of Maudsley was a most helpful discussant of the manuscript perhaps especially because our views diverge somewhat. Donna Malan, Caroline Wilson, and Deane Walter provided exceptionally dedicated secretarial assistance. A succession of permanent and acting Departmental Chairmen, Professors Ripley, Bakker, Hampson, and Eisdorfer were consistently generous in allowing time to pursue this task. I am also strongly indebted to participants in my depression seminars, both patients and students, who fostered my groping efforts toward a still elusive integration. The quality of support provided by my splendid wife, Alethia, and children, Jonathan and Bethany, made the completion of this work possible.

Joseph Becker

January 1974

1
INTRODUCTORY OVERVIEW

Melancholia is one of the great words of psychiatry. Suffering many mutations, at one time the tenacious guardian of outworn schemes or errant theories; presently misused, cavilled at, dispossessed, it has endured into our own times, a part of medical terminology no less than of common speech. It would seem profitable to consider the history of this word, and of the states of fear and distress with which it has from the beginning been associated. (Lewis, 1934).

Pathological depressions are usually classified as *functional, primary mood* disorders (American Psychiatric Association, 1968; World Health Organization, 1968). As the term *functional* indicates, no specific cause or etiology[1] for these disorders has been determined. The qualifier *primary* signifies that other aspects of depression, especially cognitive-perceptual distortions (delusions and hallucinations), are secondary or contingent accompaniments of the mood disorder. As for the principal term *mood*, it " . . . is an ancient term which is still almost wholly nontechnical and which through centuries of usage has accumulated a variety of vague and sometimes inconsistent meanings" (Nowlis, 1963, p. 73). In formal psychological theory and research, mood refers variously to inferred dispositional tendencies with motivational properties, to objectively observable responses (facies, gait, posture, speech), and to a self-reported, experiential state. The presence of a mood state must always be inferred or interpreted. Even when mood refers to an objectively observable state, the referent is a *pattern* of responses (affective, physiological, cognitive, and behavioral), rather than any single response per se.

---

[1] A specific etiology is a necessary, but not necessarily sufficient, cause of a disorder (see Meehl, 1959; 1962).

MOOD AS A GENERAL PSYCHOLOGICAL CONSTRUCT

Excellent theoretical analyses of the mood concept have been made by the experimental psychologist Nowlis (1963; 1965; 1970) and the psychodynamic theorist Jacobson (1957). Nowlis (1963) views mood as an inferred construct which is useful in accounting for certain behavioral constancies during a mood's duration. He defines mood as "the effect on the self of its own configurations of activity." When mood " ... changes, there are changes in the probability of occurrence of large repertoires of behavior, [p. 76]"; the whole person is affected; experience and behavior covary in significant aspects; and spontaneity and variability are reduced. In a moderately depressed mood, for example, the individual may engage in many different behaviors, but his speech, thoughts, movements, physiological processes, and experience of time may all be slowed; his view of self (past, present, and future) and of his surroundings may all be tinged with deprecation and pessimism. As a dispositional construct a mood is not observed directly, but is susceptible to objective investigation by systematic examination and manipulation of variables that initiate, sustain, and terminate it.

When affective[2] behavior is theoretically conceived as hierarchically ordered, mood is an intermediate-level construct between emotion and temperament, which are lower- and higher-order constructs, respectively. Higher-order dispositions are of greater temporal duration than lower-order dispositions. Higher-order dispositions predispose, or increase the probability, of the organism's acquiring and displaying lower-order dispositions by providing the organized background activity with which eliciting stimuli (mood inducers) interact to evoke affective responses. Empirical validation of a hierarchy of affective dispositions is handicapped by the absence of established criteria for identifying order of disposition. Nowlis (1963) notes that the concept of mood is sometimes invoked to mask our ignorance of constraints on behavior which account for its shared characteristics.

Nowlis classifies mood inducers into habitability and organic factors and emotional provocations. The first two generate relatively persistent stimuli whose durable affects may be largely subliminal. Habitability refers largely to ecological variables such as atmospheric conditions, spatial arrangements, and qualitative and quantitative aspects of visual and auditory stimulation. Organic factors pertain to states of the internal environment such as nutritional status, muscle tonus, and endocrine balance. The eliciting stimuli of emotional provocations may be relatively brief, but they can evoke persisting psychological

---

[2] For a sound introduction to the concept of affect see Wessman and Ricks (1966, Ch. 1); for a brilliantly speculative account, see Tomkins (1962, Vol. 1, Ch. 1 & 2); for a scholarly review of emotion as a general psychological construct see Lazarus (1968, pp. 175–271); and for a conceptual analysis of anxiety as an emotional state, see Spielberger (1972, Vol. 1, Ch. 2).

processes. Elicitors may include activities and interpersonal events which provoke or interact with psychological drives, conflicts, or cognitions.

Although it is commonly assumed that moods are experienced along bipolar dimensions—that one is elated or depressed, loving or angry—this assumption is usually incorrect. Moods are generally experienced as mixtures or blends of affect. Such blends probably result from multiply determined variations in cognitive response to arousal rather than from the mixture of qualitatively different emotions with distinctive physiological substrates (Schachter, 1964).

A lively theoretical issue regarding affective phenomena merits some elaboration. Many behaviorists regard affects (emotions and moods) as intervening variables (I.V.), that is, as dispositions best understood as abstract constructs mediating between identifiable antecedent conditions and consequences. Theorists who conceptualize moods as I.V.s typically view affects as having motivational properties with a drive or activation component (Brown & Farber, 1951) and frequently a directive or steering component as well. Within this I.V. approach, the psychophysiological changes, overt behaviors, and phenomenological states associated with mood are construed as responses to, or consequences of, the antecedent conditions. In contrast to this orthodox behaviorist position, cognitive theorists, as exemplified by Lazarus (1968), view affects as patterned responses mediated by cognitive appraisals or reappraisals of the antecedent stimulus conditions. Lazarus essentially equates an affective state with the pattern of psychophysiological, behavioral, and phenomenological responses as mediated by the individual's evaluation (threatening, benign, etc.) of the stimulus conditions. However, Lazarus does not negate the utility of viewing emotional responses also as motivational mediators that elicit responses designed to cope with stimulus conditions that arouse affect. Nowlis (1965) also entertains the possible advantage of viewing mood as a complex response pattern rather than as a dispositional construct:

> ... Perhaps mood, then, is not a set of second order dispositions after all but rather the inferrable ordering, in terms of momentary prepotency, of a number of basic systems of behavior and experience: aggression, anxiety. ... Such factors, then, are mood factors insofar as their temporal fluctuations in relative strengths result in variously ordered steady state patterns which assist in the understanding, prediction, and control of a person's behavior through short intervals of time. ... it can be reasonably asserted that a waking person is always in a mood, even when affective levels are very low [p. 385].

If the reader is somewhat perplexed by these distinctions between usages of affect as a psychological construct, let him not be unduly alarmed. The somewhat ambiguous theoretical status of affective variables appears to be typical of complex behavioral phenomena. For example, Koch (1959) asserts that:

> When systematically defined independent and dependent variables are introduced or mentioned by students of the more 'complex' man-pertinent processes, it is uniformly made obvious that these are ... very far from direct 'observables,' that in

fact such variables are at an enormous distance from the scientific observation base. . . . Indeed there seems little doubt that most systematists of the person and the social context would accept without embarrassment a view of their constructs which held them all 'intervening variables.' [p. 745] [3]

MOOD AS A PSYCHOPATHOLOGICAL CONSTRUCT

Jacobson (1953; 1957) has provided a penetrating psychodynamic, clinically derived analysis of contrasts between normal and pathological moods which has substantially influenced subsequent experimental research (Nowlis, 1963; Wessman & Ricks, 1966). According to her analysis, moods pervasively influence all aspects of personality function: feelings, ideation, overt behavior, physiological processes, and especially feelings about oneself and the world. She describes mood as a "barometer of ego state," an indicator of how the individual experiences the quality of his present existence. Mood differs from affect or emotion in terms of breadth or generality; while moods are pervasive, emotions are relatively transient and specific to particular contexts.

Mood is not simply a feeling without content; it has strong cognitive and motor components. It can be thought of as a state of mind determined by temporarily prevailing emotion. Moods affect the rate and rhythm of motor activity and selectively bias thought and perception toward congruence with their prevailing quality. Usually, individuals are quite aware of their mood state, and others can reliably judge an individual's mood by observing his facial expression and motor activity in the absence of any verbal report of feelings.

Presumably major personality functions have evolutionary survival value, or they would not have evolved. Since moods diminish stimulus differentiation and response specificity and therefore distort reality, what might their adaptive value be? Jacobson speculates that moods permit modulated affective discharge in which small amounts of affect are repetitively discharged on a wide range of objects for a relatively prolonged period. This mode of discharge is adaptive, because it is less disruptive than abrupt, massive affective discharge.

According to Jacobson, individuals vary greatly in mood susceptibility, duration, and depth. Moods are regarded as a relatively primitive form of affective regulation; hence well integrated persons are assumed to be less moody. Their moods are more variegated or complex, more tied to accurate appraisal of self and external reality, less fixated temporally and qualitatively than the moods of less well integrated persons. The latter presumably have lower tension tolerance thresholds and more free floating, unneutralized tension to contend with.

[3] For an illuminating discussion of the intervening variable concept see Koch (1959, pp. 733–749).

Persons who experience marked deviations in mood seem prone to overgeneralize unduly from past experience or transsituationally. Likewise, their responses toward themselves and others tend to be poorly differentiated. Some of the variability in mood susceptibility is probably constitutional, some learned, and much of it an interaction of these two factors.

According to social psychiatrists such as Sullivan (1953), self-evaluation is largely a reflection of the appraisals of significant others during the socialization process. If the significant others, who largely serve as mediators of reality for the uncritical child, provide deviant mood identification models and reinforce deviant appraisals (e.g., excessively high or low) of the child's worth, it is not surprising that the child matures into an adult relatively fixed on skewed ways of experiencing his existence (Greenson, 1954). For example, one's ideals and moral conscience, or superego in analytic terminology, largely regulate self-esteem. If one does what one has learned to believe is right, then one tends to feel positively about oneself. If realistic standards have been acquired from parental models, then conscience, via guilt or decreases in self-esteem, provide a highly effective signaling function by alerting the self to impending unacceptable violations of internalized standards. But if indiscriminately favorable or unfavorable standards have been acquired, self-esteem is more irrationally and crudely regulated, with a strong resultant susceptibility to reality distorting moods.

The phenomenology of normal and pathological moods may overlap considerably. Most moods entail poorer discrimination between subjective and objective reality. But in normal moods the individual has greater awareness of what events induced the mood and better recognition that changed perceptions are temporary effects of the mood. Moreover, qualitative and quantitative aspects of the mood are more appropriate to the mood-eliciting events. Events that are incompatible with the mood are perceived and responded to more realistically, which may lead to a shift or termination of the mood. By contrast, pathological moods are less appropriate to reality in relation to all of these factors.

Sadness and mourning are normal moods, whereas depression is a pathological mood. According to Jacobson, all of these moods are responses to loss or deprivation of "objects" (relationships, material things, health, ideals) significant to the maintenance of self-esteem. The losses may be real or fantasied; conscious or unconscious; external, intrapsychic, or somatic. Jacobson contends that in normal mood reactions to loss (hereafter generically referred to as mourning), the relationship to the lost object was a genuinely positive one, whereas in pathological moods the relationship was conflictual or "ambivalent."

Depressions are elicited by the reactivation of conflicts in which the aggressive, hostile components and their sources are largely inaccessible to awareness. Jacobson categorizes these conflicts as unconscious conflicts (those between the self and external objects) and narcissistic conflicts (those between the self and the self's moral or nonmoral ideals). According to her developmental theory, self-representations and self-critical values and functions evolve early and are relatively less accessible to reality-induced modification than object representations of the external world. Hence moods induced by reactivation of narcissistic conflicts are apt to be especially pathological. For example, the child of harshly critical, demanding, unloving parents who were intolerant of self-assertion might well develop excessively high standards, be unduly self-critical, and so overlearn the curbing of aggressive impulses as to be largely unaware of them. Such unfortunate persons may be relatively unamenable to subsequent modifying experience. Their commitment to achieving unattainable standards and to obtaining approval from subsequent authority figures, toward whom they harbor much resentment displaced or generalized from their parents, renders them highly vulnerable to experiencing disappointing losses, frustrations, and depression.

Psychotic moods involve gross reality distortion of the eliciting event and its impact or meaning. Loss may be denied or its effect experienced paradoxically, so that the presence of a patently depressed mood may be flatly denied or a realistically grim event responded to joyously. According to Jacobson, unconscious hostile conflicts may result in paranoid as well as depressive moods. In the former hostility is projected onto the world; in the latter hostility is turned against the self, presumably as a means of retaining a positive tie with the valued object or person.

Weinshel's critique (1970) of Jacobson's milestone work (1957) modifies and elaborates several aspects of her conceptualization, which she has accepted as valid alterations (1971). He notes that although moods are complex and enduring affective states, not all complex and enduring affective states are moods. Many character traits, such as pessimism and optimism, have strong affective components and are even more enduring than moods. Weinshel classes such traits as temperament variables. They can be partially discriminated from moods in terms of their greater compatibility with one's sense of self. That is, moods tend to be experienced as transient changes rather than as manifestations of a characteristic state. Presumably traits are more constitutionally determined and/or rooted in an early, strongly fixated parental identification (Greenson, 1954).

Weinshel emphasizes the range of differentiation or developmental maturity within and between moods. They can be tension sustaining, as for example in a mood to work, as well as tension discharging. Moods have important structural, regulatory, and synthetic properties. They tend to harmonize internal and external needs and demands and to reduce the potential disruptiveness of incompatible factors. Moods may also act as communicative or transactional mechanisms, which are sustained by the interpersonal responses elicited from others. In sum, while moods can serve as relatively primitive, archaic methods of affective discharge, they can alternatively or simultaneously facilitate "optimal functioning." As to the genesis of moods as complex structures involving affective, cognitive, and behavioral components, Weinshel (1970) candidly states: "The whole question . . . is still completely unanswered [p. 315]." His genetic conjectures are refreshingly free of reified analogies. He stresses that while moods may be derivatives of significant infantile experiences of frustration or gratification, they are experienced by adults in highly elaborated form. Hence really primitive affective displays are much more likely to be reflections of personality decompensation than of mood phenomena, whose affective components tend to be subtle, muted, and tamed.

GRIEF AND DEPRESSION

A time-honored method of attempting to clarify the distinction between normal and pathological mood has been to contrast the reactions of normal grief (mourning) and pathological grief (depression or melancholia) to a significant loss. Freud (1917) contrasts the two thusly:

> The melancholic displays something else besides which is lacking in mourning—an extraordinary diminution in his self-regard, an impoverishment of his ego on a grand scale. In mourning it is the world which has become poor and empty; in melancholia it is the ego itself. The patient represents his ego to us as worthless, incapable of any achievement and morally despicable; he reproaches himself, vilifies himself and expects to be cast out and punished. He abases himself before everyone and commiserates with his own relatives for being connected with anyone so unworthy. He is not of the opinion that a change has taken place in him, but extends his criticism back over the past; he declares that he was never any better. The picture of a delusion of (mainly moral) inferiority is completed by sleeplessness and refusal to take nourishment, and—what is psychologically very remarkable—by an overcoming of the instinct which compels every living thing to cling to life [p. 246].

In a sequel worth pondering, Freud (1917) adds:

> When in his [the melancholic's] heightened self-criticism he describes himself as petty, egotistic, dishonest, lacking in independence, one whose sole aim has been to hide the weaknesses of his own nature, it may be, so far as we know, that he has come pretty near to understanding himself; we only wonder why a man has to be ill before he can be accessible to a truth of this kind. For there can be no doubt that if anyone holds and expresses to others an opinion of himself such as this, he is ill, whether he is speaking the truth or whether he is being more or less unfair to himself [pp. 246–247].

Averill (1968) has performed a fascinating, if speculative, analysis of grief and mourning as an affective response pattern from an evolutionary standpoint. According to him, grief is a *biogenetically* determined, stereotypic pattern of psychological and physiological responses to bereavement or loss of a significant object. Mourning behavior, while occasioned by the same antecedent (loss), is *culturally* determined. Clinical depressions probably entail a pathological grief reaction, which may be due to complicated situational or personality factors, or to physiologically mediated genetic abnormalities.

Averill (1968) ventures some intriguing hypotheses about the possible functional or evolutionary adaptive value of grief reactions. He points out that grief reactions seem to occur only within species in which social forms of existence are essential to survival; social ties are based on individual recognition and attachment; and intraspecific aggression is common. Presumably, such species are genetically geared to avoidance of separation from significant objects (i.e., members are prone to "separation anxiety") as a means of ensuring group cohesiveness. Unsuccessful avoidance of loss results in a grief reaction.

Support for a genetic formulation of grief reactions stems from the apparent transspecies and transcultural patterning of the grief response. The specific etiology or antecedent is reputedly the actual, fantasied, or threatened loss of a significant object. The grief reaction stereotypically passes through stages of shock, despondency, and recovery. Averill does not argue that grief is adaptive for the individual. The heightened susceptibility to physical and psychological stress and reduced social interaction in grief may lessen the likelihood of species propagation. But natural selection operates primarily to perpetuate the population rather than the individual. Separation anxiety and grief strengthen social ties which maximize group safety, nurturance, and reproduction.

Descriptive Aspects of Depression

Hopefully usages of the term mood and distinctions between normal and pathological moods are now somewhat clearer. But before presenting a brief history of the concept of depression it may be helpful to clarify some varying usages of this term. Depression is variously referred to as a sign, symptom, syndrome, reaction, disorder, and disease entity (Lehmann, 1966; Mendels, 1968). The distinction between sign and symptom is increasingly blurred in diagnostic formulations. Both are indicators of a pathological process. Signs in a purist sense are objective indicators (pallor, temperature, blood count, etc.) observable by the examiner. Symptoms are subjective indicators reported by the patient (pain, mood, dizziness). A syndrome includes multiple signs and symptoms which covary in a relatively specific manner for a particular disorder.

The most common signs and symptoms that occur in depressive syndromes are as follows:

1. Sad, lonely, apathetic, or irritable mood.
2. An exaggeratedly negative, self-punitive *self-concept*.
3. Disturbed vegetative functioning with overactive autonomic nervous system, accompanied by decreased appetite, poor sleep, constipation, and diminished sexual interest.
4. Physical complaints of aches, weakness, fatigue.
5. Altered activity level with slowing or agitation.
6. Impaired thought processes with high distractibility, indecisiveness, disinterestedness, and preoccupation with hopelessness and helplessness.

In psychopathology, distinctions between reactions, disorders, and diseases are not clear-cut. But usually, reaction and disorder imply either a psychogenic or an undetermined etiology. Many psychologists who describe themselves as "behavior modifiers" view syndromes, reactions, and disorders as essentially synonymous. Psychodynamically and cognitively oriented psychopathologists more typically construe syndromes as reflections of inferred, underlying conflicts and maladaptive cognitive-perceptual biases that operate largely outside of awareness. These differences in opinion have generated heated disputes, some of which promise to make the issues more amenable to objective investigation (Weitzman, 1967).

The term depression is used generically in this volume to refer to a functional personality disorder unless stated otherwise. In this definition the term personality disorder is preferred to the more fashionable behavioral disorder because subjective, experiential states figure so prominently in depression. Personality is a more broadly encompassing term that includes both inner experience and overt behavioral manifestations. The term disorder is used to convey theoretical neutrality as to whether clinical depressions are primarily psychophysiological reactions to life circumstances, or whether they constitute a disease entity with a specific biological substrate and largely predetermined course.

Some Historic Concepts of Depression[4]

Melancholia, the earlier term for psychotic depression, dates from Hippocrates in the 4th century B.C., who attributed the black mood to an excess of black bile and phlegm afflicting the brain. Half a century later, Aretaeus ascribed melancholia to flatulence or anger, grief, and dejection. He linked some depressions to manic states and noted that logical thought processes were not impaired in depression.

The establishment of asylums for the insane in the late 18th century permitted long-term observation resulting in Falret's and Baillarger's (Lewis, 1934) elaboration of circular manic-depressive states as distinguished from recurrent depressive episodes. Baillarger also noted the higher incidence of manic-depressive episodes in females and strongly implicated a genetic etiology. The development of psychiatric clinics at German universities during the latter part of the 19th century further facilitated the study of personality disorders. Kahlbaum (1876) differentiated psychotic manic-depressive states from less pathological "cyclothymic" mood fluctuations. He also distinguished psychotic depressions from dementia praecox or schizophrenia on the basis of cognitive impairment in schizophrenia and prognosis or outcome. He contended that depression entails a primary *mood* disturbance and has a favorable prognosis, whereas dementia praecox involves a primary *thought* disturbance and results in progressive deterioration.

Kraepelin (1913) in successive editions of his *Lehrbuch der Psychiatrie*, progressively refined and extended these earlier distinctions and thus provided the basis for contemporary classifications of psychopathology. He divided the

---

[4]For a more complete review, see Lewis (1934).

functional psychoses into dementia praecox and manic-depressive psychosis. The latter encompassed virtually any significant mood deviation, i.e., cyclothymia and depression of any degree, duration, age of onset, and repetitiveness, with or without associated manic episodes. Kraepelin preferred to classify on an etiological basis. But in the absence of identified organic etiological agents, which he was convinced existed, he was forced to classify functional personality disorders, or diseases, as he regarded them, on the basis of clinical description and course of illness. While he maintained that most, if not all, depressions are innately determined, he acknowledged that some appeared to be of psychogenic etiology. However, Kraepelin could distinguish no clinical or prognostic differences between the endogenous or innately determined depressions and the apparently psychogenically determined ones, except for the greater environmental responsiveness in the latter during the course of the disorder.

Kraepelin's significance, as Kendell (1968) aptly states, was that:

> Until this time fruitful discussion of the relationship between different types of depression was scarcely possible. There was no acceptable classification of mental illnesses in general to provide the necessary framework. Since this time discussion has been unceasing and inconclusive [p. 2].

The term depression rather than melancholia was proposed by A. Meyer (1905) because it implies greater etiologic neutrality. Unlike Kraepelin, who viewed depression as a disease entity with a specific etiologic agent and course, Meyer construed it as a maladaptive, psychobiological reaction to stress.

Psychoanalysis generated the major countervailing force to Kraepelin's assumption of a predominantly endogenous etiology for depression. Working chiefly with nonhospitalized neurotic depressives (whereas other psychiatrists worked chiefly with hospitalized psychotics), Freud (1917), Abraham (1911, 1916, 1924), and Rado (1928) argued for a significant psychogenetic component in depressive disorders. But they explicitly and repeatedly affirmed the strong possibility of an etiologic interaction between psycho- and genogenic factors. Schematically, they argued that depressives were fixated at relatively early stages of psychosexual maturity, resulting in tenuous, highly dependent, and ambivalent relations with others (strongly mixed feelings of love and hatred, with hatred usually outside of awareness). Severe frustration by or loss of the person (ideals, material possessions, status, etc.) upon whom the predepressive is excessively dependent for self-esteem results in partial regression to the earlier fixated stage of development. The predepressive's interpersonal ambivalance becomes internalized as an intrapsychic conflict. Hatred previously felt toward the external source (object) is turned against the self, as a result of a primitive identification of the self with the frustrating person. Self-punitiveness reflects an internalization of previously interpersonal operations. That is, in normal socialization, one transgresses, is punished, expresses remorse, and is forgiven. Presumably, the depressive, by punishing himself, seeks magical expiation from his suffering.

For somewhat obscure reasons, British psychiatrists became intensely involved with the issue of whether depression consists of a unitary disorder varying in severity or of several discriminable reaction types and disease entities. Only recently has this highly polemical, sometimes droll, controversy begun to generate the systematic empirical data that may effect its resolution (Kendell, 1968; 1970a,b). The most articulate advocates of the "unitary" position or "continuity hypothesis" tend to be products of Maudsley Hospital, notably Mapother (1926) and Lewis (1934, 1936). Essentially, they agree that, regardless of subclassification, depressives overlap *inter-* and *intra-*individually with respect to environmental reactivity, constitutional predisposition, degree of precipitating stress, suicide proneness, responsiveness to electroconvulsive therapy (ECT), etc. In short, depressives are quite similar with regard to every factor ostensibly discriminating among reactive, endogenous, and involutional depressives according to the "separatist" school of thought. While the unitary school presented clinical data to support their contentions (Lewis, 1934, 1936; Garmany, 1938), these observations lacked rudimentary intersubjective reliability safeguards.

British continuity advocates also incline toward belief in a constitutional predispositional factor in all depressive disorders. They accept a neurotic-psychotic severity distinction as administratively advantageous, although potentially misleading. For example, suicide proneness is strong in depression but not highly correlated with severity of depression, as some clinicians mistakenly believe.

"Separatists" such as Gillespie (1929) and Mayer-Gross (1948) generally equate neurotic or reactive depression with a Meyerian-type reaction to environmental stress; endogenous depression with a constitutionally determined disease entity; and involutional melancholia with another distinguishable disease entity. Depressive subtypes reputedly differ in premorbid personality, age of onset, and course of illness. Until recently, the separatists typically justified themselves by fiat and individual case histories.

Kendell (1968), in summarizing the British classification dispute, contends that the separatist position has been invalidated and amusingly ascribes its continuation in part

> ... to the fact that over the years the controversy had acquired many of the characteristics of a feud, with the Guelfs on the one hand and the Ghibellines on the other each deeply committed to their opposing views and each in honor bound to counter any move by the other [p. 8].

American psychopathologists, in their inimitably eclectic, pragmatic manner, have largely minimized the whole issue of classifying depressions, despite an occasional effort to point up the inherent contradictions in prevailing practice (Ascher, 1952). Attempts to order diverse depressive phenomena meaningfully have resulted in three broadly discriminable approaches, the unitary, dichotomous, and polydimensional (Lorr, 1969). Unitary advocates primarily view depression according to gradations on a unidimensional severity continuum (Lewis, 1936; Muncie, 1939). Dichotomous adherents divide depressives into reactive (environmentally determined) and endogenous (genogenically or biochemically determined) forms (Kay, Garside, Beamish, & Roy, 1969; Carney, Roth, & Garside, 1965). Polydimensional protagonists have fairly consistently identified at least six depressive syndromes (Lorr, 1969). According to the polydimensional view, these syndromes are not discrete, mutually exclusive entities; patients may display predominantly aspects of one or of several syndromes and quite probably some degree of all of them. Lorr (1969) proposes an integrating conceptualization of the three classificatory systems in terms of: (a) a general depressive factor common to all depressive states; (b) several group factors probably best reflected in the traditional reactive-endogenous dichotomy; and (c) multiple specific factors as exemplified by five frequently replicated syndromes.

Other alternatives also exist. Depressions may be a heterogeneous group of disorders with some subgroupings that conform well to a disease model. Another alternative is that a common biological anomaly may characterize all pathological depressions, the apparent heterogeneity stemming from different personality and environmental interactions with the anomaly. Even classical physical diseases elicit quite varying reactions from the host.

Clarification of issues related to the etiology, prevention, and treatment of depression is hindered by problems broadly related to adequate classification. Depressive phenomena are ubiquitous and may occur as blatant primary sources of distress, as secondary though pronounced concomitants of a host of physical and/or mental difficulties, or as basic though obscure substrates of seemingly unrelated complaints of any variety. Consider, for example, the marked semantic ambiguity implicit when individuals X and Y are both designated depressed. Person X may have no significant familial or ontogenetic history of depression. Moreover, he may function splendidly in all vital spheres of activity but, owing to a serious disappointment occasioned by transient situational factors beyond his control, he is temporarily "blue" or depressed. By contrast, Y may come from a family background loaded with depressed and suicidal first-order relatives, have experienced severe, recurrent, chronically debilitating bouts of depression, and he too might be designated as depressed.

In essence, we are pointing up the difference between a depressive state in X and a markedly depressive disposition, or characterological trait, in Y.[5] To lump these conditions indiscriminately together impedes both humane intervention and increased knowledge. Simple distraction or reassurance may be all that X requires to buoy him up; while depressives such as Y may be severely retarded and almost insensitive to environmental alterations. In order to alter Y's behavior a combination of pharmacotherapy, electroconvulsive shock, psychotherapy,

[5] See Spielberger (1966, 1972) for a detailed exposition of these distinctions with reference to anxiety.

family therapy, behavioral modification, environmental manipulation, and eugenics counseling may be required.

Lehmann (1966) provides a useful example of the advantages of even present crudely accurate diagnosis. However, recent findings (Winokur, Clayton, & Reich, 1969) indicate that he may be unduly optimistic about the long-term effects of depression:

> ... once the physician has diagnosed a depression as manic-depressive psychosis, depressed phase, he can predict with 80 percent probability that there will be at least one other attack. . . . He can also predict that such attacks will probably be limited to a few weeks or months and that they will not interfere to any significant extent with the patient's life course or career. Further, he will be able to estimate the probability that the offspring of a manic-depressive person will develop the same condition as from 10 to 20 percent. . . . [pp. 11–12].

The two following chapters deal with current problems in the development of an empirically validated classification system for depressive phenomena.

2
CLASSIFICATION AND
MEASUREMENT OF DEPRESSION

It is very hard to classify one's ignorance in a satisfactory manner (Brill, 1965).

GENERAL ISSUES IN THE CLASSIFICATION
OF FUNCTIONAL PSYCHOPATHOLOGY

To some, taxonomy may smack of tedious, sterile pigeon-holing. But, as Meehl (1959) observed, any nomothetic reference to a person places him in conceptual space. In part, nihilistic views on taxonomy may reflect an earlier era of despair about the efficacy of treating functional disorders. Since many psychopathologists were convinced that functional disorders had an as yet undetermined organic etiology, treatment efforts were considered futile (Bockoven, 1963). Instead, much professional effort went into relatively fruitless diagnostic exercises. The usefulness of psychodiagnostic classification remains controversial. Some, like Szasz (1957) and Rogers (1951), argue the meaninglessness of the very concept of psychopathological entities, while others, like Menninger (1959), contend that there is a single continuum of psychopathology. These views are probably not shared by most psychopathologists who regard improved classification as vital to the advancement of their field (Klerman, 1971). What are the objectives of classifying disorders? Basically, to simplify the interpretation of complex data so as to facilitate their use in controlling, preventing, and understanding disorders. To accomplish these goals investigators attempt to determine the necessary and sufficient antecedent conditions of the disorder, its bio-psycho-social correlates, and its consequences. The more reliable the diagnostic groupings, the less the error variance in research and the greater the possibility of valid inferences about what measures might prevent the occurrence or ameliorate the debilitating features of the disorder.

Ideal Classification Systems

The quality of taxonomy within a scientific domain reflects its level of scientific maturation. There is virtually universal dissatisfaction with the present status of taxonomy in psychopathology, especially in regard to the functional disorders (Katz, Cole, & Barton, 1965). In an ideal classification system (Hempel, 1961), each diagnostic subclass (e.g., manic-depressive) would be explicitly defined by a concept which embodies a set of characteristics that stipulate the necessary and sufficient conditions for class membership. Subclasses would be mutually exclusive, so that all members of a class, and only such members, would share its necessary and sufficient characteristics (specific etiology and syndrome manifestation). Concepts within scientific vocabularies are designed to facilitate adequate description, explanation, and prediction of the relevant phenomena; "to understand a phenomenon scientifically is to show that it occurs in accordance with certain general laws or theoretical principles" (Hempel, 1961, p. 6). Classification systems reflecting early scientific development are based chiefly on descriptive qualities and simple empirical relations. Advanced systems increasingly rely on inferred, theoretically postulated entities, characteristics, and processes.

Hempel (1961) includes among the criteria of fruitful scientific concepts "clear uniform criteria of application."

> Science aims at knowledge that is *objective* in the sense of being intersubjectively certifiable, independent of individual opinion or preference, on the basis of data obtained by suitable experiments or observations [pp. 7–8].

Hempel rejects the notion that concepts must have no surplus meaning beyond their operational definition. In principle, hypotheses and theories should be testable by observational data. But all observation entails some judgment; reliable classification requires maximal explication and objectification of classificatory criteria.

Given a reasonable degree of objective definability, the most crucial determinant of a concept's value is its "systematic import." That is, how extensively and strongly does the concept relate to other variables within the system; and how well does it facilitate the development of general laws and theoretical principles which further scientific understanding?

Only within a logical system such as mathematics can the properties of a classification system rigorously fulfill ideal criteria. The more complex the biobehavioral phenomena to be classified, the less absolute the possibilities for mutually exclusive categorization. In psychopathology, classificatory types become ideal reference points rather than corresponding to actual cases. The latter become increasingly described in dimensional rather than typological terms; hence the clinical use of terms like borderline psychotic, schizo-affective, and mixed neuroses, or the factor analyst's designation by factor scores.

Classification of Psychopathology is Intrinsically Difficult

Lest the unfortunate impression be conveyed that psychopathologists' limited progress with satisfactory classification reflects their ineptitude or dereliction, it is somewhat comforting to reflect on Kety's (1965) evaluation of the inherent difficulties involved. Kety is a distinguished biochemist and former Chief of the Laboratory of Clinical Science at the National Institute of Mental Health.

There are many problems in psychiatry which are much more formidable than those which the rest of biology has ever faced and one can enumerate certain of them:

There is a considerably larger subjective element in the primary data of psychiatry than in that of the other branches of medicine. Radiologic evidence for pulmonary fibrosis is considerably more objective than the indications of affective state even though the interpretation of both types of evidence requires subjective judgments. Psychiatry also deals more with functional rather than structural alterations in underlying processes, and functional changes are more difficult to observe and to validate than are structural alterations. Interpersonal relationships are of considerably greater importance in psychiatry than they are in other branches of medicine, and these are not easy to define or control.

There is what appears to be the important distinction between the digital data of biology and the analog data of psychiatry. I can't help but feel that these problems, which are real and which undoubtedly help to explain the somewhat slower pace at which classification has occurred in psychiatry than in other branches of medicine or biology, do not constitute qualitatively different problems from those which are faced in these other areas, and that somehow the basic principles of nosology, nomenclature, and classification which have been found useful in other sciences are equally useful in psychiatry [p. 193].

In short, the problems in reliable psychopathological classification are multiple. For example, discrete etiological agents may generate highly overlapping symptomatology (Blumenthal, 1971), and the evaluation of signs and symptoms usually entails a significant value component. The judgment whether someone is cognitively loose, excited, withdrawn, insensitive, affectively flat, etc., involves considerable subjectivity, especially within moderate ranges of deviance from essentially idiosyncratic norms. The "patient's" cultural background and proximate contextual factors may greatly complicate the interpretation invariably required of clinical observations. As Ferster (1965), a noted Skinnerian, notes, a man may move slowly because he has a retarded depression or because he is not in a hurry. The facts do not speak for themselves. Diagnostic reliability problems are compounded by training biases weighted toward emphasis on accurate dynamic inference rather than objective description. Grinker's group (Grinker, Miller, Sabshin, Nunn, & Nunnally, 1961) reported that psychiatrists agree more positively on the inferred "feelings and concerns" of patients than on their objective behavior. Less formally trained personnel seemed able to record overt behavior more accurately than psychiatric residents.

Current diagnostic systems reflect kaleidoscopic conglomerates of descriptive, etiologic, prognostic, and phenomenologic variables (Zubin, 1967). Diagnostic reliability between investigators tends to be mediocre, whether defined by interrater agreement, re-evaluation over time, or distribution of diagnoses between comparable samplings. Tables 1 and 2, compiled by Zubin (1967), are self-explanatory in this regard.

Much of the difficulty doubtless stems from disorders in which there is no specific etiology, or in which the etiology accounts for limited variance. There is always the question of classification for what purpose? The clinician is apt to be chiefly interested in disposition, or in what treatment is likely to have what outcome. The researcher is more interested in etiology, prevention, and elucidation of normal structure and function. Classification which is highly valid for one purpose may not be for another. Even within camps, a clinical classification that predicts well for the effects of drug therapy may predict more or less well than other classifications for the effectiveness of psychotherapy, behavior modification, or electroconvulsive therapy. Depending upon how classification goals, universe of patients, and subcategories of disorders are specified, it is possible to demonstrate widely disparate taxonomic reliabilities and validities. Classifications designed to answer highly specific prediction problems with the aid of advanced techniques like discriminant function analysis and multiple regression can usually be refined to yield higher reliabilities and validities than classifications designed to identify natural groupings of etiology, syndrome, and outcome. But such analytic procedures are not guarantors of productive outcomes. Lubin (1965a), for example, presents a telling critique to overzealous advocates of a strictly pragmatic approach to classification by treatment response:

> Would you consider it important to classify together headaches, rheumatism, and bruises because they all respond to aspirin? In the same way, what about the fact that both meningococcal meningitis and syphilis respond to penicillin? Basically we will probably progress faster and further if we stick to the nosological procedures that have been so effective in physical medicine. Remember that there are basic questions of biochemistry, genetics, neurophysiology, etc., involved in psychiatric classification. If we insist on a purely pragmatic approach, psychiatry will never be able to root itself firmly in the bases of biological science [pp. 324–325].

Abandonment of a quest for specific etiologies for specific disorders would almost certainly be premature. Persistent efforts to identify high variance determining specific etiologies for a number of syndromes have paid off handsomely in the instances of pellagra, paresis, and phenylketonuria, all of which include significant behavioral pathology.

Common Misunderstandings about Classification Requisites

According to Meehl (1959, 1962), both critics and advocates of the Kraepelinian, or what Lorr (1961) terms the "conventional class model," often

TABLE 1

Percentage Agreement on Diagnosis by Observers

	Ash 1949(2)	Seeman 1953(55)	Schmidt 1956(54)	Kreitman 1961(32)	Beck 1962(6)	Sandifer 1964(53)
DESCRIPTION:						
Location of study	US	US	US	GB	US	US
Med. facility[a]	1	1	2	3	3	2
N of patients	52	6	426	90	153	91
Sex	M	–	MF	MF	MF	MF
Sampling	Sel.	Sel.	Succ.	Succ.	Ran.	Sel.
Class. type[b]	X(1, 2)	–	X(1)	Y	X	X(1)
Interval[c]	0	0	2	1	0	0
Agreement[d]	B	A	A	A	B	B
GENERAL CATEGORIES:						
Organic			92	85		
Functional psychosis			80	71		71
Characterological			71			74*
Psychoneurosis				52		
Av. agreement. gen. cat.	64†#		84	78	70	
ORGANIC PSYCHOSES:						
Acute brain synd.			68			46
Chronic brain synd.			80			66
Mental deficiency			(42)			73
Psychosis of old age				78		
Paresis		49†				
Other				62†		
FUNCTIONAL PSYCHOSES:						
Schizophrenia		80†	75†‡	(0)	53	74
Affective			(35)	65†		
Involutional			57		40	26
Manic depressive (depressive)		82†				36
Psychotic depressive						22
Hypomanic		29†				
Paranoid reaction						13
Other reaction						(17)
NEUROSIS AND PERSONALITY DISORDERS:						
Psychoneurosis			(16)			56
Reactive depressive				18†	63	
Anxiety state				27†	55	
Psychophysiological reaction						40
Pers. pattern disturb.			(8)			
Pers. disorder						66
Pers. trait disturb.			(6)		38	
Sociopath			58		54	
AV. AGREEMENT ON SPECIFIC CATEGORY	38†#	66†	55	63	54	57

Legend to Table 1
[a]Type of medical facility: 1 = Clinic, 2 = Psychiatric hospital, 3 = Psychiatric unit of general hospital.
[b]Type of Classification: X= APA Diagnostic & Statistical Manual, 1952; (1) abbreviated, (2) with additions; Y = Special.
[c]Interval between interview: 0 = Simultaneous (or within a few minutes), 1 = 1 week, 2 = 2 weeks, 3 = 1–2 months.
[d]Kinds of agreement: A = Criterion, B = Average group.
Symbols: – = Unspecified; ( ) = N < 8; † = Calculated on data reported in another form; # = 3 psychiatrists, 2 at a time;
* = The combined av. of character disorders and psychoneuroses; ‡ = Criterion agreement, reworked by present writer.
Schmidt & Fonda's 51% agreement refers to specific subtypes of schizophrenia.

TABLE 2
Consistency of Diagnosis over Time

	Hunt 1953(23)	Norris 1959(48)	Langfeldt 1960(33)	Kaelbling 1963(27)	Babigian 1965(3)
DESCRIPTION:					
Location of study	U.S.	G.B.	Norway	U.S.	U.S.
1st med. facility[a]	2	2	3	4	1, 2, 5, 8
2nd med. facility[a]	6	4	7	4	1, 2, 5, 8
N of patients	794	6263	200	218	4512
Type of patient[b]	A	B	C	B	C, D, B
Sex	M	MF	MF	MF	MF
Sampling	Succ.	Succ.	Sel.	Succ.	Sel.
Class. type[c]	Y	W	V	X	X
Interval[d]	–	2	4	3	1
Time of diagnosis[e]	ad.	ad.	ad.	di.	ad.
Independence of diagnosis	No	No	No	No	Yes
ORGANIC PSYCHOSES:					
Chronic brain synd.					92
Mental deficiency		70*			
General paralysis		89*			
Senile dementia		53*			
Cerebrovascular		29*#			
Epileptic	72*	92*			
Alcoholic		64*			
Other		60*			
Total organic		53*		65*†	
FUNCTIONAL PSYCHOSES:					
Schizophreniform			55*		
Schiz., schizo-affective				28*	
Nuclear schizophrenic			87*		
Total schizophrenic	37*	68*		66*	70
Involutional				10*	
Manic depressives		69*Δ			
Affective				43*	46
Paranoid		29*			
Mixed		31*‡			
Total functional	59			43*§	
PSYCHONEUROSES:					
Anxiety	18				
Hysteria	15				
Situational	0				
Mixed	6				
Depression				42*	
Unclassified	16				
Total psychoneuroses	24	46*		49*	
PERSONALITY AND CHAR. DISORDERS:					
Emotionally instable	47				
Inadequate personality	34				
Schizoid personality	62				
Pers. pattern disturb.				10*	
Pers. trait disturb.				46*	
Sociopath				38*	
Total pers. and char. disorders	74	46*		58*	

Legend to Table 2

[a]Type of medical facilities: 1 = Univ. hospital psychiatric emergency dept.; 2 = Observation unit (impatient); 3 = University hospital psychiatric clinic; 4 = Psychiatric hospital; 5 = Private practice; 6 = Psychiatric ward, general hospital; 7 = Follow-up in community; 8 = Outpatient dept. of univ. hospital.

[b]Type of patients: A = Naval psychiatric patients, B = Inpatients, C = Clinic outpatients, D = Private patients.

[c]Type of classification: X = APA, Y = Special Navy classification, V = Langfeldt's adaptation of Kraepelin, W = Amended ISC.

[d]Interval between contacts: 1 = 1 week to 4 weeks, 2 = 2 weeks to 4 weeks, 3 = 1 day to 26 weeks, 4 = 7 to 10 years.

[e]Time of diagnosis: ad. = Admission, di. = Discharge.

Symbols: # = Includes organic psychoses not otherwise specified; † = Combination of alcoholism, acute brain syndrome, and alcoholic intoxication; § = Excludes psychotic depression; ‡ = Includes a symptomatic and confusional psychoses and those with no diagnosis specified; Δ = Includes involutional psychosis; * = Reworked data; – = Not specified.

entertain the erroneous assumptions that (*a*) diseases are present or absent; (*b*) nearly all signs and symptoms of a disorder always occur; (*c*) personality disorders are mutually exclusive, unlike physical disorders; and (*d*) each disorder has a specific etiologic or pathogenic agent. Meehl argues that the Kraepelinian system survives because it has enough clinical predictive validity to warrant its continued usage.

Meehl (1959) points out that diagnostic unreliability may stem from at least three sources: (*a*) diagnostic error, that is, the signs and symptoms may be elicitable but undetected; (*b*) the diagnostic entity is validly conceptualized, but no signs or symptoms were elicitable (he cites, for example, postmortem reviews by a skilled medical internist indicating that 29% of his cases were undiagnosable prior to postmortem); or (*c*) the nosological entity may be nonexistent or inadequately conceptualized. Psychopathologists have nothing corresponding to postmortems to enable them to sharpen their conceptual and diagnostic capabilities. Furthermore, validation of diagnostic categories can only be accomplished indirectly by construct validation, not by operational test. That is, evidence for the validity of a diagnostic category implicitly resides in a network of hypothesized laws concerning the category. Even evidence from these laws constitutes only a "family of indicators of unknown relative weights. [p. 110]." This state of affairs is not as radically different from aspects of physical diagnosis as some might believe; few physical diseases have pathognomonic indicators, (that is, definitive signs or symptoms); indeed, few physical diseases are invariantly reflected in specific signs and symptoms.

If a somewhat unreliable syndrome description constitutes the only extant knowledge of a disorder, patently it makes no sense to ignore the phenomenon. Perhaps discomfortingly for some psychologists, who as Meehl (1959) points out often act as though they do not really believe in environmental-organic interaction, recent etiological research increasingly supports Kraepelin's hypothesized primary biological etiology for at least some functional psychotic disorders (Heston, 1969; Mednick, 1970; Rosenthal, 1971; Winokur, Clayton, & Reich, 1969). Many of the chief critics of Kraepelinian classification are psychodynamically oriented, and Meehl (1962) challenges these advocates to adduce evidence that knowledge of psychological structure and dynamics permits better prediction of the course and outcome of their disorders than crude life history data or Kraepelinian diagnosis.

Meehl contends that many psychologists have difficulty in fairly assessing data which indicate that functional disorders have a specific hereditary etiology because they misunderstand the implications of a specific etiology. Essentially the term implies a necessary, but not necessarily sufficient, condition for the occurrence of a disorder. It does not imply any of the following common misconceptions:

1. The etiological factor always, or even usually, produces clinical illness.
2. If illness occurs, the particular form and content of symptoms is derivable by reference to the specific etiology alone.

3. The course of the illness can be materially influenced only by procedures directed against the specific etiology.

4. All persons who share the specific etiology will have closely similar histories, symptoms, and course.

5. The largest single contributor to symptom variance is the specific etiology (Meehl, 1962, p. 828).

KRAEPELINIAN CATEGORIES VERSUS
FACTORIAL DIMENSIONS

While sophisticated clinicians such as Meehl (1959) defend the intrinsic worth of the traditional Kraepelinian typology, others (Lorr, 1961; Zubin, 1967) seriously question its utility. Critics of traditional typologies argue that the mutual exclusiveness or the discontinuity of categories does not veridically reflect the tendency of all syndromes to be present in all patients, but in varying degrees and combinations. These protagonists argue for a configural, factor analytically derived dimensional schema. These differences are clearly noted in the proceedings of a recent conference sponsored by the American Psychiatric Association and the National Institute of Mental Health (Katz, Cole, & Barton, 1965). In this symposium, most clinicians uneasily adhered to a Kraepelinian style typology which assumes discontinuities between disorders. In contrast, their research colleagues tended to favor dimensional approaches with implied continuities on psychopathological parameters. Clinicians often derogate dimensionalist approaches, largely because they can only be as good as the clinical ratings upon which the ascertained factors and clusters are based. Furthermore, clinicians criticize the general lack of ordering or hierarchical significance among identified factors. All signs and symptoms are not of equal import, regardless of their frequency of occurrence. Clinicians also criticize the cross-sectional time-boundedness of the observational rating base and the obscuring of interactions and interdependencies between factors (Lehmann, 1965). Sophisticated theoretical statisticians such as Rao (1965) and Torgerson (1965) share much of the clinician's reserve about the contribution of factor analytic approaches to classification thus far. Torgerson argues that it is premature to opt for a typological versus dimensional classification. The prime task yet to be accomplished is identification of the underlying structure of disorders; some may involve continuities, some discontinuities, and other mixtures of the two. Lubin's (1965a) remarks as a discussant on the quantitative papers in the APA-NIMH Symposium are informative, amusing, and sobering:

> The four papers presented here, on the methodology of developing new typologies, cluster together very well in terms of their presenting symptoms, dynamic etiology, and temporal transactional sequence. In each case, the first statistical procedure was to carry out a factor analysis. In fact, several factor analyses usually were done. These factor analyses generally provided linear combinations of the original scores or ratings. The linear combinations were then used to compute correlations and covariance matrices between selected patients (although in one case, the factor analysis was abandoned and the original scores were used).

Next the intercorrelations between the patients were attacked with a variety of weapons: cluster analysis, powered vectors, higher order correlations, congruency coefficients, etc., more than one of these methods generally being applied. In this way, clumps of patients were hacked out of the correlation matrix, and a new typology was born.

This period of colossal computation was followed in most cases by a certain amount of skepticism as to the usefulness of the results (Lubin, 1965a, pp. 322–323).

Faced then with a functional disorder like depression, which probably has a variety of sources and which is expressed in a multiplicity of ways, what approaches for attempting to identify meaningful, homogeneous subgroupings exist? Basically there appear to be four approaches and combinations thereof, and most extant classification systems nonsystematically combine aspects of all four approaches.

1. The cross-sectional approach seeks consistent groupings of signs and symptoms.

2. The longitudinal, natural history approach examines the interrelations of factors like age of onset, duration, severity, periodicity, and outcome.

3. The treatment-response approach determines whether identifiable subgroups respond differentially to various therapeutic interventions.

4. The etiological approach usually is combined with one or several of the above.

Variants of such approaches are currently best exemplified in the work of Robins, Munoz, Martin, & Gentry (1972) and Winokur, Clayton, & Reich (1969) which is discussed subsequently.

The American Psychiatric Association's system for classifying affective disorders, which is presented in Appendix A, combines various aspects of these approaches. This system provides a useful example because of its attempted theoretical neutrality and common usage (the American Psychiatric Association Diagnostic Manual (1968) is essentially identical with the World Health Organization's eighth revision of the Classification of Mental Disorders). Note, however, that the poor diagnostic reliabilities for affective disorders summarized by Zubin are based on an earlier, similar diagnostic system.

Severity of Depression Ratings

The implicit rationale underlying severity of depression measures is that increased severity is associated with a higher frequency and a greater intensity of depressive symptoms. Many scales for rating the severity of depression have appeared recently. This increase reflects the growing awareness by clinicians that such scales have greater reliability than global clinical judgments; an increased acceptance by behavioral scientists of subjective self-reports as valid data; and research interests broadened from depression as a primary nosological entity to depression as a ubiquitous personality variable. Severity of depression estimates based on such measures are more economical and less susceptible to variations in observer bias and skill than estimates based on unstructured interviews.

The American Psychological Association (1954) has provided guidelines for evaluating the psychometric utility of diagnostic assessment scales in terms of reliability and validity. Because the severity of depression scales have been insufficiently evaluated against these reliability-validity criteria, they have to be compared descriptively rather than critically.

Personality theory and research increasingly distinguish between affective states and traits (Spielberger, 1966, pp. 3–23). An affective state refers to the momentary here-and-now feeling status of the individual, as exemplified by the statement that "Mr. Smith is depressed now." By contrast, an affective trait refers to a lower threshold for experiencing depressive states, which tends to result in frequently experienced depressive states. It is quite possible, then, to be in an acutely depressed state, although one has low trait depression, and conversely to be in a nondepressed state, although one has very high trait depression. Affective states fluctuate, whereas dispositional traits are relatively constant. Although research on anxiety trait-state differences has been fruitful (Spielberger, Gorsuch, & Lushene, 1969), this approach has not been extended to depression. A number of depressive state measures are available, but most confound trait and state. Before briefly discussing severity of depression measures, some mention should be made of the content item relationship of anxiety and depression state measures. Generally they show considerable item overlap; indeed many of the items in Spielberger et al.'s (1969) trait anxiety measure STAI Form X-2 read more like depression than anxiety items. The two conditions frequently occur together clinically. Both states seem to be triggered by failure-related threats to self-esteem. Many clinicians conjecture that anxiety reflects a mobilization to cope with threat, whereas depression reflects a passive despair, a sense of futile inevitability about an adverse outcome. That is, cognitive interpretation of the nature and portent of the threat critically determines the affective response elicited. Costello & Comrey (1967) have developed brief orthogonal depression and anxiety measures. When further developed, these may prove highly useful in examining the interactive effects of varying degrees of these two basic affective states. While Beck's Depression Inventory (Beck, Ward, Mendelson, Mock, & Erbough, 1961; Beck 1967; Beck, in press) also confounds depressive state and trait, it correlates well with other depressive measures and negligibly with other anxiety measures; hence it too may prove useful in sharpening discrimination between anxious and depressive phenomena. One further note of caution before reviewing the depression scales: when Becker & Nichols (1964) intercorrelated a number of depression measures, they found more variance attributable to the method used than to the ostensibly identical variables assessed by the different measures (Campbell & Fiske, 1959).

The two most frequently used self-rating severity of depression measures are the Zung (1965) and the Beck scales (Beck et al., 1961; Beck, 1967; Beck, in press). Both confound trait and state depression. Zung has devised a Self Rating Depression Scale of 20 items covering affect and physiological and psychological depressive concomitants or equivalents. Items are rationally derived but expressed in verbatim patient language. Items are rated on a four-point scale, half-positively and half-negatively keyed toward depressive content. The scale correlates .70 with the MMPI Depression Scale and differentiates diagnostic categories at statistically significant levels. Its status as a measure of severity of depression is supported by higher initial scores for depressive inpatients than outpatients, and by the decreased scores of inpatients upon discharge. No effort has been made to increase its discriminatory power by item analyses and refinement. Psychometrically it is a relatively crude but useful tool for group assessment (Zung, 1965; Zung, Richards, & Short, 1965).

Beck's Depression Inventory (Beck, et al., 1961; Beck, 1967; Beck, in press) is probably the best developed and most widely used self-report depression measure. The scale consists of 21 categories of symptoms and attitudes clinically related to depression. Each category contains a set of severity graded self-evaluative statements that are rated 0 (neutral) to 3 (maximum severity). Validity and reliability data are more thoroughly reported for this depression scale than any other. Development of this scale stemmed from an interesting series of studies on diagnostic reliability. Briefly, the first phase consisted of Board Certified psychiatrists independently diagnosing psychiatric outpatients in terms of broad (neuroses, psychosis, personality disorder) versus specific nosological categories. Agreement on the former was 70%, and on the latter 56%. With diagnosis disregarded, still better agreement was obtained on severity of depression ratings based on the rating of 22 explicit signs and symptoms. Since the goal was a research instrument that could be used across institutions, these a priori clinically derived items were used as a basis for a self-rating inventory. Analysis of Depression Inventory (DI) scores from several large psychiatric samples (200 and 606) indicated good reliability as indexed by internal consistency and stability criteria: split-half Spearman-Brown corrected Pearson $r = .93$; all items significantly related to total score at the $p < .001$ level per item; and highly significant test-retest correlations with clinicians' independent severity of depression rating. Validity data are likewise encouraging. Clinicians' ratings of severity of depression were made independently of knowledge of scale scores, which were categorized as none, mild, moderate, and severe. Mean scale scores for each respective category were 10.9, 18.7, 25.4, and 30.0, respectively. These differences are significant ($p < .001$). and the study has been essentially replicated with similar results in Great Britain (Metcalfe & Goldman, 1965). The DI correlates well with other measures of depression such as the MMPI, Lubin's Depression Adjective Check List, and the Hamilton Rating Scale (1967). It is sensitive to clinical change. Scores are unrelated to race, age, and intelligence, but females and the less well educated tend to obtain higher scores. Factor analysis of the Beck DI by orthogonal rotation to simple structure yielded the four interpretable factors of Vital Depression, Self-Debasement, Pessimism-Suicide, and Indecision-Inhibition (Pichot & Lempérière, 1964). Experimental studies that generally support the construct validity of the Beck DI are reviewed in a subsequent chapter. As noted before, a particular virtue of the Beck DI is its apparent ability to discriminate depression from anxiety. Many ostensible measures of anxiety correlate at least as highly with other measures of depression as with others of anxiety.

The promising Self-Rating Depression Inventory for Severity Use (Hunt, Singer, & Cobb, 1967) has the particular advantage of items that cover a wide range of depressive symptomatology sensitively and in simple language highly suitable for survey purposes. Initial studies of internal consistency, stability, and validity are encouraging, but the instrument has not been used enough to compare its effectiveness with the Zung and Beck Scales. It may prove complementary to these measures, since the former is highly loaded with vegetative symptoms and the latter perhaps more suitable to clinical than to survey populations.

The MMPI Depression Scale (Hathaway & McKinley, 1942) is one of the older self-rating depression scales still in use. This 60-item scale is based on 49 items that discriminated hospitalized manic-depressive depressed patients from normals, and 11 items that discriminated the former from other psychiatric patients. The scale has been criticized for its factorial complexity (O'Connor, Stefic, & Gresock, 1957; Comrey, 1957) and lack of dimensionality (Dempsey, 1963; 1964). Similar scores on this scale can reflect quite different depressive states qualitatively and quantitatively. The scale does reasonably well for predicting mean score differences between nosological groups, but for individual differences within groups it does poorly. Dempsey has devised a 30-item modification of the original scale termed the D_{30}. Items were selected by contextual analysis; to be acceptable they had to relate consistently in the same direction to the major underlying dimension within normal and abnormal samples of both sexes. Despite halving the number of items, the D_{30} scale showed improved split-half ($r = .88$) and test-retest ($r = .92$) reliability over the original. This scale seems promising for discriminating severity of depression within nonpathological groups, provided its confounding with social desirability is taken into account (Edwards, 1965).

There are a number of self-report state measures of depression. Hildreth (1946) developed the Battery of Feeling and Attitude Scales based on the responses of hospitalized servicemen to the query, "How do you feel?". The scales tap feelings about immediate affective state, amount of energy, future outlook, and attitudes toward work, people, and one's mental status. Each scale has 10 items ranged in increasing weighted value from negative to positive by a modified Thurstone scaling procedure. The psychometric properties of these measures are largely unknown. Wessman & Ricks (1966) designed a set of Personal Feeling Scales for repeated self-reports over time. Each scale has 10 graduated items selected on an a priori rational basis for unidimensionality and equal subjective interval. The Elation vs. Depression Scale provides a typical affective state measure. Again the psychometric properties of these scales are largely undetermined, although their scores have related meaningfully to other variables in several studies (Becker & Nichols, 1964; Wessman & Ricks, 1966). Lubin (1965b; 1966) has devised a set of parallel or alternate form adjective check lists for measuring transient or state depression. The Depression Adjective Check Lists (DACL) intercorrelate highly and discriminate between normals, nondepressive psychiatric patients, and diagnosed depressives. They show fairly high concurrent validity with Beck's Depressive Inventory and the MMPI-D Scale. Promising predictive validity is indicated by the DACL's responsiveness to change in sensitivity training groups (Lubin, Dupre, & Lubin, 1967). However, the normal controls used in developing these lists were significantly younger than the patient groups. Refinement of the lists by selecting more adequate controls might enable it to discriminate among clinically depressed patients in terms of severity. DACL scores did not distinguish between outpatient and hospitalized depressives. An interesting replicated but unexplained finding with the DACL is the interaction between sex of subject and psychiatric status. Normal males score higher (more depressed) than normal females; nondepressed psychiatric patients do not differ by sex; and depressed females score higher than depressed males. These scales require negligible time to administer, seem to be nonstressful, and show good split-half reliabilities. Their utility in studies requiring repeated measurement should be considerable, especially if their discriminatory power can be increased. Other useful state measures are Nowlis' (1965) Adjective Check List and the Clyde Mood Scale (1963). Nowlis (1963) contends that state measures are less biased by defensiveness and response biases than trait measures.

The most widely used observer rating instrument is Hamilton's Rating Scale for Depression (Hamilton, 1960; Hamilton & White, 1959). This scale is designed for use with diagnosed depressives. Raters are urged to use all available information, including interview, records, and collateral informants. To enhance objectivity, Hamilton urges that two raters independently evaluate the same material whenever possible. Factor analysis of this scale yields three factors; the first corresponds to retarded depression, the second to agitated depression, and the last to psychopathic depression, a hitherto little acknowledged syndrome. Factor scores derived from the third factor are related to treatment outcome. Psychopathic depressives tend to be younger, more aggressive, and lower in frustration tolerance than other depressives. This instrument of course requires the greatest possible clinical sophistication for optimal effectiveness.

The Depression Rating Scale is essentially a state measure of depression using both patient's self-reports and observer's interview observations (Wechsler, Grosser, & Busfield, 1963). Since this scale was designed to assess treatment-related changes in severity of depression, its items cover all major symptom areas typically associated with depression: physical functioning, motor activity, motivation, mood, intellectual functioning, self-esteem, and guilt. It was devised so that ratings can be made readily from a standard psychiatric interview.

DIFFERENTIATION OF DEPRESSION
AND SAMPLE VARIABILITY

The major issues in the classification of depression are whether it is a meaningful nosological entity and whether there are meaningful subtypes of depression. These issues are empirically as well as theoretically important. Efforts to replicate research findings on depression are frequently unsuccessful. These failures, in part, are probably due to variability in the attributes of depressives between and within research samples (Katz, 1969).

Research concerned with the reduction or assessment of variability within research samples of depressives has followed several methods. One method skirts the issue of depression as a nosological entity and confines itself to the assessment of severity of depression. Another approach separates relatively pure cases of depression from those in which depression is secondary to another disorder.

Depression inventory measures would be more useful as research instruments if their dimensional aspects and suitability as repeated measures (Hargreaves, 1969) were more systematically developed. Factor analyses of such measures suggest four underlying dimensions: central mood disorder, self-accusation, psychomotor disorder, and somatic dysfunction (Katz, 1969). Any of these depression related factors may be associated with other diagnostic entities, and none are essential to a diagnosis of depression. If depression inventories had reliable subscales to represent each of these factors, intersample comparability could more easily be established or more homogeneous research samples selected. Also, such inventory construction would permit analyses of relations between subscale components and correlative psychological and biological variables within studies.

Primary versus Secondary Depression

Robins and his associates at Washington University are attempting to reduce diagnostic heterogeneity by distinguishing "primary" from "secondary" depression (Robins & Guze, 1969; Robins, Munoz, Martin, & Gentry, 1972). To justify a diagnosis of affective disorder, patients must have a dysphoric or euphoric mood, a predetermined number of somatic and psychological symptoms, and a definite onset of the deviant mood. When an affective disturbance meets these three criteria, its classification as primary or secondary or undiagnosed depends mainly on chronology. If prior episodes have been affective disorders only, or if the presenting disorder is the first diagnosable psychiatric disturbance, then the designation is primary affective disorder. If another major diagnosable psychiatric disorder has preceded or accompanies the affective disorder, then the designation is secondary affective disorder. And if another undiagnosable or poorly defined psychiatric disturbance or major medical illness preceded or accompanies the affective disorder, then the affective condition is classed as undiagnosed or uncertain.

The approach of Robins et al. (1972) is designed to determine ultimately whether depression is a meaningful entity. According to them, the establishment of a valid psychiatric entity requires five phases: "clinical description of the syndrome, laboratory studies, delimitation from other syndromes, follow-up studies, and family studies (Robins et al., 1972, p. 34)." They contend that several disorders, such as schizophrenia, hysteria, and anxiety neuroses, meet these criteria reasonably well.

The principal advantages cited for this primary-secondary classification approach are its simplicity, eschewal of etiologic and severity assumptions, and requisite clear-cut criteria for diagnosable psychiatric disorders. However, no reliability data on the application of this method have been provided. Whether reliable ascertainment of prior psychiatric states is adequately achieved remains moot for the present.

Robins et al. (1972) investigated the relative incidence of primary-secondary depression among 314 randomly selected patients from an urban Mental Health Center emergency room. Although 72% complained of a dysphoric mood, only 39% were diagnosed as primary or secondary depressives. The ratio of primary to secondary depression was 5:3. This high incidence of depression among an essentially indigent sample is inconsistent with traditional psychiatric beliefs.

MULTIVARIATE STUDIES OF DEPRESSION AS A NOSOLOGICAL ENTITY

Most recent efforts to validate the Kraepelinian designation of depression as an entity use some form of cluster analysis (Everitt, 1972). This technique groups rating scale scores of individuals on the basis of their similarity. Unfortunately, different cluster analytic techniques may yield unlike clusters from the same data. For example, different techniques do better at clustering data that have spherical score distributions or elongated parallel distributions. If several clustering techniques yield similar clusters, confidence in their validity is somewhat greater. As Everitt (1972) notes:

> The problem of deciding the 'best' number of groups into which to partition a set of data must really be considered unsolved . . . 'groups' found may only be extremes from a single distribution [p. 144].

Depression versus Schizophrenia

Everitt, Gourlay, & Kendell (1971) performed four cluster analyses with two cluster analytic techniques (class 1 and Normap) on two series of 250 admissions each to a London and New York psychiatric hospital. Data were obtained as part of the U.S.-U.K. Diagnostic Project (Zubin & Fleiss, 1971), which is discussed subsequently. These data are unusually reliable symptom and diagnostic ratings made by trained investigators using the Present State Examination (PSE) and a semistructured mental status exam (Cooper, Kendell, Gurland, Sharpe,

Copeland, & Simon, 1971). Seventy items were preselected from a pool of 728 for cluster analysis, because they best discriminated between patients with neurotic and psychotic depressions and between those with affective and schizophrenic psychoses. Principal component analyses preceded the cluster analyses. Clusters derived from the British data were more consistent with classical Kraepelinian categories than the American data. Four small, reasonably well defined groups emerged in each of the four cluster analyses: manics, psychotic depressives, paranoid schizophrenics, and chronic schizophrenics. But in all four analyses more than 60% of the patients clustered in one or two poorly defined groupings composed of members from all of the ten major diagnostic categories plus addicts and personality disorders. These findings failed to clarify the issue whether a categorical (typological) or dimensional system of classification is optimal. Everitt et al. (1972) put the matter succinctly:

> ... we have no mathematical criteria for deciding whether the variance within any given body of data is better represented by a typology or by a dimensional system. Cluster analysis is bound to produce clusters, and factor analysis is in practice only capable of defining dimensions. Discriminant function analysis can test the validity of an existing categorical classification and refine its criteria, but it cannot generate new groupings [p. 411].

The investigators share the view that a combination of a dimensional and typological system will eventually emerge.

One of the most difficult clinical diagnostic discriminations to make is frequently that between psychotic depression and schizophrenia. Many patients, sometimes designated schizo-affectives, have manifestations of both disorders. Such cases are variously regarded as a third diagnostic category, a genetically determined combination of depression and schizophrenia, or a reactive combination of the two. Still other clinicians contend that if any schizophrenic manifestations are present, the diagnosis should be schizophrenia. Empirical studies indicate that the prognosis of schizo-affectives is intermediate between the better one for depression and the poorer one for schizophrenia. Kendell & Gourlay (1970) have moved from polemics to investigation in an effort to determine whether psychotic depression and schizophrenia are poles of a continuum or discrete entities. The subjects were again carefully diagnosed patients from the U.S.-U.K. Diagnostic Project; 146 were diagnosed as affective psychotic and 146 as schizophrenic. Items for a discriminant function analysis were drawn from the Present State Examination and semistructured history interview previously cited. Again, only items which significantly discriminated between the two groups were selected for a discriminant function analysis, in order to maximize the likelihood of obtaining a bimodal distribution of patients. Discriminant function analysis determines a weighted linear function for a set of variables that best discriminates between two samples. A bimodal distribution would support the classical notion of psychotic depression and schizophrenia as entities rather than poles on a continuum (Beck, 1967). An unanticipated trimodal distribution was obtained initially, with 9% of the cases misclassified. A second analysis with more cases (366, including 117 of the original ones) yielded a normal distribution, with 7% of the cases misclassified. These findings provided no support for depression and schizophrenia as distinct entities although, as the investigators contend, additional items related to treatment response and degree and durability of recovery versus deterioration might yet produce a more bimodal-like distribution. Most of the misclassified cases were American patients, but whether this was due to rater unreliability or ambiguous symptomatology was not determined.

Depression versus Anxiety States

Depression and anxiety frequently occur together as well as separately. Psychopathologists identified with the "unitary" school have favored grouping these disturbances together under the heading of "affective states." In contrast, the "separatists" who have advocated a reactive-endogenous split in the classification of depression also tend to favor a categorical separation of depression and anxiety states (Kelly & Walter, 1969).

Few empirical attempts have been made to discriminate depressions from other types of neuroses. Zubin & Fleiss (1971) report that a factor analysis of the 700-item mental status exam used in the U.S.-U.K. Diagnostic Project yielded relatively independent anxiety (21 items) and depression factors (45 items). The anxiety items pertain to specific anxiety fraught situations and to physiological concomitants of anxiety rather than to nonspecific uneasiness or fear. Very good interrater and repeated interview reliabilities are reported. A comparison between the factor scores on the two scales for 63 depressive neurotics and 14 anxiety neurotics yielded no group difference in depression scores, but anxiety scores were significantly higher ($p < .001$) for the anxiety neurotics. This result has no direct implications for the entity versus continuum issue, but it suggests that depression ratings from current clinical status interviews are unlikely to support an "entity" position.

Only one major investigation has systematically sought to determine whether anxiety and depression, the two affective disorders, are discriminable entities (Roth, Gurney, Garside, & Kerr, 1972; Schapira, Roth, Kerr, & Gurney, 1972). The data analyses in this project are similar to those recommended by Moran (1966) for the delineation of a psychopathological syndrome. Therefore, this study is reported in considerable detail.

Subjects in this project included 145 patients admitted to psychiatric units in the city of Newcastle-upon-Tyne with a primary mood change in which anxiety or depression predominated. Patients received a structured interview soon after admission which covered the range of symptomatology for depression and anxiety; family history; childhood; medical history; sexual, occupational, and social adjustment; and premorbid personality. An interrater reliability evaluation of ratings on 29 patients indicated adequate agreement for research purposes, the lowest reliability coefficient being +0.86. Subsequently the Maudsley Personality Inventory was administered and at discharge the patient's treatment was noted and his clinical state assessed. Patients were categorized as depressed (62), anxious (68), or uncertain (15). Four years after the project began, the 126 available subjects were reinterviewed jointly by two project members who were unaware of the initial diagnosis. This one follow-up interview spanned the period from the time of initial hospital discharge to the time of interview in six-month intervals. It covered further treatment, breakdowns, hospital readmissions, stresses, health, social adjustment, and present clinical status. An average reliability coefficient of +0.85 per item was obtained on a subsample of 21 patients.

Initial chi square analysis of the pre-follow-up data indicated a sizable overlap in the incidence of many symptoms. But interesting differences did emerge. For example, depressives frequently reported severe anxiety and anxious patients reported depression. However, anxiety in depressives tended to be episodic rather than persistent, and the same relation obtained for depression in primary anxiety states. Most of the symptoms which discriminated depressions from anxiety states were characteristic of endogenous depression (e.g., depression worse in A.M., low reactivity of depression to environmental change, early wakening, retardation, and delusions), which comprises about 15% of diagnosed depressives. This finding reinforces the likelihood that obtained differences between the groups are most generalizable to hospitalized depression and anxiety state populations only. Other investigators might have classified a number of the anxiety state cases as reactive depressives. Distinctions between endogenous and reactive depressions are elaborated in the next chapter.

Anxiety state patients more frequently manifested ($p < .001$) panic attacks, increased vasomotor response, emotional lability, severe agoraphobia, depersonalization, derealization, and perceptual distortions than depressives did. Anxiety state patients also had more disturbed backgrounds: their first-order relatives more frequently had neurotic and personality disorders; their parental relations were poorer; they had more -childhood neurotic traits and poorer school adjustments. In short, depressives tended to be more "stable, mature, and independent." Their lower neuroticism scores ($p < .001$) on the Maudsley Personality Inventory supported this conclusion. Also, anxiety state patients had an earlier age of onset, preceded by more stress, and more prolonged disturbances.

A principal components analysis of 58 items from the pre-follow-up data yielded a bipolar first-order factor accounting for 14.4% of the variance. Positively loaded items were associated with anxiety states and negative loadings with depression. Factor scores on the first component were calculated by summing the weighted item scores for each patient, and the score distributions were plotted. The difference in factor score means between the two groups was highly significant ($F > 100$), which suggests a bimodal distribution.

The investigators acknowledge the close resemblance of their first bipolar factor to ones reported in numerous other studies whose subjects included diagnosed depressives only.

Subsequently 13 of the 58 items with the highest coefficients of individual determination were used in a discriminant function analysis with the initial clinical diagnosis as the dependent variable. Weighted and summed scores of the patients on the 13 items again yielded a bimodal distribution that reflected the two clinical groups. Items were then used to construct a diagnostic index whose prognostic validity was tested by comparing the follow-up improvement ratings and total symptom profiles of the two groups. The obtained group differences support the predictive validity of the scale: depressive patients were more improved than anxiety patients ($p < .05$), and symptom patterns differed at the four-year follow-up. The two group improvement score curves which were plotted over six-month intervals follow parallel U-shaped courses. These curves turn sharply downward until six months to a year after discharge, then are relatively flat for a year to a year-and-a-half, and only then begin to climb to their level at hospital discharge four years previously. While the anxiety state improvement curve is flatter than the depression curve, the overall course of the curves appears similar by visual inspection. The best overall predictors of improvement were an absence of premorbid hysterical traits, a brief course of illness, and degree of recovery at the time of hospital discharge.

Even if the investigator is unprepared to accept the existence of depression and anxiety state as diagnostic entities, the 13-item discriminant function analysis derived diagnostic index provides a score on an anxiety-depression dimension which allows objective comparison of these patient characteristics across studies.

There is much inevitable capitalization on chance at this phase of the project. As a methodological approach there is much to commend, but evaluation of its substantive merits must await replication locally and elsewhere.

Additional studies on the unitary versus separatist affective disorders issue are quite interesting but inconclusive. They are reported in some detail because they probably have important implications for failures to replicate previous psychophysiological findings on depressives. Kelly & Walter (1969) argue for three subtypes of anxiety states: acute, phobic, and chronic. They contend that classical endogenous symptoms are "invariably absent" in chronic anxiety states. They compared data on autonomic responsivity mostly of hospitalized groups of chronic anxiety, agitated depressive and nonagitated depressive patients, and controls in an experimentally induced stress situation. The principal response measure was basal forearm blood flow (FBF), which they contend is a valid and reliable physiological index of anxiety. Both basal and stress levels of forearm blood flow were obtained, as well as self- and observer-anxiety ratings during both conditions. Between-group mean differences on the FBF were highly significant ($p < .001$), and their rank order (chronic anxiety state, agitated depression, nonagitated depression, and controls) was consistent with the study's rationale. Only the FBF levels of the latter two groups did not differ from each other. Data for self- versus observer-anxiety ratings were presented graphically only but appear quite similar. The more extensive self-rating anxiety data indicated minor differences between patient groups during the basal phase, with all clinical groups significantly higher than the controls. Apparently the stress induction was successful, since self-reported anxiety increased in all groups, and no differences were obtained between groups under that condition.

The writers concluded that a distinction between anxiety and depression is supported. They buttressed this argument with the contention that FBF is uninfluenced by depression, as indicated by the lack of difference in basal scores between nonagitated depressives and normal controls. The agitated depressives who had much internal tension and motor restlessness scored intermediately between the chronic anxiety states and the other groups, as would be expected if FBF is a valid anxiety measure.

In contrast, Noble & Lader (1971) argue that depression has an inhibitory effect on FBF rather than no effect. They note that the agitated depressives obtained the highest mean self-reported basal anxiety score, yet their mean basal FBF score was significantly ($p < .001$) lower than the anxiety group. Even the nonagitated depressives had a basal self-report anxiety mean only slightly below the anxiety group, yet their FBF scores were also substantially below the anxiety group's ($p < .001$). Furthermore, Noble and Lader provide pre- and post-ECT FBF data in an experimental paradigm similar to Kelly and Walter's which substantiates the likelihood that depression has an inhibitory effect on FBF. They speculate that hypothalamic dysfunction accounts for many autonomic anomalies in endogenous depression.

Evidence for the distinctiveness of anxiety and depression as classificatory entities is inconclusive. But it clearly behooves investigators of physiological variables associated with affective disturbances to obtain independent quantitative assessments of anxiety and depression which will permit covariance adjustments of their dependent variables.

A Cautionary Note on Multivariate Methods

Maxwell (1972) has noted that the distributional properties of psychiatric rating data usually violate critical statistical assumptions related to bivariate normal distributions. Only when this assumption is met can " . . . correlation coefficients between pairs of variables be estimated independently of the variate means [p. 19]." But many symptoms occur rarely, or raters are concerned only with pathological magnitudes of symptoms. When zero ratings predominate, correlation coefficients may be very inflated. Maxwell cites data from several relevant studies to indicate how commonplace positively skewed distributions occur with psychiatric ratings. He reanalyzes the data of Everitt, Gourlay, & Kendell (1971) using his own factor model, which allows for errors of measurement. A large, meaningful factor, "retarded depression," and two meaningful associated group factors, "general anxiety" and "self-depreciation," emerge, but they occur in both the schizophrenic and affective samples! Other factors paralleling those of Everitt et al. are shown to be artifactual. Even the factor loadings on the three meaningful factors are questionable because of the nonnormality of most of the variables involved. Maxwell is more optimistic about constructing rating scales for adequately dimensionalizing neurotic symptoms than he is for psychotic ones, which tend to be intrinsically present or absent.

In sum, the question of whether depression is a meaningful diagnostic entity remains unresolved. Nor is any definitive analytic method for resolving the issue apparent. Although all current approaches appear to have vulnerable premises, perhaps enough convergence will emerge to permit conclusions reasonably worthy of confidence. At most, only some subtypes of depression are likely to warrant characterization as entities. Attempts to identify such subtypes will be presented in the following chapter.

3
SUBTYPES OF DEPRESSION

Last night, in concluding his talk, Dr. Eli Robins quoted Kendell to the effect that in our current state of knowledge of depression, there are no answers. This reminded me of the remarks attributed to Gertrude Stein on her deathbed: semi-comatose, she was heard to mumble, 'The answer, the answer, the answer.' Then, in a moment of lucidity, she opened her eyes and asked, 'What is the question?' (Klerman, 1969, p. 331).

ISSUES IN THE SUBCLASSIFICATION OF DEPRESSION AS EXEMPLIFIED BY THE ENDOGENOUS-REACTIVE DISPUTE

Most research on the subclassification of depressives has focused on the question of whether valid endogenous and reactive subtypes exist. However, since the terms refer primarily to etiology, and the etiology of depression is unknown, Lewis (1971) contends that the use of these terms is inappropriate.

Historical Overview

The etiological distinction between endogenous and reactive disorders was introduced into psychopathology by Mobius in 1893 as a reaction against the practice of classification based on clinical description and tissue pathology. Kraepelin likewise rebelled against the traditional diagnostic methods, but he turned to prognostic classification criteria as more subject to empirical validation than etiological factors. Kraepelin's distinction between endogenous and psychogenic depressions was on the basis of emotional reactivity during the depression rather than on the presence or absence of an identifiable precipitant. Endogenous depressives were alleged to be nonreactive to external events or to the discussion of sensitive issues during the course of their illness; they might or might not have an identifiable precipitant; this was inconsequential. Psychogenic depressives, on the other hand, were reputed to be emotionally affected by concurrent events and issues. In the absence of identifiable genetic or constitutional anomalies which ostensibly underlie the predisposition to endogenous disorders, the term endogenous remains a hypothetical construct for depression. If the original etiological import of the term were adhered to, it could only be invoked by the elimination of all possible exogenous causes (organic or psychological). In order to make our ignorance of causation more explicit, some psychopathologists have preferred the terms cryptogenic or idiopathic to endogenous.

In several landmark studies which used a strictly clinical approach, Lewis (1934; 1936) investigated the reactivity aspects of hospitalized depressives at Maudsley Hospital. He concluded that it was impossible to distinguish validly among depressives on the basis of episodic precipitants, intercurrent reactivity, or outcome. Patients varied in reactivity during the course of their illness, outcomes were variable, and none of these factors seemed systematically related to any other. According to Lewis, the only valid distinctions among depressives consistent with available data are in terms of severity and chronicity (1938; 1971).

The interest of psychopathologists in the classification of depression waned until about 1960. Renewed interest was spurred by: new treatment developments (electroconvulsive therapy and antidepressant drugs) that were alleged to have differential effects on endogenous and reactive depressives; advances in neurochemistry, particularly with regard to relations between the catecholamines and the affective disorders; and the development of high speed computers which facilitated the use of multivariate statistical techniques, especially factor analysis. Good responders to electroconvulsive therapy as well as good responders to antidepressant drugs tend to have severely depressed moods, diurnal mood fluctuations, insomnia, retardation and/or agitation, and good premorbid and interepisodic social adjustment. Such clinical configurations are usually referred to as endogenous, despite the lack of consistent evidence for differences among depressives in regard to precipitants and etiology.

Contending Positions

Most of the endogenous-reactive (E-R) studies reviewed in the following sections are not, then, directly concerned with the etiology of either endogenous or reactive disorders, despite their use of these etiological terms. Rather, they are chiefly concerned with whether depression is unitary or binary, that is, a single syndrome or two syndromes (endogenous and reactive); and whether the syndrome or syndromes is/are categorical or dimensional, that is, whether they are discrete entities (categorical), or whether they are normally distributed and occur in varying combinations with each other or with other syndromes (dimensional). Eysenck (1970) has proposed this useful and illuminating conceptualization. The four possible positions, then, are: unitary and categorical, unitary and dimensional, binary and categorical, and binary and dimensional.

Eysenck contends that the factor analytic criteria for resolving the unitary versus binary issue are clear-cut, provided items which reflect endogenous and reactive variables are reliably rated on a representative sample of depressives. The unitarian position would predict the generation of a single, general factor with positive loadings only (if higher item ratings reflect greater depression), whereas the binary position would predict (in an unrotated solution) a general factor with positive loadings only, plus another bipolar factor which accounts for at least as much of the variance as the first factor. Items for one form of depression would load positively, and items for the other form would load negatively.

As for the categorical versus dimensional issue, Eysenck (1970) contends that factor analysis is not appropriate and its use involves

> a misunderstanding of the issues involved, and the logic of the statistical methods. . . . Kendell's compromise solution of a single continuum running from reactive to endogenous depression is shown to be inadequate statistically, and irrelevant psychologically [p. 249].

Eysenck views the empirical support for the binary position as very strong, at least within the clinical populations sampled. Efforts to resolve the categorical versus dimensional issue have largely rested on assigning factor scores to patients and examining their distribution along a single continuum, thus collapsing the two obtained dimensions (endogenous and reactive) into one. Binary-categorical advocates have predicted a bimodal distribution of factor scores, and unitary-dimensional advocates have predicted a normal distribution of factor scores (obtained results have usually accorded with the investigator's proclivities). Eysenck dismisses this approach as illogical. He argues that the endogenous and reactive poles must be treated as independent factors. Each case must be assigned an endogenous factor score and a reactive factor score, and these scores must be plotted in two-dimensional space, with one axis representing endogenous depression and the other reactive depression. Such an approach would more accurately reflect the relative independence of the two syndromes, as well as their tendency to shade into each other and to occur together in the same patient in varying degrees.

Some Methodological Problems in E-R Factor Analytic Studies

Eysenck (1970) astutely describes the formidable sampling problems in the identification of depressive subtypes thusly:

> . . . even more detrimental to any evidential value of such distributions is the unsolved problem of selection. Kendell used successive admissions, whereas the Newcastle workers seem to have selected (in part) purposely clear cases of either endogenous or reactive depression (at least what they say leaves this possibility open; their words are not entirely clear on this point). But even successive admissions are

biased by a great variety of factors which influence individual decisions by consultants involved in this procedure; admissions certainly do not represent fairly all applicants. And all applicants are not a proper sample of all persons who might be considered to be suffering from depression. Thus the final distribution of scores, along this meaningless continuum, will depend very strongly on selection procedures (the nature of which is largely unknown) used on samples themselves self-selected (or G.P. selected) on principles equally unknown, from a universe entirely unknown! It does not require much knowledge of statistics and sampling procedure to see that this method is unlikely to give us a population very representative of anything, other than itself [p. 246].

Eysenck is referring to the common practice among binary advocates of preselecting clear-cut cases of endogenous and reactive depression for their experimental samples. It would be quite surprising if factor analyses of ratings on such samples did not yield a bipolar factor. And furthermore, if such a factor were rotated to yield two independent factors from which factor scores were derived and plotted, it would not be surprising if the distributions clumped together in more categorical than dimensional form. However, as an initial tactic for identifying items that are likely to be discriminating with large unselected depressive samples from a variety of settings, the method has merit. Unfortunately investigators of depressive subtypes still tend to rely exclusively on cross-sectional rather than repeated measures and thus fail to take cognizance of Lewis' observation that the reactivity level of a depressive may fluctuate markedly within and among depressive episodes.

Several common problems in E-R factor analytic studies pertain to item specification and rater stereotypes. As Koch (1959) indicated, many variables in the psychological literature are really intervening variables. By the same token many items in the studies under consideration are so grossly specified as to encourage "halo" effects from rater stereotypes. The Costello & Belton (1970) review of observer based sleep studies of depressives provides ample support for this concern. As previously noted, Grinker et al. (1961) found that psychiatrists and residents achieve higher reliability on inferred "feelings and concerns" of depressed patients than on their overt behavior. The higher reliability of the former tends to be influenced by observer stereotypes. It is difficult to obtain clinically astute judges who are unaware of the implicit assumptions of the study. Ideally one would wish for highly objective, pertinent variables rated by clinically sophisticated judges who are naive about the objectives of the investigation. A partial solution is the use of patient self-ratings (Pilowski, Levine, & Boulton, 1969). The foregoing does not imply that investigators using multivariate methods have been unaware of these problems. On the contrary, virtually every difficulty cited is mentioned by at least one of them. Increased adequacy of design is clearly evident over time.

Before turning to the substantive E-R findings, a few elementary cautions about interpreting factor loadings may be helpful. A factor can be construed as a construct and the individual items on which the patient is rated as variables. The size and sign of the factor loading (+1 to −1) indicate how strongly and in what direction the variable is related to the factor. Note, however, that a low factor loading implies only that an item is not distinctively associated with a factor; such items may frequently accompany the symptom pattern. Conversely, a very high loading may denote an item which is distinctively but rarely associated with the factor.

Substantive E-R Findings

Mendels & Cochrane (1968) reviewed seven factor analytic studies of depression which used unrotated factors and identified one of such factors as endogenous depression. They caution that this factor may reflect a severity dimension. The reviewers reported eight items which had been used in at least four studies and which had always loaded positively and significantly on the endogenous factor. The eight items that loaded positively on endogenous depression were psychomotor retardation, nonreactivity to environment, loss of interest in environment, visceral symptoms, lack of a precipitating event, middle-of-the-night insomnia, and lack of self-pity. Other variables that clinicians commonly associate with endogenous depression and that also related positively to the endogenous factor, but not as strongly, were increased age, previous episodes, weight loss, early wakening, guilt feelings, lack of inadequate or hysterical premorbid personality, and suicidal tendencies. Somewhat surprisingly, diurnal mood variation (low in a.m., better in p.m.) and high familial incidence of affective disorder did not relate to endogenous depression. However, if all items that are used in at least two studies and that load significantly in at least one are examined, only 15% perfect agreement (i.e., the items always loading significantly and in the same direction) is obtained (Costello & Belton, 1970). In evaluating Costello & Belton's justifiable skepticism about E-R factor analytic studies, it must be borne in mind that most samples involve severe hospitalized depressives, whose constricted range of variability inevitably curtails the size of covariations obtained. Also, the social consequences of the disorder are likely to generate phenotypic similarities regardless of possible genotypic differences. For example, low energy and dysphoria probably diminish social interaction, constrict the range of interest, and foster self-preoccupation. Indeed, Kraines (1957) speculates that endogenous depressive episodes may generate reactive exacerbations. Important social losses may occur when significant others are frightened, discouraged, or repelled by the depressive illness. Some E-R dichotomous advocates ingeniously argue that, if anything, the interstudy variability indicates that raters are not unduly influenced by stereotypes (Kay, Garside, Beamish, & Roy, 1969).

Many of the factor analytic studies of depression have been unduly weighted with inpatients and have included relatively few items associated with reactive depression. An exception is one by Rosenthal & Gudeman (1967) done at Massachusetts Mental Health Center with 100 consecutively admitted depressed females: 50 inpatients and 50 outpatients. Patients were rated on a seven-point scale for 48 clinical items including signs and symptoms, premorbid personality traits, personal and clinical history. Rating reliability safeguards were somewhat better than in most studies. Interobserver agreement on 35 patients (r = .90 overall) was obtained with one observer unaware of the hypotheses. The first two factors extracted accounted for 20% of the matrix variance and corresponded to endogenous and reactive depression, respectively. Item loadings on these two factors for signs and symptoms are shown in Table 3. Note particularly items that load highly and in an opposite direction between Factors I (Endogenous) and II (Reactive). In contrast with the endogenous depressive pattern, the reactive pattern includes a positive tendency toward hypochondriasis, demanding and complaining behavior, self-pity and blaming the environment, hostility and irritability, reactivity; and a negative tendency toward psychomotor retardation, guilt and self-reproach, suicidal impulses, and feelings of worthlessness. In general, these item loadings correlate well with those previously reported by Rosenthal & Klerman (1966) and Hamilton & White (1959). The reactive pattern is associated with presence of precipitating factors (r = .31, p <.01) and unrelated to severity of the disorder, whereas the endogenous pattern is weakly but negatively related to precipitants (r = −.23), and positively related to severity. Rosenthal & Gudeman (1967) are commendably aware of possible biases in their data, and their clarity of presentation is exemplary. Their conclusions are quite compatible with Eysenck's:

> We feel that our results do not imply a division of the depressive population into two mutually exclusive patient groups which together encompass the entire depressive population. A patient's high factor score on one factor does not necessarily imply a low factor score on the other, and patients may exhibit blends of the two patterns. In our study, the patient distribution on each of the factors is essentially normal, and only the top 10–20 per cent of patients along each distribution curve have clinical pictures recognizably typical for the pattern. We feel therefore, that these factors describe patterns of reaction rather than patient groups [p. 489].

A recent study that incorporates some of Eysenck's criticisms and suggestions (Kiloh, Andrews, Neilson, & Bianchi, 1972) partly supported his binary-dimensional position. One hundred forty-five inpatients from a general hospital psychiatric unit in Sydney, Australia, were interviewed. Their responses to the same 35 items used in a previous study (Kiloh & Garside, 1963) were factor analyzed by the principal components method. Good replication with the earlier results were obtained. Rotation provided two factors which correspond to endogenous and neurotic depression. Factor scores were plotted on a bivariate surface with the two axes reflecting the two depressive dimensions. The scatter plot suggested that endogenous depression may be a categorical entity, since the factor scores of patients clinically diagnosed as endogenous depressives clustered around the endogenous axis. The factor scores of neurotic depressives approximated a normal distribution which is suggestive of a dimensional condition. The investigators speculate that primary neurotic depressives probably do not manifest endogenous symptoms, whereas endogenous

TABLE 3

Factor Loadings

Item	Factor I	Factor II
Hypochondriasis	.06	.63
Anxiety, psychic	.37	.54
Demanding and complaining behavior	-.01	.53
Self-pity and blaming the environment	-.31	.52
Anxiety, somatic	.23	.50
Hostility and irritability	-.04	.40
Fatigue	.39	.35
Weight loss	.25	.34
Insomnia, evening	.26	.31
Symptoms worse in the mornings	.12	.29
Reactivity of the depression	-.67	.26
Visceral symptoms	.53	.20
Muscular symptoms	.27	.18
Insomnia, morning	.42	.17
Loss of concentration	.55	.14
Loss of interest	.51	.09
Severity of depressed mood	.53	.09
Fluctuation	.29	.03
Agitation	.53	.00
Quality of the depression	.61	.00
Symptoms worse in the evenings	.31	-.03
Obsessive-compulsive symptoms	.41	-.04
Somatic delusions	.19	-.06
Genital symptoms (loss of libido)	.39	-.09
Insomnia, middle	.52	-.09
Paranoid symptoms	.04	-.19
Worthlessness	.61	-.20
Suicidal symptoms	.43	-.26
Guilt and self-reproach	.54	-.34
Retardation	.57	-.35

Source: Rosenthal and Gudeman (1967).

depressives may develop neurotic symptoms in response to their endogenous condition. The investigators (Kiloh et al., 1972) seem to prefer the term neurotic to reactive because they are characterizing a "diffuse entity" in which the clinical manifestations are highly colored by the patient's individual defenses against "his own neuroticism and concurrent environmental stress" [p. 194]. They view the restricted expression of endogenous depression as consistent with a genetic or biochemical etiology.

Predictive Validity of the E-R Factors

Attempts to predict treatment outcome from an endogenous-reactive classification have been moderately successful. However, few of these studies have used adequate double-blind safeguards. Usually the same investigators classify the patients, make the predictions, and evaluate the effectiveness of treatment (McConaghy, Joffe, & Murphy, 1967). Possibilities of unwitting rater bias are thus very high. The treatment effectiveness as well as the outcome ratings may be influenced by the raters' hypotheses. Evaluation of the effectiveness of predicting treatment response from an endogenous-reactive classification is complicated by the high proportion of depressives who improve without specific treatment. Lehmann (1968) asserts that about 25% of *hospitalized* depressives improve significantly within 3 weeks of admission without specific treatment of any kind; administration of a placebo drug increases the rate to nearly 50%. About 60-70% of unselected depressives respond favorably to antidepressant drugs, and 80% to electroconvulsive therapy. Not surprisingly Lehmann (1968) states,

> ...I am not yet convinced of the clinical significance of the many findings which have been reported supporting the choice of a particular antidepressant drug on the basis of existing symptoms, life history, personality structure, etiology of the depression, or other predictions [p. 18].

E-R and treatment. Binary advocates contend that endogenous depressives respond better to antidepressant drugs (monoamine oxidase inhibitors and tricyclic compounds) and electroconvulsive therapy (e.g., Carney, Roth, & Garside, 1965; Carney & Sheffield, 1972; Kay et al., 1969), whereas reactive depressives fare better with support, suggestion, psychotherapy, and psychic energizers. These findings are by no means uniform (Klerman, 1966). A recent controlled study, for example, reports that even nonclinically depressed college students with elevated depression scores on the MMPI respond favorably to a brief course of the tricyclic compound imipramine (DiMascio, Meyer, & Stifler, 1968).

E-R and precipitating events. Alleged differences between endogenous and reactive depressives with regard to environmental precipitants have also been challenged anew (Leff, Roatch, & Bunney, 1970; Paykel, Meyers, Dienelt, Klerman, Lindenthal, & Peffer, 1969). Essentially these studies have investigated three questions: do stressful events tend to precede the onset of depression; if so, do the stresses have any specific character; and can clinically diagnosed endogenous and reactive depressives be distinguished by amount and type of premorbid stress. Leff et al. (1970) criticize prior studies for relying on inevitably superficial information obtained during the early, acute phase of the depression. Subjects in Leff et al.'s study were 40 consecutive depressive admissions to an NIMH research ward. Criteria for admission were severe depression and the willingness of the patient's spouse or parent to be interviewed weekly. Patients were also interviewed weekly. Thirteen patients were diagnosed as endogenous and 27 as nonendogenous (note: not necessarily as reactive); the classification criteria were fairly explicit but no information on how the criteria were rated or on their reliability are presented. Nor are there data on when the classification decisions were made, or whether the decision makers were familiar with the hypotheses or findings. Two time points of interest prior to hospitalization were identified: the time when the patient began to function less well, and the time when he began to manifest signs or symptoms of depression. Again no reliability data on these determinations are given. The occurrence and timing of stressful events were derived from the observations of the total research team: psychiatrist, social worker, and nurse. Stressors selected for analysis were those which occurred most frequently during the year prior to the patient's diminished level of functioning. In order of decreasing frequency, these stresses included: threat to sexual identity or adequacy, changes in marital relations, geographical moves, compelled to face denied reality, physical illness, failure in job performance, failure of children to meet parents' goals, increased responsibility, damage to social status, and death of an important person. Leff et al. tried to avoid identifying events as stressors if much interpretation was required, but scrutiny of their list raises some doubt about their success in this worthy endeavor. Again, no reliability data are provided on the ascertainment of stressors.

Lest the writer seems unduly critical of this particular study, he should acknowledge that its findings accord well with his own preconceptions or biases. Unfortunately its methodological shortcomings are quite typical of those in the area. As a consequence, conflicting results that are subsequently presented allow little rational basis for deciding on the relative merits of the issues involved.

Leff et al. (1970) report a mean of four premorbid stressors per patient, with no quantitative difference between endogenous and nonendogenous depressives. Furthermore, the number of stressors was unrelated to severity of depression (hardly surprising in view of the constricted range of severity) or to treatment responsivity. Stressors tended to cluster in the month prior to the onset of the depressive episode, which tended to be gradual. Additional data were gathered on family background. An interesting lead was that 23 of 36 patients had early same-sex parental deprivation in the form of parental death, illness, absence, or gross inadequacy: 18 of the 28 patients who were rated as stressed by a threat to their sexual identity or by sexual inadequacy were parentally deprived. Again, how independently these determinations were made and, if the determinations are valid, how specific they are to depressives, is indeterminate. Leff et al. make some interesting speculations about why the spouses of their depressive sample were not also afflicted with depression, inasmuch as many shared the same stressors as the patient. They conjecture that many of the stressors were initiated by the nonafflicted spouses (e.g. proposed moves); they used denial and projection more effectively; they responded with anger rather than depression when their sexual adequacy was threatened; and only three of 16 spouses reported early same-sex parental deprivation. Some of the most interesting data provided in the Leff et al. paper are the six case histories of endogenous depressives. These cases seem clearly to meet the clinical criteria for endogenous depression specified by those who question the role of precipitants in endogenous depression (e.g. Hudgens, Morrison, & Barchha, 1967) and to provide a reasonable likelihood that distressing events did contribute significantly to the onset of the depressive episodes.

No attempt was made by Leff et al. to explain why the stress reaction was depressive in form. Numerous studies indicate that illness of many forms tends to be preceded by stress (Engel, 1962). Thus even if it can be unequivocally established that high stress precedes the onset of depression, this by no means precludes an interaction with other life history factors and/or a biological predisposition.

Using quite different patient samples and methods, Paykel et al. (1969) obtained results similar to those of Leff et al. They investigated life change events in 185 depressives and 185 matched controls using a modified Social Readjustment Rating Scale (Holmes & Rahe, 1967). Patients were a consecutive series of depressive admissions to a wide range of psychiatric settings in the New Haven area; they were interviewed only when much improved clinically. Controls were drawn from an epidemiological sample in the same geographic area and were matched for age, sex, marital status, race, and social class with the depressives. Life change events were rated for six months prior to onset of depression in patients and six months prior to interview in controls. As usual, no reliability data on anything are provided. Depressives who ranged in severity from mild to severe reported three times as many stressful life change events as controls ($\overline{X}$s 1.69 and .59, respectively). Eight stressful events were significantly more frequent in depressives: increased marital arguments, marital separation, new type work, changed work, serious illness, death of family member, serious illness of family member, family member leaves home ($p <.01$ for the first 3 items and $p <.05$ for the other 5); the similarity to Leff et al. (1970) is noteworthy. *Post hoc* categorizations of the data indicated that undesirable stresses in general and losses (e.g., death, separation, demotion, etc.) in particular best discriminated depressives from controls ($p <.01$). Paykel et al. contend that few of their depressives were endogenous. But Thomson & Hendrie (1972) used similar methods to Paykel et al. in a comparison of life change events in endogenous and reactive depressives prior to onset of their episodes and found no differences between them, although both groups had more change than a polyarthritic and normal control group.

Hudgens et al. (1967) contend that a loose analogy between the emotions of sadness and elation and between the affective disorders of depression and mania has led to the questionable assumption that both are influenced by life events. This assumption may operate as a self-confirming hypothesis. Hudgens et al. (1967) compared 40 hospitalized patients with primary affective disorders with 40 individually matched medical patients. Group matched variables were similar to those of Paykel et al. A standard interview supplemented by hospital records and collateral informants provided the data on life stresses during the age of risk for affective disorders and especially for the six months prior to onset of symptoms of the current illness. Once again, no reliability data are given. Hudgens et al. concluded that there was no overall difference in amount of premorbid stress between the groups, nor had unusual stress preceded prior episodes of affective illness. Even the 10 affective patients with considerable stress within the six months preceding their present episode had had periods of equivalent stress during the age of risk without incurring episodes of affective disorder. Loss situations in particular were studied, but no group differences were identified. Affective patients had more marital discord and frequent moves during the year prior to admission, but these factors were interpreted as effects of their illnesses. Certainly these investigators touch on a critically difficult issue: the determination of when stressful events are antecedent or consequent to early states of an affective disorder. While they do not classify their depressives as endogenous, they too explicitly challenge the validity of the distinction. The conclusions of these investigators (Hudgens et al., 1967) are a commendably modest and appropriate summary of the present state of knowledge in this domain:

> It would seem premature to state that a connection definitely does or does not exist between a presumed cause and an illness (depression) of whose essential nature we are ignorant [p. 145].

The minimum conclusion that can be drawn from these studies of precipitants and the onset of depression is that presence or absence of a precipitant is probably not a reliable discriminator between endogenous and reactive depression; Paykel et al. assert that both groups have them, and Hudgens et al. that neither have them. Grinker et al. (1961) examined precipitating events as a peripheral aspect of their study of patterns of depression in hospitalized depressives. These investigators, who might be characterized as very empirically and descriptively oriented, but nonetheless highly sophisticated psycho-dynamically, concluded that

> Although psychiatrists, especially those with psychoanalytic orientation, glibly pinpoint exact precipitating factors and formulate psychodynamics with great assurance, neither could be stated with confidence by the research group [p. 227].

However, they qualify this position to conform more closely with Leff et al. and Paykel et al. in nothing that, "We found almost invariably a series of events that led up to the clinical illness" [p. 236].

It is very easy to criticize the foregoing studies on precipitants by invoking such canons of scientific respectability as the desirability of explicit criteria and of independent, objective ratings by observers who are uninformed about the nature of the hypotheses. These are laudable goals and should be striven for to the greatest practicable extent. But consider the intrinsic difficulties in a fair assessment of Leff et al.'s contention that critically relevant information can only be elicited by detailed and prolonged inquiry inevitably guided by certain assumptions. Leff et al. and Paykel et al. generally reflect a psychodynamic, interpersonal orientation, and they find support for it; Hudgens et al. reflect a biogenetic orientation, and they find support for it. Perhaps a partial methodological solution is to have data gathered and rated by several observers whose orientations are predetermined and systematically varied, in order to examine their effects on information elicited and on ratings assigned to such information. The cost and effort of such ventures are not to be underestimated, yet they seem essential if inquiry is to yield reliable, valid, and significant findings.

E-R and psychophysiology. Numerous investigations have attempted to differentiate neurotic and psychotic depressives on the basis of such physiological aspects as sedation threshold (Shagass & Jones, 1958; Ackner & Pampiglione, 1959), fasting blood level of acetyl methyl carbinol (Anderson & Dawson, 1962), salivary rates (Strongin & Hinsie, 1939; Loew, 1965), crying (Davis, Lamberti & Ajans, 1969), cortical excitability (Shagass & Schwartz, 1962), and body build (Rees, 1960). All such measures were initially reported to differentiate the two groups, but subsequent independent studies usually failed to replicate the original findings or markedly attenuated their magnitude. As Beck noted (1967, p. 71), many of the reported differences between depressive subgroups are probably due to age disparities, since neurotics tend to be younger and psychotics older; these age differences inevitably affect many biological parameters. Also, many of these studies are confounded by the rater's awareness of the diagnosis and hypothesis. Whether reanalysis of these data in terms of E-R and with scores adjusted for age would alter the findings is uncertain. There appears to be considerable overlap in the usage of neurotic and reactive and of psychotic and endogenous, but the pairings are not synonymous.

E-R summary. While some (the "Newcastle" group) argue that the E-R data support a dichotomous distinction (e.g. Carney, Roth & Garside, 1965), others are more cautiously reserved (Mendels & Cochrane, 1968), while still others are frankly skeptical (Kendell, 1968; Kendell & Gourlay, 1970; McConaghy, Joffe, & Murphy, 1967; Stern, McClure, & Costello, 1970). There seems to be an emerging consensus that endogenous and reactive depressives represent distinguishable patterns of disorder. Although most depressives show an admixture of the two patterns, it is nonetheless possible to diagnose reliably a fairly high proportion of depressives as predominantly endogenous or reactive and to make useful treatment predictions on that basis (Carney & Sheffield, 1972; Kay, Garside, Beamish, & Roy, 1969; Rosenthal & Klerman, 1966; Rosenthal & Gudeman, 1967). It appears that high priority should be given to replacement of the E-R terms by etiologically neutral ones, and more importantly, that Eysenck's suggested use of independent endogenous and reactive ratings should be used in further tests of their construct and predictive validity.

OTHER APPROACHES TO IDENTIFYING
DEPRESSIVE SUBTYPES

Treatment Derived Subtypes

One group of investigators has focused on the interaction of hospitalized depressive subtypes and response to drug or pharmacotherapy. Overall and his associates devised the Brief Psychiatric Rating Scale (BPRS), composed of 16 depressive symptoms commonly used to differentiate among depressives. A powered vector analysis of the scale yields a profile of three depressive subtypes designated as anxious depression, hostile depression, and retarded depression. Results of a typical study are presented in Table 4 (Overall, Hollister, Johnson, & Pennington, 1966). Subjects were 77 male depressives in seven Veterans' Administration Hospitals. The two drugs compared in a double-blind study were an antidepressant tricyclic compound, imipramine (Tofranil), and an antipsychotic phenothiazine, thioridazine (Mellaril). Scores in the table reflect mean changes obtained by subtracting posttreatment BPRS scores from pretreatment scores. Note the lack of overall (or main) effect for response to drug treatment. However, when the response of particular groups to particular drugs is examined (interaction effects), significant differences appear. Imipramine is more effective for retarded depressives and thioridazine for anxious depressives; they do not differ in effectiveness for hostile depressives. However, Hollister, Overall, Johnson, Shelton, Kimbell, & Brunse (1966) note that

> A significant degree of spontaneous improvement in depressed patients was evident in that one-half the potential sample of patients was lost because of clinical improvement after one week of placebo medication (atropine) prior to being placed into the study [p. 468].

Lest psychogenetically biased readers take undue comfort, Klerman & Cole (1965) suggest that atropine may not be a desirable placebo for comparison with

TABLE 4
Mean Improvement in Depressive Mood
for Patients Classified into
Three Depressive Profile Categories

Depressive subtype	Drug therapy	
	Imipramine	Thioridazine
Anxious	3.6	5.2
Hostile	4.0	3.7
Retarded	3.8	1.5

Source: Overall, Hollister, Johnson, & Pennington (1966).

antidepressant drugs, because it shares many of their physiological main and side effects, at least in animal studies [pp. 118-119]. To further confound generalizations, whereas Hollister et al. produce reasonably consistent findings, these findings were quite unsupported by Raskin, Schulterbrandt, Reatig, & McKeon's results, (1970).

The largest drug study with depressives to date was done by the Collaborative Depression Study Group under the aegis of NIMH's Psychopharmacology Research Branch (Raskin et al., 1970). This study has many of the methodological flaws ably summarized by Costello & Belton (1970), plus a tremendous attrition rate of 60%; nonetheless the large number of treatment settings, patients, diagnostic subtypes, and measurements is a partly redeeming feature. Patients were randomly assigned to chlorpromazine, imipramine, and placebo groups at 10 hospitals of various kinds. Raskin et al. reported imipramine to be somewhat more effective with retarded depressives as long as it was administered, but one week after its discontinuance its effects were much inferior to placebo and two weeks afterward its effects were no different from placebo or chlorpromazine, an antipsychotic phenothiazine. Contrary to Overall et al., Raskin et al. found imipramine to be more effective than placebo or chlorpromazine for anxious depressives during and after the medication phase of treatment. Hostile depressives did best on placebo during "medication," but after its withdrawal those who had been on imipramine did best. However, the large number of subjects, 555, made even small consistent differences statistically though not necessarily clinically significant. Thus at best, only 10% of the variance in treatment outcome could be associated with a particular drug. A combined predictor of drug, diagnosis, overall subtypes (anxious, hostile, retarded), age, sex, and pretreatment symptom score would probably account for no more than 50% of the variance among the criterion scores. The investigators conjecture that additional measures of premorbid competence (Garmezy, 1965) and of social and psychiatric history (Roff & Ricks, 1970) might have improved the prediction of which drugs are most suitable for which patients. It should be noted that patients were not explicitly classified as endogenous and reactive, but rather as psychotic and neurotic. Conceivably dimensional ratings on endogenous-reactive classification factors might have yielded a stronger relation between subgroup, drug treatment, and outcome.

Polydimensional Classifications of Affective Disorders

As indicated before, empirical classifications of depression are multiple. The polydimensional or multifactorial orientation has become increasingly common (Paykel, 1972). These classification attempts are not widely sampled because their potential fruitfulness is still unclear. Some of the thorny methodological problems in validating such typologies are ably discussed and demonstrated by Fleiss, Lawlor, Platman, & Fieve (1971). For example, none would dispute that confidence in the reliability and validity of a typology is increased when the typology is replicated with additional subject samples and with additional variables. Evidence that the several groups have a differential treatment response is also regarded as supportive. But additional variables for validation purposes are rarely sought that are statistically independent of those used in the original cluster analysis. More concretely, if one group is characterized by psychoticism and cross-validation is with other measures of psychoticism, all that may be demonstrated is a correlation between measures of psychoticism. By the same token, if one group is characterized by acute insomnia and one of the treatments happens to be a sedative, this group will probably show considerably diminished insomnia. Improvement on a specific symptom may provide some incremental support for the validity of a type but is not definitive evidence for an entity or subtype. Fleiss et al. also have sensible suggestions for visual inspection of the distribution of factor scores before a numerical typological analysis is conducted. Multimodal and asymmetric distributions increase the likelihood that subtypes generated are nonartifactual.

Grinker et al. (1961) factor analyzed staff ratings of 96 hospitalized depressives and 10 nondepressed psychiatric controls. Feelings and concerns and behavior of patients were rated and analyzed separately and then intercorrelated. Valid questions have been raised about the orthodoxy of aspects of the analysis (Wittenborn, 1965), such as the small number of subjects relative to the number of items rated, dichotomous ratings, and high factor intercorrelations. Nevertheless, the partly replicated results (Friedman, Cowitz, Cohen, & Granick, 1963) of this landmark study are well worth considering. In an unusual analysis, factor scores derived from the factor analysis of the patient's feelings and concerns and the patient's behavior were factor analyzed to yield factor patterns of depression. These patterns are described as follows:

Factor Pattern A

On feelings and concerns these persons are above the average of all patients in Factors I, III, and IV. They are dismal and hopeless, with loss of self-esteem, and to some degree feel guilty. Their behavior is withdrawn, isolated, and apathetic; speech and thinking are slowed; there are evidences of cognitive disturbances. However, they are *not* hypochondriacal, anxious, clinging, and love-seeking, nor do they have many somatic symptoms.

These traits describe a person who is moderately sick and close to the common stereotype of depression. The absence of large amounts of gloomy affect and the apathy, uncomplaining attitude without efforts at projection, attempts at restitution, or clinging demands for love give the appearance of an 'empty' person who has 'given up.' Yet the moderate degree of hopelessness in spite of the withdrawal and apathy does not suggest the so-called psychotic depression.

Such a profile recalls from empirical experience a premorbid compulsive personality precipitated into a depression by internal changes or by aging and the attendant external alterations of sexual, familial, and economic roles, hence occurring in middle life. These patients respond poorly to psychotherapy and usually receive electric shock therapy or other somatotherapy. They have a tendency to relapse and usually have several hospital admissions during their lifetimes.

Factor Pattern B

Patients in this pattern have high loadings on feelings and concerns factors indicating dismal, hopeless attitudes and low self-esteem, considerable guilt feelings and almost as much anxiety as possible, but little more than average use of an external event as a focus of blame and for feelings of being rejected. In current behavior two factors dominate: agitation and clinging demands for attention. There are lower than average loadings on all other behavioral characteristics such as slowed speech, impaired thinking, hypochondriasis, and psychosomatic symptoms.

This pattern suggests a fairly well-integrated premorbid personality whose equilibrium has been broken by some external event which cued off a mobilization of repressed aggression. The resulting guilt feelings and self-punishment mobilize attempts at restitution to make up for wrongs done, rationalized by recall of many past incidents. At the same time there is considerable pleading for help and affection. The projective mechanism of blaming others is only slightly used.

Patients within this pattern are helped by support and kindness although they temporarily feel better after externally furnished punishment. In the height of their agitation they are sleepless, anorexic, and suicidal. Their clinging demands lead their families to institute early hospitalization. Such patients complain bitterly, demand drugs insatiably, and are benefited by tranquilizers. Some can endure the anxiety signalling eruption of repressed hostile feelings and do well in psychotherapy.

Factor Pattern C

These patients do not exceed the average scores on the feelings and concerns trait list except for Factor V indicating a feeling of not being loved. Thus they have less than average depressed affect, guilt, or anxiety. In current behavior they are outstanding in their agitated, demanding, hypochondriac complaints, associated also with psychosomatic symptoms. Cognitive functions seem disturbed.

The striking aspect of this pattern is the low loading on dismal and hopeless affect in contrast to the active irrational complaining attitudes. This is the picture of the hypochondriac, where attention is diverted to his own body although seemingly rationalized by some observable somatic manifestations.

Herein lies the difficult differential diagnosis from complainers who are somehow aware of an inner destructive process in spite of negative medical examinations. Many of these 'know' of their illness before it is discovered, too late. In general patients with the hypochondriacal syndrome have been seriously disturbed all their lives, often with a variety of 'borderline' symptoms or with some schizoid features. They are precipitated into depression by actual external losses or by approaching aging. They seem to benefit, but only temporarily, by support, reassurance, and drugs. Electric shock treatment often worsens the condition. In rare cases prolonged psychotherapy is helpful.

Factor Pattern D

This pattern is characterized by high loadings on feelings and concerns traits of gloom, hopelessness, and anxiety with some guilt feelings; but these patients do not cling or demand attention. They thus resemble the B factor pattern. But they are distinguished by current behavior characteristics most of which are low, except for Factor 4 describing demanding provocative behavior. These patients are not withdrawn, continually seeking affection, hypochondriacal, nor do they have somatic symptoms. They are the 'angry depressives' whose behavior does not suggest an etiologic component of 'repressed aggression.'

The premorbid personalities of these patients are typically narcissistic and overaggressive. They 'rule the roost' at home, in business, or in their social settings. Precipitated by frustration or inability to continue this pattern for external reasons they become depressed and attempt to influence the environment through their illness. Suicidal thoughts are frequent and serious. They are difficult management problems for hospital personnel and treatment is fraught with dangers and disappointments. The former constitutes the eruption of rage expressed by suicide. The disappointment is inherent in the never-ending compulsion to be on top or to be the best, which interferes with psychotherapy [pp. 219–221].

Factors derived from the feelings and concerns ratings and the behavioral ratings, as well as their loadings on the depressive patterns, are shown in Table 5. Note that nothing corresponding to an endogenous-reactive dimension emerges from any of the analyses. Data were also obtained on the usual demographic data, premorbid personality, and precipitants. These related somewhat to behavior ratings in males especially, but were generally nondiscriminating. In addition to rating the patients, staff did Q-sorts on the items to identify their own stereotype of a typical depressive. These staff Q-sorts correlated highly only with Factor A of the factors derived from staff ratings of patients. A prime instigator to the Grinker et al. study

TABLE 5

Average Scores on 10 Current Behavior and 5 Feelings and Concerns
Factors for Each of 4 Factor Patterns and for All Patients

Factor	Average score				
	Factor pattern				All patients
	A	B	C	D	
Current behavior					
1 Isolated and withdrawn	.76[a]	.25	.54	.07	.45
2 Speech and thought slowed	.67[a]	.13	.38	.13	.36
3 Apathetic	.95[a]	.65	.71	.35	.76
4 Demanding and provocative	.32	.03	.51[a]	.61[a]	.21
5 Hypochondriac	.16	.18	.69[a]	.04	.20
6 Cognitive disturbances	.56[a]	.15	.59[a]	.09	.30
7 Agitation	.39	.70[a]	.90[a]	.46	.53
8 Thought confusion	.40	.13	.49[a]	.10	.16
9 Psychosomatic symptoms	.14	.13	.49[a]	.10	.16
10 Clinging, demanding	.02	.86[a]	.36	.00	.41
Feelings and Concerns					
I Dismal, hopeless, "bad"	.58[a]	.66[a]	.38	.66[a]	.49
II Projection to external events	.24	.42	.35	.42	.32
III Guilty feelings	.43[a]	.62[a]	.26	.49[a]	.36
IV Anxiety	.69[a]	.94[a]	.58	.92[a]	.65
V Clinging appeals for love	.36	.36	.48[a]	.32	.38

[a]Loadings of factors characteristic of pattern.
Source: Grinker, Miller, Sabshin, Nunn, & Nunnally (1961).

was their conviction that clinicians' conceptions of depressives are strongly stereotyped by classical clinical descriptions and orthodox psychoanalytic formulations. Their findings supported this assumption. If anything, increased experience was related to increased stereotyping, although this was confounded by deficiencies in hospital records. Residents and ward personnel especially rate patient behavior more reliably than staff.

The factors from the "Feelings and Concerns" ratings were interpreted as follows: the first factor reflects the essence of depression; the second a projective defense against it; the third a resolve to make restitution; the fourth reflects anxiety; and the fifth an attempt to emotionally bind others, deny anger, and recoup love.

The behavior factors were less clear-cut than the Feelings and Concerns, which Grinker et al. attribute to a training bias to infer and interpret rather than to observe and describe.

With regard to the factor patterns, most depressives exhibit aspects of all four, but a sizable number clearly fit either Pattern A or a combination of A and B. None were pure instances of C or D. The hope is that these patterns can be related to epidemiologic, psychodynamic, personality, biological, and clinical findings.

Friedman et al.'s factor analytic study (1963) showed an unusual regard for explicit diagnostic criteria and rater reliability checks. Since the patterns identified closely parallel those of Grinker et al., they will not be discussed except for several interesting peripheral aspects. No depressives below the mid 30's met Friedman et al.'s criteria for psychotic depression. This finding led the investigators to speculate that psychotic depression may be related to aging effects on metabolic processes that interact with psychological factors. Also, a high proportion of depressives loading heavily on their Pattern D—demanding and complaining—were Jewish females, a finding supported by an additional investigation at Hillside Hospital, New York. Pattern D patients reported an unusually high incidence of fathers and brothers lost through death and separation. They seem exceptionally vulnerable to separation anxiety, possibly due to a combination of object loss and symbiotic ties with extremely self-centered, exploitive mothers.

Lorr (1969) bases his integrative summary of factor analytic studies of depression on eight independently conducted studies using a variety of interviews, ward observation, and patient self-report techniques. Six syndromes are essentially replicated in at least three studies. These factors are listed in decreasing order of strength of evidence for their validity in Table 6. In reviewing studies that purport to identify an endogenous-reactive dimension, Lorr argues that all report a general unrotated factor and a second bipolar unrotated factor equated with the endogenous-reactive dichotomy. This second factor, he contends, is an artifact of the method used for extracting principal components. If the two factors were rotated relative to each other, variables loading positively on both unrotated factors

TABLE 6

Studies Identifying the Depressive Syndromes

Syndrome	Authors							
	[a]F	G	H	L	O	P	R	W
Anxious self-blame	X	X	X	X	X	X	X	X
Functional impairment	X			X	X	X	X	X
Retardation		X	X	X	X		X	
Depressive mood		X	X	X	X	X		
Somatic disturbance	X	X		X	X	X		X
Somatic preoccupation		X	X		X		X	

[a]Friedman, Grinker, Hunt, Lorr, Overall, Pichot, Raskin, & Weckowicz.
Source: Lorr (1969).

would load on the first rotated factor, and variables loading positively on one unrotated factor and negatively on the other would load on the second rotated factor. The first rotated factor would reflect psychotic depression and the second an independent neurotic factor. The first five syndromes in Table 6 are intercorrelated in decreasing or "hierarchical order," indicating an underlying general factor, psychotic depression, as shown in Figure 1 (Lorr, Sonn, & Katz, 1967). The paucity of neurotic depressive factors may be due to the underrepresentation of milder depressives in many studies; many use only hospitalized depressives. Lorr views this speculative but

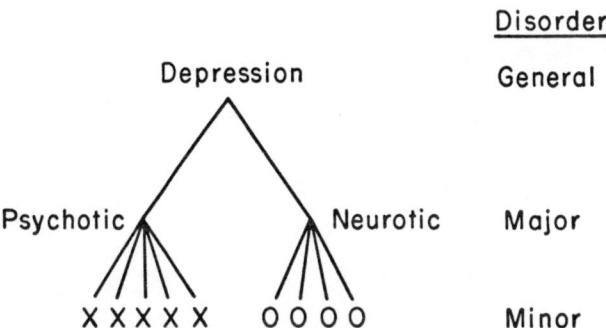

FIG. 1. Hierarchical conception of depression. (*Lorr, M. The depressive syndromes and the endogenous vs. reactive dichotomy: An integration. Paper delivered at the American Psychological Association Meetings, 1969. Available from the author at Catholic University of America.*)

appealing synthesis as analogous to the issue of how intelligence is structured. In the latter case, most psychologists accept the utility of a hierarchical model including a general, group, and specific factors. Lorr's position seems to provide a challenging alternative to Eysenck's as a possible means of reconciling the dichotomous and unitary viewpoints.

4
EPIDEMIOLOGY[6]

A loose and insincere use of language leads not only to intellectual confusion but to the shirking of vital issues or the acceptance of specious formulae. Words were never a more common means than they are today of concealing ignorance and persuading even ourselves that we possess opinions when we are merely vibrating with verbal reverberations (Ogden & Richards, 1930).

DEFINITION AND OBJECTIVES
OF EPIDEMIOLOGY

Epidemiology is concerned with the frequency and distribution of disorders in relation to the physical, biological, and social characteristics of the environment and host. Its objectives are: (a) to clarify etiological factors; (b) to facilitate the development and assessment of preventive measures; and (c) to determine the availability, utilization, and effectiveness of methods and facilities used for treatment and remediation. Morbidity (frequency rates) and mortality (death rate) are assessed in relation to ecological and demographical variables such as geographic locus, climate, season, rural-urban residence, migratory rates, race, ethnicity, socioeconomic class, religion, age, sex, and marital status. Epidemiological methods have made noteworthy contributions to the amelioration of health problems such as pellagra, lung cancer, and cholera (Gruenberg, 1965). Unfortunately, epidemiological studies of personality disturbances have been less fruitful. Opler (1967), a distinguished investigator in this area, terms incidence and prevalence studies thus far as "useless" for

[6] For a comprehensive review of epidemiological studies of depression, see Silverman (1968).

etiological purposes [p. 265]. Opler's position may be pessimistic, but it is certainly tenable.

DIAGNOSTIC UNRELIABILITY REVISITED

Accurate case identification is patently critical in epidemiological studies. Perhaps the most basic problem in epidemiological studies of depression is the lack of consensus on reliable, objective case criteria. Psychiatric classification is still largely based on ostensive rather than operational definition. Illustrative cases are described rather than objective, empirically substantiated indices of theoretical states specified. The problem of poorly specified diagnostic criteria is inevitably compounded by inter- and intra-observer inconsistency. Observers differ in training, personal biases, and acumen. Their judgments may vary as a function of the age and sex of the interviewee; the site of the interview (clinic or home); the time of day, week or year; the effects (favorable or otherwise) of experience; and concern for the patient's welfare (Gruenberg, 1965; Hempel, 1961).

For example, a recent study was conducted on diagnostic consistency within Monroe County, New York (Babigian, Gardner, Miles, & Romano, 1965). Subjects were patients who were initially diagnosed as having an affective disorder, and who had then been transferred to the care of another service or practitioner. Initial and subsequent diagnostic agreement was only 46%. Private practitioners significantly underdiagnosed psychotic states, probably because of the social stigma.

Mediocre diagnostic reliability for depression may be partly due to its changing form of expression. Grinker et al. (1961) contend that current textbook descriptions differ little from the classical ones of Kraepelin and Bleuler. Numerous clinical reports of altered expression led to a systematic comparison of the symptoms and complaints of contemporary depressives with classical descriptions (Harrow, Colbert, Detre, & Bakeman, 1966). Harrow et al. interviewed and rated state hospitalized female depressives and schizophrenics on several scales that assess classical depressive phenomena. While the direction of the results generally affirmed classical descriptions, there were notable exceptions. Current depressives expressed little guilt (e.g., that they deserved to be punished for moral transgressions) in absolute magnitude or relative to schizophrenics. Neither did depressives view themselves as inadequate or evil persons prior to the onset of depression. Furthermore, they were not pessimistic about the outcome of their difficulties, although they voiced much despair and hopelessness about their present state. They complained of gross insufficiency, but attributed this to their depressive affliction rather than to their personal shortcomings. Classical descriptions, of course, stress the depressive's sense of worthlessness, futility about the future, and feeling of receiving his just deserts. The investigators were well aware of possible alternative explanations for their findings. For example, in order to control for the typical age differences between depressives and schizophrenics, they selected atypically younger depressives and older schizophrenics. The difference between obtained and expected results may also be due to a lowered threshold for severity of disturbance that leads to hospitalization. Present urban environments probably allow for less deviance than before, and mental hospitals may no longer be as stigmatized. Furthermore, patient management both prior to hospital admission and during its initial stages is probably more effective in affording symptomatic relief. Harrow et al. (1966) noted a marked improvement in most depressive symptoms during the first week of hospitalization. Most classical cases described in the literature were seen in other national environments, were hospitalized in private institutions, and may well have exemplified depression in its severest form.

While it is extremely important to be aware of the shortcomings in extant data, formulations must proceed with what is available. If independently conducted studies have unknown or mediocre diagnostic reliability and methodological flaws of various types, but yield convergent results, it is senseless to dismiss them out-of-hand. Such results at least suggest promising leads for more rigorous investigation.

Sandifer (1972) strikes an unusually optimistic note on prospects for the reduction of diagnostic unreliability. He presents pilot results which indicate that crosscultural agreement on diagnostic stereotypes is quite good, as well as ratings on the presence and severity of particular symptoms. Disagreements occur chiefly when classification requires a judgment on the relative weight that should be assigned to symptoms. Thus a patient who is alcoholic, depressed, and anxious might be variously diagnosed as an alcoholic, depressive, or anxiety state, depending on the contingent relations ascribed by the rater. Sandifer reports that agreement on the rank order of importance of symptoms is highly correlated with agreement on diagnostic labeling when the latter is assessed by a deviance scale which he has devised. In short, absolute agreement on diagnostic categories may leave much to be desired, but sources of disagreement are at least susceptible to investigation.

DIFFERENCES IN INCIDENCE AND PREVALENCE BETWEEN THE UNITED STATES AND UNITED KINGDOM

Kramer (1965, 1969) presents some intriguing comparisons of first admission rates to mental hospitals for the United States versus England and Wales. Data are presented for overall admissions and for specific diagnoses by age and sex over two time spans. Overall admission rates are quite similar between the several countries (1965, p. 108), even by sexes, except when analyzed by specific diagnosis as shown in Figure 2. Three marked divergences are apparent. The

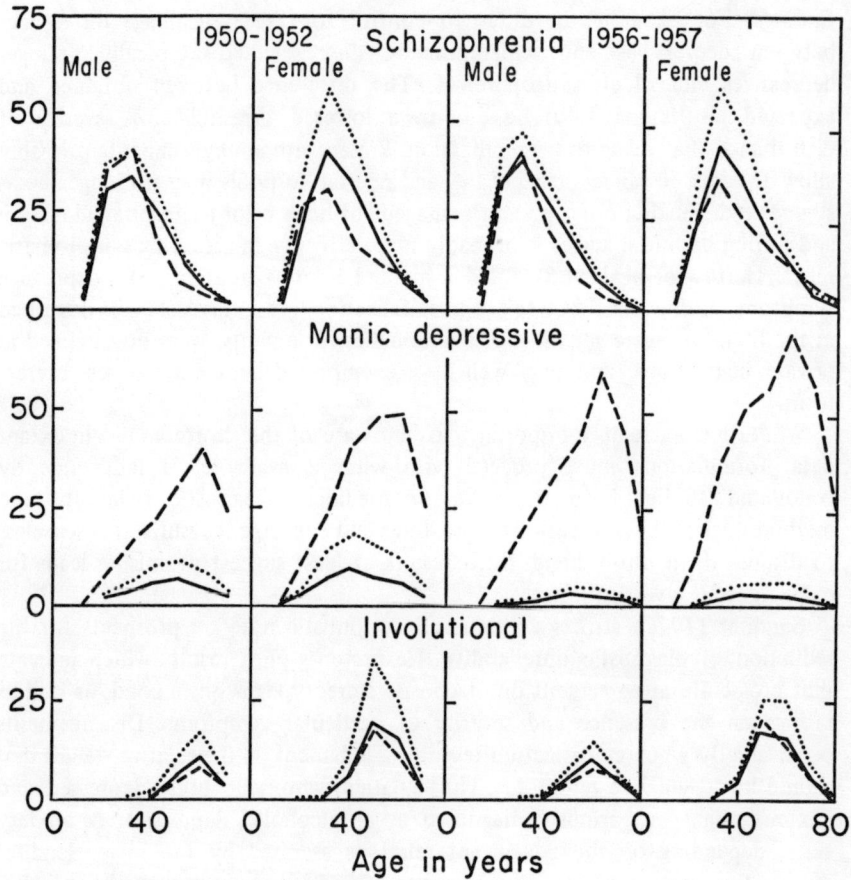

FIG. 2. Age-sex-specific first admission rates per 100,000 population to public mental hospitals in the United States (1950, 1957) and in England and Wales (1952, 1956), and public and private mental hospitals combined in the United States (1950, 1957): functional psychoses. [*Kramer, M. Classification of mental disorders for epidemiologic and medical care purposes: Current status, problems and needs. In M. M. Katz, J. O. Cole, W. E. Barton (Eds.) The role and methodology of classification in psychiatry and psychopathology. Washington, D.C. Public Health Service Publication No. 1584, U.S. Government Printing Office, 1965, Pp. 99–116.*]

English and Welsh manic-depressive first admission rate is 18 times that of U.S. public hospitals, or 9 times combined U.S. public and private hospital rates. British manic-depressive admissions peak at a later age (55-64) than U.S. admissions, and the British rate of admissions is continuing to climb (from 1950–52 to 1956–57), whereas the U.S. rate is declining.

In order to ascertain the sources of these diagnostic disparities between the United States and the United Kingdom a joint research project was initiated between Maudsley Hospital in London and the Biometric Research Unit in New York (Zubin & Fleiss, 1971). A structured interview was administered to 250 consecutive hospital admissions in New York and a like number in London. Project interviewers were systematically trained to rate 700 items, and unusually high reliability was established. Diagnosis of the New York patient sample by indigenous (nonproject) American psychiatrists indicated that schizophrenia was 3½ times more prevalent than affective disorders, whereas diagnosis of the London sample by indigenous British psychiatrists indicated that affective disorders were only ¾ as prevalent as schizophrenia. Rediagnosis by the project psychiatrists using the structured interview strikingly reduced the disparity in prevalence between the two samples. They found that schizophrenia was 80% as prevalent as affective disorder in the New York sample and 40% as prevalent in the London sample. Even this disparity is sizable, and its source is undetermined. Project psychiatrists identified subgroups of patients in each sample who had virtually nothing other than marked depressive symptoms. Of these clear-cut depressives only 20% of the New York sample were correctly diagnosed by nonproject American psychiatrists, although 50% received antidepressant treatment; whereas 60% of the London sample were correctly diagnosed by British psychiatrists and 84% were receiving antidepressant treatment (Gurland et al., 1972). Diagnostic classification based on the systematic structured interview showed good concurrent validity with British psychiatrists' diagnoses and good predictive validity for length of hospitalization.

TEMPORAL TRENDS IN INCIDENCE AND PREVALENCE: IS DEPRESSION DIMINISHING IN WESTERN SOCIETIES?

There is a widespread impression that the incidence of severe depressive states in the United States has decreased in recent decades, whereas the incidence of schizophrenia has increased. Incidence refers to the rate of new cases occurring in a specified population during a specified time period. The data in Table 7, which presents first admission rates to public mental hospitals in the United States for the preceding three decades, support the contention of diminished incidence. Several aspects of this table require further explanation. The term "age adjusted" refers to the population at risk for a particular disorder. For example, if the incidence of psychotic depression is compared in two communities whose populations differ in age distribution, while the occurrence of such depressions is relatively age-specific, the incidence rates must be corrected for the population differences within the age-at-risk. Note that the data in Table 7 do not purport to reflect the "true" incidence of these disorders within the population. True incidence rates would require community surveys. Many psychotic depressives are untreated or treated in settings other than public

TABLE 7

Age-Adjusted[a] First Admission Rates and Percent Change to Public Mental
Hospitals 1940, 1950, and 1960 for Selected Diagnoses

Diagnosis	Rates per 100,000			Percent change		
	1940	1950	1960	1940–50	1950–60	1940–60
All mental disorders	90.2	94.6	101.3	4.9	7.1	12.3
Brain syndromes	42.3	38.8	25.4	-8.3	-34.5	-40.0
Diseases of the senium	22.0	24.5	19.0	11.4	-22.5	-13.6
Syphilitic	7.6	3.2	.6	-57.9	-81.3	-92.1
Other (excluding alcoholics)	12.7	11.1	5.8	-12.6	-47.8	-54.3
Functional psychoses	30.0	32.6	33.7	8.7	3.4	12.3
Schizophrenics	17.2	22.0	25.3	27.9	15.0	47.1
Affective (including involutionals)	11.2	9.5	7.4	-15.2	-22.1	-33.9
Other	1.6	1.0	1.0	-37.5	0	-37.5
Disorders associated with alcoholism	9.3	11.4	15.0	22.6	31.6	61.3
Brain syndromes	4.8	4.2	5.4	-12.5	28.6	12.5
Addiction	4.5	7.2	9.6	60.0	33.3	113.3
Psychoneurosis	2.9	4.7	7.7	62.1	63.8	165.5
Personality disorders	1.8	2.8	10.5	55.6	275.0	483.3
Mental deficiency	1.4	1.2	3.1	-14.3	158.3	121.4
All other	2.5	3.1	5.8	24.0	87.1	132.0

[a]U.S. 1950 civilian population 10 years of age and over was used as a standard.

Source: U.S. Department of Health, Education, and Welfare, PHS, NIMH; "Patients in
Mental Institutions, Part II, 1940, 1950, 1960"; "State and County Mental Hospitals."

Prepared by: Hospital Studies Section, Biometrics Branch, National Institute of Mental
Health, October 1964.

Source: Katz et al. (1965).

mental hospitals. With increased societal affluence, the proportion of depressives seen in private mental hospitals, general hospitals, outpatient clinics, and in private practice may well have increased substantially. Thus, whether the 34% decline in affective psychoses from 1940 to 1960 is genuine or simply reflects changing diagnostic patterns and reporting systems is unclear.

Arieti (1959) attributes the reputed decline in affective psychoses in the United States and Western Europe to a shift from an inner-directed to an other-directed cultural orientation (Riesman, 1950). Becker, Spielberger, & Parker (1962) have noted striking similarities in the central conflicts ascribed to cultures in transition from inner- to other-directedness and those ascribed to manic-depressives by socioculturally oriented psychiatrists (Cohen, Baker, Cohen, Fromm-Reichmann, & Weigert, 1954). Arieti was considerably influenced by Eaton & Weil's (1955) study of Hutterite communities in the United States. They reported an extremely high prevalence rate for manic-depressive psychoses among the atypically inner-directed Hutterites. However, Eaton and Weil neglected to allow for the unusually large proportion of elderly persons (i.e., persons-at-high-risk) within the Hutterite communities (Kramer, 1957).

It is difficult to reconcile Arieti's contention of a diminished incidence of depression in Western societies with English data which demonstrate a 75% rise in first hospital admissions of depressives from 1952 to 1960 (Lehmann, 1971). There was no change in the admission rate for schizophrenics during that period.

Regardless of temporal trends, the enormity of the public health problem posed by depression is amply reflected in the following sophisticated estimates by Lehmann. He estimates the prevalence rate of clinical depression in Western society at about 3-4%. Approximately 1 in 5 of these are treated professionally, 1 in 50 are hospitalized, and 1 in 200 commit suicide. The lifetime expectancy rate is estimated at 10%, which is 10 times greater than for schizophrenia. The prevalence rate for hospitalized schizophrenics is always greater, because schizophrenia is a more chronic disorder. Even so about 10% of manic-depressives spend more than 4 years in hospitals. The death rate from all causes for female depressives is twice, and for males triple, the normal rate. The difference in suicide rates is even more impressive. Pokorny (1964) reported a depressive suicide rate 25 times greater than the expected level among male Texans, and Temoche, Pugh, & MacMahon (1964) reported a rate 36 times the expected level in Massachusetts. The suicide rate for depressive disorders exceeds that of any other disorder. Manic-depressives seem to have an extraordinarily high suicide rate, estimated as high as 14% in contrast with .01% for the general population in the United States (Robins, Murphy, Wilkinson, Gassner, & Kayes, 1959). At present these data serve little more than to confirm the magnitude of depression as a public health problem.

CONVERGENT EPIDEMIOLOGICAL FINDINGS

Three reasonably consistent epidemiological findings on depressives have emerged, although not without challenge. First, the incidence of depression tends to be much higher among females than among males (Sorensen & Stromgren, 1961; Taylor & Chave, 1964). Second, the age, sex, marital status, and socioeconomic distribution and prognosis of depressives differs from schizophrenics; depressives tend to be older at onset, to be more frequently female, married, and higher ranking and more heterogeneous socioeconomically (Munro, 1966), and to have a more favorable prognosis (Silverman, 1968). Third, if suicide is viewed as the mortality (death) rate for depression, then depression is among the leading causes of death in the United States; among all forms of personality disturbance, only alcoholics have a comparable mortality rate (Silverman, 1968). For reasons that are largely obscure at present, suicide in Western cultures, at least, is more frequent during spring and in white, Protestant males (Farberow & Schneidman, 1961).

QUALIFICATIONS AND SOME PROMISING
MISCELLANEOUS FINDINGS

The contentions that depression occurs more frequently in the aged and females have been challenged as possibly overgeneralized dogma buttressed by tradition and the class bias of observers. Much depends on the depressive population sampled.

Depression and social class. Several studies by Schwab and his associates nicely illustrate the complexity of teasing out the influence of sociocultural variables on depression when the diagnosis is so susceptible to bias (Schwab, Bialow, Holzer, Brown, & Stevenson, 1967a, 1967b). Schwab et al. rated 143 consecutive medical admissions to a University of Florida teaching hospital. Subjects were multiply rated for depression (Beck Depression Inventory, Hamilton Rating Scale for Depression, a protocol rating from case records, and provisional staff diagnosis), and for Srole's measure of socioeconomic class (SES) (Hollingshead & Redlich, 1958). Twenty-one percent of the sample were designated as clinically depressed, using Beck's cutting score of 13 on the Depression Inventory. The four depression rating scores were summed and patients with scores in the highest 20% of the range were designated as depressed. There were no overall differences in age, sex, socioeconomic, or marital status between the depressed and nondepressed groups. But when the groups were examined within and between socioeconomic groups, interesting differences emerged. Patients were grouped into the SES categories of upper (highest 20%), middle (55%), and lower class (25%). Lower class depressives were younger ($p < .05$) than nondepressives; there were no differences within the other two classes. There were no significant sex by social class interactions, although more middle-class females tended to be depressed, whereas more lower-class males tended to be depressed. Marriage tended to be more frequent in middle and upper class depressives and less frequent in lower class depressives. Most interesting was the difference in rated depression by social class depending upon the method of rating. By provisional medical diagnosis, depression was most frequent in the upper class; by protocol rating there were no class differences; and by the objective rating scales (BDI and HRS) depression was most frequent in the lower class! Schwab et al. speculate that depression manifests itself differently by social class, and that generally middle class physicians are more sensitively attuned to its detection in middle and upper class patients. Some support for class-specific manifestations of depression were obtained: upper class depressives usually showed a loss of interest in life; middle class depressives evidenced loneliness, guilt, and crying; and lower class depressives expressed futility and self-hatred: the latter findings were similar to those of the Midtown Manhattan Study (Langner & Michael, 1963) on lower class depressives.

Depression in northern American blacks. It has frequently been asserted that Blacks have a lower incidence of depression than Caucasians. The generality of this claim is strongly challenged by a recent study in New Haven, Connecticut (Tonks, Paykel, & Klerman, 1970). A large sample (875) of psychiatric patients from a variety of in- and out-patient settings were screened. Thirty-two percent (218) were diagnosed as depressed and of these 16.5% were Blacks. Since Blacks constitute only 11% of the greater New Haven area, they were somewhat overrepresented. Blacks and Caucasians did not differ in age, but there was a higher proportion of Black females, and Blacks were lower in socioeconomic class. The two groups differed in the incidence of 10 depressive symptoms, but when incidence was adjusted for social class, differences were attenuated. Clinical ratings on the Hamilton scale were factor analyzed and two factors emerged: one relating to severity of depression and the other to a bipolar neurotic-endogenous dimension. Blacks had lower factor scores on the first factor and did not differ on the second. However, Tonks et al. conjecture that the severity difference may have been due to the insensitivity of Caucasian interviewers to depressive manifestations in Blacks. When Blacks and Caucasians were individually matched for global severity of depression, social class, sex, and age, the only symptom differentiating the groups was helplessness ($p < .01$). Blacks expressed less helplessness than Caucasians. The two racial groups did not differ on objective personality measures like the MMPI or Maudsley Personality Inventory. Previous reports of differences in the racial incidence of depression have also been questioned on statistical grounds by Rawnsley (1968).

Earlier epidemiological studies that indicated a low incidence of depression in preliterate societies have not been uniformly supported. Likewise, studies of differential incidence as a function of rural-urban differences, ethnic group, and migration present a welter of conflicting results.

A recent study of depression in northern India provides an interesting example of the difficulties in comparing the incidence and severity of depressive symptoms cross-culturally (Teja, Narang, & Aggarwal, 1971). The high incidence of somatic complaints as opposed to psychological complaints in some less technologically advanced cultures is attributed to the greater likelihood that physical difficulties will be seriously regarded by peers and treatment sources. Also, the extent of guilt feelings may be underestimated because in such cultures it often takes the form of shame. Perceived failures in northern India are less likely to be ascribed to personal shortcomings than to ". . . possible bad deeds in a previous life, a consequence of one's 'Karmas' (actions)" [p. 258] .

Support for the notion that individual self-accountability may be an important contributing factor to the incidence of depression is suggested by differential rates within African ethnic groups. West African societies with higher self-accountability appear to have a higher incidence of affective disorder than Eastern and Southern etnic groups which have less self-accountability (Rawnsley, 1968).

Several provocative and testable hypotheses have emerged from the epidemiological literature. Stainbrook (1954) contends, for example, that societies with an extended family structure engender less intense interpersonal frustration, provide more possibilities for obtaining rewards and avoiding punishment, and attenuate the severity of losing significant others. He predicts therefore that the incidence of depression should be lower in such societies. Cohen (1961) ventures a related hypothesis, although it is perhaps more difficult to test. He asserts that members of cohesive groups who cannot fend off impulses that threaten group cohesiveness are particularly prone to depression. Their need to preserve the group causes criticism to be turned against the self. He thereby seeks to explain the traditional view that depression is more prevalent in females, higher socioeconomic strata, and closely-knit traditional societies. Wittkower & Rin (1965) contend that transcultural data support Cohen's hypothesis. Arieti (1959) speculates that inner-directed societies are most apt to generate family constellations in which children experience an overwhelming sense of personal responsibility which they feel incapable of fulfilling. The limited data available on the socialization milieus and family configurations of depressives (Finley & Wilson, 1951; Hamilton & Mann, 1954) lend modest support to these speculations.

OUTCOME AND PROGNOSTIC STUDIES

Generalizations from outcome studies on depressive disorders are difficult to evaluate because of the following (Robins & Guze, 1969): most samples include inpatients only; few separate depressive subtypes; subject or inclusion criteria and outcome criteria are rarely specified; and the methods of follow-up vary widely in intensity and objectivity. Data from 21 follow-up studies have been collated by Robins and Guze. Detailed analysis of these papers is beyond the scope of this volume, so that only rough averages and the range of major findings are presented. About 4½% (2%-7%) of the initial affective diagnoses are changed to schizophrenia; the first or index episode lasts about 7 months

(6.0–13 mos.); about 55% of the index cases have one episode only (21%–93%); some 13% undergo a chronic, unremitting course (1%–28%); 72% improve or recover (58%–92%), while 28% do not recover or die; in larger studies, 15% of deaths were suicides (13%–17%) with no differences obtained among reactive, endogenous and involutional depressives; the interval between a first and second attack is longer (about 6 years) than between the second and subsequent attacks, which is about 3 years; the duration of succeeding attacks does not seem to vary. Bipolar depressives are more susceptible to relapses than unipolars. These widely varying results prompted Robins to undertake his studies which differentiate primary and secondary depressives.

Developmental maturity and prognosis. Reliable prognostic indicators would permit more rational treatment and planning for depressives. So far efforts to ascertain such predictors have chiefly sharpened conceptual distinctions between depression and schizophrenia (Bromet, Harrow, & Tucker, 1971). For schizophrenics (especially males) the level of premorbid social development and the severity of social dysfunction accompanying the onset of psychosis usefully predict short and long term outcome. The higher the level of social development, and the greater the initial dysfunction, the shorter the hospitalization and the better the social reintegration tend to be. Zigler & Phillips (1961, 1962) contend that level of premorbid social functioning as well as symptoms of turning against the self (e.g., guilt and anxiety) are effective prognostic indices for all hospitalized functional disorders. Bromet et al. (1971) tested this hypothesis with hospitalized depressives and schizophrenics separately. Their finding confirmed the Zigler-Phillips position for schizophrenics, but failed to support its extension to depressives. The only promising short term predictor for depressives was severity of dysfunction accompanying the onset of the disorder, which is negatively related to short term hospitalization. Bromet et al. perceptively point out that poor premorbid functioning in the schizophrenic may be symptomatic of a severe from of the disorder. Only if viewed in that light does severity predict similarly for the two disorders. Premorbid social-developmental deficiencies in depressives, if they exist, are probably much more subtle than in schizophrenics.

Socio-demographic variables and treatment response. Few studies have examined sociocultural variables in relation to treatment outcomes for depressives. Grosser's (1966) study provides a useful exemplar of typical problems and findings. Subjects were 322 mostly native-born (84%), Caucasian, severely depressed, hospitalized patients undergoing somatic therapy at three state hospitals within the Greater Boston area; two-thirds had prior hospitalizations. Subject source constricted the range of socioeconomic class: 71% were in Hollingshead's (1957) classes IV or V, and 11% in Class III. However, the sex ratio (2F:1M) and age (median = 45) distribution were typical for public mental hospitals in the United States. Marital status (80% married), religious identification (60% Catholic, 22% Protestant, 4% Jewish), and ethnic background accorded well with regional norms for the general population.

Despite the high proportion of intact marriages, these may have been quite troubled, since the mean number of children within this predominantly lower class Catholic sample was only 1.6. Interviews with husbands of depressed patients indicated that many were hostile, indifferent, or inadequate. Similar impressions of such spouses have been expressed by Jacobson (1956) and can be inferred from Lewinsohn & Atwood (1969). Social histories were obtained from collaterals of patients, but the advanced age of the patients raises serious questions about their reliability (Fontana, 1966). According to Grosser's global impressions, the case history data seemed more compatible with Bibring's (1953) notions about depressives as obsessionally preoccupied with the attainment of rigidly held standards than with any alternative explanations.

The types of somatic therapy used with Grosser's depressive sample and their effects are shown in Table 8. Patients were randomly assigned to treatment conditions and a double blind technique used (except for ECT). Minimal and optional additional drug dosages were predetermined (Greenblatt, Grosser, & Wechsler, 1964). By the end of the eight week experimental period 73% of the patients had improved moderately at least. Overall results yielded few relations between sociocultural variables and depressive diagnostic subgroupings or treatment outcome. Essentially, three positive findings emerged, although these were quite possibly due to chance factors. Education related to outcome only for the least effective forms of treatment, placebo and isocarboxazid. Patients with an intermediate educational level, 7th to 12th grade, fared best with these weak treatments. Protestants showed greatest overall improvement on the somatic therapies and Jews the least. Data analyses were incomplete at the time of this interim publication, so that the effects of Protestants' being more

TABLE 8

Global Ratings of Improvement by Educational
Attainment for All Treatments

Treatment	Less than 12th grade		12th grade or better		Total	
	N	%I	N	%I	N	%I
EST	35	71.4	29	79.3	64	75.0
Isocarboxazid	40	37.5	24	12.5	64	28.1
Phenelzine	13	53.8	28	46.4	41	48.8
Imipramine	33	48.5	36	50.0	69	49.3
Placebo	28	67.9	27	14.8	55	41.8
Desmethyl-imipramine	9	44.4	5	60.0	14	50.0
Total	158	54.4	149	43.0	307[a]	48.9

[a]Level of educational attainment for 15 patients was not ascertainable.
Source: Grosser, 1966.

frequently married, female, and of higher socioeconomic status than the rest of the sample had not been determined. Patients experiencing their first hospitalization tended to improve most, while those undergoing their second hospitalization were least improved. Grosser speculates that sequence of hospitalization is related to the patient's level of optimism about outcome. After the second hospitalization, the patient's level of aspiration seemed to shift downward from cure to social remission, and increased optimism may facilitate improvement. Grosser cogently elaborates the frequently elided significance of variables such as education and religion. As he suggests, educational level may be a marker for a host of underlying attitudinal, ability, and reality-support-demand factors; religion too may reflect a composite of socilization practices and value orientations. While economy factors frequently necessitate the investigator's treating variables like education and religion in simplistic fashion, too often the implicit compromises are lost sight of. Grosser's stimulating paper underscores the imperative need for large sized samples to assess the interactions of sociocultural variables with treatment effects.

In sum, the contributions of epidemiology to the understanding and remediation of depression remain a "promissory note" (Lewis, 1964). Stainbrook's critique of the cross-cultural literature on depression in 1954 remains apposite today:

> Unfortunately, the uncertainty of statistical reliability, the changing concepts of nosography, the lack of consistent common agreement about the operations of diagnosis-making, the controversies over etiology, the skew of the population studied, and, in general, the inadequate conceptual specification of the total field of forces determining the observed behavior all militate very effectively against the productive use of the data of the past [p. 39].

5
PSYCHODYNAMIC THEORIES OF DEPRESSION[7]

Yet it is not so important to ask who was lost as what was lost. The answer to this question is: tell me what the [depressed] patient idealizes in himself and others and I will tell you what he has lost (Safirstein & Kaufman, 1966, p. 230).

The title of this chapter is something of a misnomer. Most of the psychodynamic papers reviewed are pretheoretical, hypothesis-generating speculations based on nonsystematic clinical observation. They are rather extensively and uncritically presented for several reasons: depression is a very real and immense problem; most extant psychological formulations of depression are psychodynamic, and limited research indicates sufficient validity in these formulations to justify familiarity with them. The relatively uncritical presentation is largely because of the inevitable repetitiveness that would otherwise result. Frequently, loose analogies are reified, observations are sketchily reported in somewhat abstruse, idiosyncratic language, and generalizations are posited without due concern for reliability or validity. In most of the papers reviewed, sample characteristics such as number, sex, age, severity, ethnic, racial class, etc., distributions are rarely clear.

Readers are strongly urged to familiarize themselves with some of the clinical case material in the primary source papers. Even such material is a pallid substitute for direct, intensive, prolonged exposure to depressive thought, feeling, and action. Without exposure to such primary data, it is difficult to get a

[7] The considerable redundancy in the following section is quite deliberate. The psychodynamic Zeitgeist is not readily grasped by behavioristically trained students, yet it continues to exercise a powerful influence on contemporary psychopathology and to provide a fertile source of hypotheses.

proper feel for psychodynamic formulations, much less any sense of evaluative competence.

In Fenichel's able summation of the psychoanalytic theory of depression, he described depression as the "... most frequent and also most problematic mechanism of symptom formation [1945, p. 386]." As the following discussion indicates, this dubious accolade continues to be well merited.

EARLY CLASSICS

Many of the concepts used in psychodynamic formulations lack face validity. Freud was acutely aware of this conceptual and communicative difficulty; he wrote;

> ... It is true that notions such as that of an ego-libido, an energy of the ego-instincts, and so on, are neither particularly easy to grasp, nor sufficiently rich in content; ... But I am of the opinion that this is just the difference between a speculative theory and a science based on empirical interpretation. The latter will not envy speculation its privilege of having a smooth, logically unassailable foundation, but will gladly content itself with nebulous, scarcely imaginable basic concepts, which it hopes to apprehend more clearly in the course of its development, or which it is even prepared to replace by others. For these ideas are not the foundation of science, upon which everything rests: that foundation is observation alone [1914, p. 77].[8]

By way of a schematic overview, the most salient aspect of depression is the individual's decreased self-esteem. According to psychodynamic theory, self-esteem is regulated by the availability of "narcissistic supplies,"[9] first mainly in the form of food, and then of love. Self-esteem is increasingly, but never completely, internally regulated. As conscience or the superego evolves, self-esteem is largely regulated by the feeling that one has "done the right thing." Most psychodynamic theories seem to regard normal, neurotic, and psychotic depressions as a quantitative continuum correlated with the reality appropriateness of the depressive's efforts to restore his self-esteem. Normal depressions frequently follow prolonged stress, deprivation, and frustration. The depressed normal continues to seek realistic mastery over his difficulties. The depressed neurotic regressively seeks to restore self-esteem by eliciting support from others in response to his manifest need. Such love may also be sought to alleviate guilt generated by an accusatory conscience. The more regressed psychotic depressive internalizes his efforts to restore self-esteem. Forgiveness, love, and nurturance are sought only secondarily by manipulating external sources; primarily the effort is to ingratiate one's own conscience by self-punitive atonement. The patient contends that he has lost everything

---

[8] For an explanation of how the psychoanalytic concepts of instinctual drives and energies can be accommodated with general systems theory see Engel (1971).

[9] Stimulus inputs that enhance self-love or satisfaction. The term narcissism is used in multiple ways by psychodynamic writers; see e.g., Brenner (1955) and Rapaport (1967).

because he does not deserve anything. Rather than feeling hated by others, as in paranoia, he may contend that he is not hated as much as he deserves to be.

The core of classical psychoanalytic theory on depression is contained in papers by Abraham (1911; 1916; 1924), Freud (1917), and Rado (1928). Abraham, who had excellent scientific training as an embryologist, based his initial observations (1911) about depression on six heterogeneous cyclothymics. These cases were of both sexes, varying in severity from "light" nonpsychotic mood fluctuations to "severe and obstinate psychosis." Observations were gathered within the context of analytically oriented treatment. Several of Abraham's initial observations have had lasting impact on theories of depression. He noted the tendency of depressives to form intensely ambivalent "object-relations" (i.e., relations of both love and hatred toward significant others). The hatred aspect of the ambivalence is typically repressed or at least out of focal awareness. The strength of the repressed hatred has several untoward effects. The capacity to love is seriously impaired. "Hate paralyzes love." While largely unaware of his hatred, the depressive is aware of his limited capacity to love, hence the frequent depressive complaint of feeling impoverished. Furthermore, the unacceptable hatred arouses guilt, which in turn generates anxiety, self-depreciation, and depression. Abraham (1911) distinguished depression from related feelings of grief by ascribing the former to repressed hatred and the latter to appropriate sadness over an actual loss of a valued object (person, thing, ideal.)[10] He adumbrated parallels between the love-hate ambivalence of depressives and obsessive-compulsives and between the use of projection within depression and paranoia. His emphasis on cognitive disturbance in depressives foreshadowed Beck's recent contention that depression is primarily a thought disorder. He compared paranoid and depressive projection as follows: the paranoid's formula is "I (a man) love him" (a man); by reaction formation this becomes "I do not love him, I hate him" but this too must be further rationalized by projection to "I do not love him—I hate him—because he persecutes me." In the case of the depressive, the basic formula is "I cannot love people; I have to hate them"; this perception is repressed and projected externally to "People do not love me, they hate me because of my inborn defects, therefore I am unhappy and depressed." Although the heterosexual relations of depressives appear to be conventional, Abraham contended that the depressive's strong narcissism is accompanied by much underlying confusion about sex-role identity. He posited a direct relation between intensity of repressed hatred, amount of guilt, and severity of depression. The sadistic impulses ascribed to depressives are inferred from their dreams, fantasies, and symptoms. Many of the latter have an extremely annoying quality. To the extent that depressives are aware of their sadistic tendencies, they attribute them to their physical or psychological imperfections rather than

---

[10] For an excellent up-dating of similarities and differences between depression and sadness, see Smith (1971).

to their hatred for others. An unconscious wish to be revenged for their deficiencies is postulated. Abraham speculated that depressives may obtain masochistic pleasure from preoccupation with passively accepted sadistic impulses turned inward by repression. He became relatively optimistic about the treatability of depressives despite his initial skepticism. The therapeutic weight he ascribed to cognitive reorientation is suggested by his emphasis on the effectiveness of being able to explain "... certain ideas that completely dominated the patient [p. 155]."

In his next paper on depression, Abraham (1916) attempted to explicate the implicit wish content (or motivation) of certain depressive delusional ideas within the framework of psychosexual developmental phases. Specifically, he dealt with the depressive's frequent refusal of food and fear of starvation. Depressives commonly rationalize this refusal as a wish to die. But Abraham discounted this explanation as implausible, because it is a slow and uncertain method of self-destruction. Abraham explained this self-starvation as symptomatic of a regression to a very early "oral-cannibalistic" developmental stage, in which the most deeply repressed wish is to devour the frustrating love object. Refusal of food reflects a defense against acting out such an impulse, and an attempt at expiation for harboring such odious impulses.[11] Oral devouring fantasies are reputed to be especially common among psychotic depressives. In attempting to further differentiate depressive from obsessive-compulsive ambivalence, in both of which sadism is greater than love, Abraham contends that regression is less profound in the latter. The obsessive's sadistic impulses are gratified by tormenting real objects, unlike the psychotic depressive, who symbolically destroys the frustrating object.

Freud's paper "Mourning and Melancholia" (1917) is regarded as a major contribution to psychodynamic theory generally, as well as to the theory of depression specifically. This paper extended and applied the psychodynamic concepts of "narcissm" and the "ego ideal" to depression and foreshadowed the concept of the superego, identification, and object-relations.[12]

According to Freud, a significant loss (of a person, ideal, or abstraction) may precipitate either normal mourning or morbid melancholia. The two states share many attributes, such as dejection, constricted interest, and lowered activity. But they differ in that melancholics tend to be much more severely self-depreciating. They accuse themselves of being worthless, inadequate, helpless, and morally despicable. As Freud put it, for the mourner the world is impoverished, for the melancholic the ego is impoverished. Not all of the melancholic's self-accusations may be unwarranted, as the previous quotation from Freud indicated. However, this statement should not be construed as

---

[11] However, Arlow & Brenner (1964, p. 64) indicate that cannibalistic oral imagery and feeding difficulties can readily mask conflicts related to much later developmental issues.

[12] For those unfamiliar with psychodynamic terminology, Holzman's (1970) introductory volume would be a helpful supplement to this chapter.

Freudian congruence with Mowrer's view (1961) that severity of depression is proportionate to the amount of real moral transgression which has not been acknowledged or expiated. Rather Freud maintained that the more conscientious the person, the more susceptible he is to melancholia (1917, p. 247). Freud astutely noted a logical inconsistency in the melancholic's self-depreciation.

> ... they are far from evincing towards those around them the attitude of humility and submissiveness that would alone befit such worthless people. On the contrary, they make the greatest nuisance of themselves, and always seem as though they felt slighted and had been treated with great injustice [p. 248].

How to explain the paradox of the loss of a significant relation, resulting in loss of self-regard and felt impoverishment so unhumbly asserted? Freud (1917) contended that:

> If one listens patiently to a melancholic's many and various self-accusations, one cannot in the end avoid the impression that often the most violent of them are hardly at all applicable to the patient himself, but that with insignificant modifications they do fit someone else, someone whom the patient loves or has loved or should love ... we perceive that the self-reproaches are reproaches against a love object which have been shifted away from it onto the patient's own ego. Their complaints are really plaints in the old sense of the word. They are not ashamed and do not hide themselves, since everything derogatory that they say about themselves is at bottom said about someone else [p. 248].

When a significant relationship is disrupted, as in bereavement, the ego undergoes an acutely painful process of conflict resolution: the conflict between wish-fulfilling desires to deny the loss and reality demands to acknowledge the loss. Normally, energy invested in the psychic representations (schemas, cognitions) of the lost object's memories and expectations ("object-cathexes") are gradually freed and displaced to substitute objects. But in melancholia, loss is followed by a so-called "pathognomonic introjection." Energy from the ambivalently invested lost object is abruptly withdrawn from the object-representation, but instead of the freed energy being displaced to other objects, the ego identifies with the lost object (by introjection via oral incorporation). "Thus, the shadow of the object fell upon the ego (Freud, 1917, p. 249)." The original ambivalence or conflict in the interpersonal or object-relation between the ego and the external object is transformed into an intrapsychic conflict. On one side of the internalized conflict is the conscience and ego-ideal (or in subsequent terminology, the superego), on the other, the ego now modified by identification with the ambivalently regarded lost object.

The vulnerability of the melancholic's object cathexis to regressive identification is attributed to its developmentally immature or "narcissistic" basis. Supposedly, the melancholic's psychosexual development has not matured to the extent that he is capable of reciprocal, unambivalent love of an accurately perceived other person. Rather, he is still substantially fixated at an earlier developmental phase characterized by strong self-love and by ambivalent relations toward others. These relations are largely predicated on attraction toward others perceived as like himself, or experienced as highly indulgent of his needs ("narcissistic object-choice"). Under sufficient stress, such narcissistic object-choices may regress to an even more primitive stage of object relations which is by identification with the object. To the extent that such identification occurs, self-identity is lost.

According to Freud, after the pathognomonic introjection, the regressed and identification-altered ego is sadistically treated by the ego-ideal as, prior to regression, the unconsciously hostile aspect of the ego would like to have treated the external object with which it is now identified. The primitive torment unleashed against the altered ego results in regression to the "anal-sadistic" and "oral-cannibalistic" developmental stages. In these early developmental stages the wish to incorporate objects by devouring them prevails. Incorporation permits union with the source of narcissistic supplies (milk, love, etc.). But oral incorporative aims and fantasies often have a sadistic-destructive nature because of their objectively destructive character. Psychotic depressives reputedly have strong oral fixations due to constitutional predispositions or to unusually strong oral frustrations or gratifications. Since the boundaries between self and external objects are still quite permeable during the late oral stage, fears of being devoured frequently accompany wishes to devour. Freud agreed with Abraham that melancholics' reluctance to eat stems from their conflictual cannibalistic impulses.

Regression is never total. Part of the melancholic's sadistic ambivalence toward the object is still directed externally despite introjection. The acute suffering of the melancholic may yield secondary gains from the guilt and discomfort aroused in external objects.

Affective disorders tend to remit spontaneously, which is perplexing to most psychologically oriented theorists. Freud conjectured that a reality testing process analogous to, but not identical with, mourning occurs. In normal mourning, the struggle is between the wish to deny the loss and the realistic need to acknowledge it. Energy attached to the memories and expectations associated with the object are more readily detached and displaced to substitute objects, because these associations are more available to consciousness. In melancholia, the sadistic ambivalence toward the object is repressed. After introjection and regression, the sadistic ambivalence is available to awareness only by indirection and distortion, that is, as a struggle between ego and conscience. Given the intrinsic impairment of reality testing under these regressed conditions, the detachment of energic investments in object-representations proceeds less rapidly than in mourning.

The next landmark in psychodynamic theorizing about depression was Abraham's paper "Manic-depressive States and the Pre-genital Levels of the Libido" (1924). He remarked that he had studied only male manic-depressives intensively, but did not ". . . attribute very great importance to" this fact (1924, p. 421), since such patients tend to be bisexual.

Whereas Abraham's previous paper (1916) was largely devoted to documenting the existence of an early oral-cannibalistic developmental phase, this one (1924) sought to verify the dual importance of Freud's concepts of introjection and oral regression, ". . . the introjection of the love object is an incorporation of it, in keeping with the regression of the libido to the cannibalistic level [p. 420]." His principal contribution to general psychodynamic theory in this paper was the differentiation of the anal developmental phase into an earlier, more primitive anal-expulsive, and a later, less primitive, anal-retentive one. This distinction is critical to psychodynamic notions, since susceptibility to psychotic regression is a function of level of fixation. Personalities fixated before the late anal phase are reputed to be much more susceptible to psychotic regression than those fixated at more advanced levels: melancholics exemplify the former, and obsessive-compulsives the latter.

According to Abraham, obsessive-compulsives and melancholics share the character traits of anally fixated characters: excessive punctuality, orderliness, obstinacy, and parsimony. Both their interpersonal relations and sexual orientations tend to be ambivalent mixtures of love-hate and homo-heterosexuality. Both treat their love objects like pieces of private property, a hallmark of "anal-eroticism." Anal-erotic pleasure is gained mainly by the retention and expulsion of feces, which are highly regarded by the child. Initially, they are perceived as part of the child, and subsequently as his personal property. Since the mode of relating to people is related to the predominant modes of dealing with libidinal impulses (anal-erotic in this instance) of the dominant libidinal zone,[13] anally fixated people tend to relate to others as they do to their own feces. Abraham drew the analogy that just as the anal functions are related to retaining and expelling, so object relations during this phase center upon controlling and destroying. He ingeniously, if sometimes outrageously (Masserman, 1970, p. xii–xiv), draws on anthropology, linguistics, and patients' fantasies to argue for an unconscious equation of loss, destruction, and defecation on the one hand, and preservation, control, and anal retention on the other.[14]

The argument for differentiating the anal stage into an early, predominantly expulsive and later, predominantly retentive phase derives from the critical difference with which obsessive-compulsives and melancholics respond to loss. While the obsessive-compulsive may intensify his obsessionalism or compulsivity, he does not give up his relations with reality. By contrast, the melancholic relinquishes most of his external relatedness, and theoretically regresses in part to the oral-cannibalistic state. According to Abraham, the frustrating object is unconsciously destroyed and expelled like feces, then orally reintrojected. He

[13] See Erickson, 1950, pp. 72-97, for an unusually lucid, relatively jargon-free exposition of these postulates.

[14] Should this sound absurdly speculative to the reader, he should read the original article and attempt alternative explanations of the material as an intriguing exercise.

differed from Freud in contending that the self-reproaches of the depressive are not only accusations against the introjected object, but also against the previously introjected cruel conscience as well. According to Abraham the etiology of melancholia consists in: (a) a constitutionally strong oral eroticism (b) that predisposes to oral fixation because of intense experiences of oral gratification and frustration, (c) a severe injury to infantile narcissism (self-regard) from successive disappointments in love (by parental figures), (d) the most important of which occurs before the oedipal situation has been resolved.[15] The significance of the latter point resides in the contiguity of strong incestuous impulses toward mother, hatred of father, and weak repressive controls, all within the context of still active oral-cannibalistic impulses. This combination results in a sadistic introject of mother and father as the basis of the superego. Love objects are partially experienced as repetitions of the oedipal objects; therefore the melancholic's reproaches are directed not only against the recently introjected object, but against the original parental introjects as well. While the theoretical interpretations of Abraham's abundant clinical material are certainly questionable, his type of data must be encompassed within a comprehensive theory of depression.

Freud's next contribution to the psychodynamics of depression appeared in "Group Psychology and the Analysis of the Ego" in a section entitled, "A Differentiating Grade in the Ego" (1921, pp. 129–134). This paper marked a further waystage in the evolution of his theory from a topographical model (unconscious, preconscious, conscious) to a structural model (id, ego, superego) trichotomized on the basis of mental functions. Earlier the "differentiating grade in the ego" was referred to variously as the conscience, critical agency, and ego ideal, and subsequently as the superego. The functions ascribed to this construct include self-observation, moral conscience, censorship of dreams, and chief agent of repression. According to Freud, each structural differentiation of the personality provides a particular vulnerability to disruption. The ego-ideal evolves from the ego:

> ... it is the heir to the original narcissism in which the childish ego enjoyed self-sufficiency; it gradually gathers up from the influences of the environment the demands which that environment makes upon the ego and which the ego cannot always rise to.... [1921, p. 110].

Guilt reflects tension between the ego and the ego-ideal. Some degree of tension between the systems is inevitable. Freud contended that festivals like the Saturnalia and Mardi Gras are culturally devised means for the periodic alleviation of such tension without guilt. When the ego-ideal is unusually strict, spontaneous ego rebellions without external precipitants may occur. The

---

[15]The "tough-minded" who find the oedipal concept to be anathema may find Lindzey's (1967) Presidential Address to the American Psychological Association quite informative.

severity of such rebellions may range from normal mood fluctuations to full-blown endogenous depressions or manic-depressive episodes. Temporarily successful rebellions in depressives resulting from excessively severe punishment of the ego by the superego may result in "triumphant" manic phases.

Freud's last significant contribution to the psychodynamics of depression per se appeared in "The Ego and the Id," in which he elaborated the process of "defusion" (1923, p. 54). This process refers to an unbinding of the previously fused ambivalent cathexes into their libidinal and sadistic components as an accompaniment of the pathognomonic introjection. Object-libido is transformed to narcissistic libido and object-sadism into a "pure culture" of "death instinct."

Freud is somewhat ambiguous about the fate of these defused instinctual impulses, except that the pure culture of the death instinct "holds sway" in the superego. That is, the sadistic impulses previously turned against the external object in muted form because of the fusion with libidinal or loving, conserving impulses become available to the superego for punishment of the introject-modified ego. According to Freud, the proneness of depressives to instinctual defusion, and the resultant paralysis of their ability to work and to love, accounts for their chronic pessimism and despair.

Much of the traditional psychotherapeutic effort to encourage the expression of hostility by depressives stems from Freud's (1923) notion that the sadism of the death instinct is either blended with libido and expressed outwardly as aggression, or is turned inwards. "It is remarkable that the more a man checks his aggressiveness toward the exterior the more severe—that is aggressive—he becomes in his ego-ideal [p. 54]."

Rado (1928) reformulated the psychodynamic theory of depression within Freud's structural framework. His chief innovation was the concept of a dual pathognomonic introjection associated with regression to an archaic developmental phase which involves the splitting of objects into "good" and "bad" representations.

According to Rado, developmentally early perception is dominated by the pleasure principle, so that only pleasurable experiences achieve conscious psychic representation. With maturation, pleasurable and painful experiences are both perceptualized but as discrete entities, objects, or personifications. Hence the pleasure-conferring mother is perceived as the "good mother," who is discrete from the dysphoric-inducing "bad mother." The infant's wish to experience only a "good mother" fosters its renunciation of unacceptable impulses toward the parents. In order to sustain the feeling of being loved and of loving, the child internalizes the proscriptive controls of the parents. That is, it acquires an awareness of criticism and of guilt as an anticipatory dread of the consequences of violating parental standards. The psychic representation, imago, or schema of the hatred invested "bad mother" tends to be repressed, while the love invested "good mother" becomes a wish-idea precursor of conscience. To reify considerably, this internalized conscience-ideal is accorded unqualified love, despite its equally unqualified proscriptive rights. This proscriptive right is delegated by the ego to avert threatened loss of love. Conscience formation on this basis is more passive and primitive than the variant which occurs later with the resolution of the oedipal situation. The determinants of this premature evolution of conscience are not clearly stated by Rado. Predepressives have strong narcissistic cravings, along with a low tolerance for narcissistic frustrations. Even trivial disappointments precipitate a marked loss of self-esteem. Craving for narcissistic gratification is so acute that it impedes or precludes substitutive or sublimatory activity. Normally, self-esteem is increasingly regulated by one's own self-evaluations and achievements, but in predepressives, self-esteem continues to be regulated primarily by gratifications from others. Thus, predepressives avidly court others' favor.

> But as soon as they are sure of the affection or devotion of another person and have entered into a fairly secure relation with him or her, their behavior undergoes a complete change. They accept the devoted love of the beloved person with a sublime nonchalance, as a matter of course, and become more and more domineering and autocratic, displaying an increasingly unbridled egoism, until their attitude becomes one of full-blown tyranny. They cling to their objects like leeches and feed upon them, as though it were their intention to devour them altogether [1928, pp. 422-423].

This process operates largely out of awareness, so that retaliation or withdrawal by the exploited object is experienced by the predepressive as a "grave injustice" which is responded to with "embittered vehemence." If the predepressive's rebellion against the (perceived as) neglectful object fails to reinstate narcissistic gratifications, his aggression is redirected toward himself, and the depressive reaction ensues.

Rado terms the psychotic depressive reaction an oral-narcissistic reparation mechanism. Two parallel psychic processes constitute this mechanism, one of which is melancholic atonement. In this atonement process the ego is massively contrite:

> ... that which it could not accomplish by rebellion it now tries to achieve by remorseful self-punishment and expiation. The ego does penance, begs for forgiveness and endeavors in this way to win back the lost object" [p. 423].

Melancholia is viewed as a "... great despairing cry for love." Rado minimizes any manipulative aspects of such despairing behavior.

The psychogenesis or learning history for the pattern of contrition after rebellion is rooted in the consequences of violating parental standards. Despite the internalization of parental standards as controls, violations are inevitable given the child's inability to perceive parental standards accurately, the parents' inconsistency, and the transient intense drive states that overwhelm the child's inhibitory capacities. Violations of parental standards tend to be followed by punishment, and by pleas for forgiveness and reconciliation. This process becomes internalized so that even transgressions unnoted by the parents are responded to with expiatory guilt or self-punishment and reconciliation between self and conscience. As with much "overlearned" behavior, this reparative process becomes automatized to the point of unawareness. The intimate linkage between guilt, atonement, and forgiveness provides the paradigm for the depressive reaction.

> Instead of the early process of putting matters right in actual fact with the parents, we have the purely psychical process by which he puts them right with his super-ego, as happens later in melancholia [1928, p. 425].

Surprisingly, Rado minimizes the significance of a directly learned association between the sequence of guilt, atonement, and forgiveness and melancholic atonement; it ". . . cannot possibly owe its enormous importance simply to the experiences of the growing child in the course of his training [p. 425]." Rather, he attributes the associative strength of the sequence to prototypical infantile feeding experiences: notably the sequence of hunger, rage, and feeding. Aggressive reactions to frustrations originate in the primitive rage of the hungry infant. If not immediately gratified, this rage leads to exhaustion, helplessness, and tormenting hunger, followed by feeding, "alimentary orgasm," and feelings of "narcissistic bliss." As hunger led to feeding, so self-punishment as expiation should lead to loving acceptance. But again Rado emphasized that love is sought primarily from an intrapsychic source, the internalized parental introject, or superego, not from the external object whose disappointment precipitated the rebellion and depression.

While Rado essentially concurred in Freud's concept of pathognomonic introjection, he accepted the face validity of the depressive's self-reproaches somewhat more than Freud:

> . . . we have only to listen attentively and then we easily arrive at the inner meaning of his self-reproaches. He feels guilty because by his aggressive attitude he has himself to blame for the loss of the object [1928, p. 429].

The second parallel psychic process in the depressive reaction is a modified version of Freud's pathognomonic introjection. Rado's conception of this process stems from his notions about regression to the archaic, subjectively preambivalent stage of splitting objects into "good" and "bad" representations. According to Rado, when the pathognomonic introjection occurs, the object is split: the "good" aspect is introjected into the superego and the "bad" aspect into the ego. The modified superego then exercises its right to be angry with the altered ego. In accordance with the regressed cognition of the depressive, the goal of the superego's attack on the ego is to purge the ego's bad object. Elimination of the bad object rids the ego of its ambivalence, leaving only the good object, which is the state sought by the archaic pleasure principle. The resultant narcissistic restoration of self-esteem may result in a manic episode which is followed by an obsessively tinged remission. Obsessional defenses (reaction formation, intellectualization, undoing, isolation) derive from the sadistic-anal instinctual fixation of the depressive and serve to curb the intensity of his ambivalence.

In a subsequent paper (1951), Rado attempted to relate variations in depressive reactions to differences in the relative strength of their expiatory self-punitive and coercive-rage components. If the former predominates, a retarded depression ensues; if the latter, an agitated depression.

ENGLISH SCHOOL OF PSYCHOANALYSIS

Melanie Klein's theoretical contributions (1934; 1940; 1945) on depression have been influential, stimulating, and controversial. Her advocacy of certain "radically orthodox" psychodynamic concepts has alienated many psychopathologists. Several critiques (Bibring, 1947; Rosenfeld, 1959; Zetzel, 1953) of Klein's contributions on depression are very helpful in clarifying this highly abstruse material.

The flavor of Klein's conceptualization (1934) of the infant's early mental life is well conveyed by the following excerpt:

> In the very first months of the baby's existence, it has sadistic impulses directed, not only against its mother's breast, but also against the inside of her body: scooping it out, devouring the contents, destroying it by every means which sadism can suggest. . . . From the beginning the ego introjects objects 'good' and 'bad,' for both of which the mother's breast is the prototype for good objects when the child obtains it, for bad ones when it fails him [p. 282].

These constructions derive chiefly from Klein's analyses of children's fantasies. Klein's "radical" positions include adherence to Freud's concept of an innate death instinct and beliefs in the infant's innate unconscious knowledge of sexual differences and of parental coitus. She postulates a much earlier development of oedipal conflicts and superego functions than most psychodynamic personality theorists. In Klein's theory, early infantile development proceeds through so-called paranoid and depressive positions whose resolution critically determines subsequent personality integration, interpersonal relations, and vulnerability to personality disorders. The developmental positions are termed paranoid and depressive because their characteristic anxiety-situations and defenses are reputedly analogous to those in adult psychoses.

The paranoid phase precedes and overlaps the depressive phase. During the early months of life when the paranoid position is dominant, the internal and external worlds are perceived in fragmentary fashion, as "part-objects." Little differentiation exists between internal and external or real and fantastic part-objects. By incorporation or introjection, the infant continuously internalizes aspects (people, things, situations, events) of the external world, and by projection it externalizes aspects of its internal world. These processes occur within the context of intense sadistic impulses, deriving from the death instinct. Psychic or internal reality consists of innate and internalized part-objects or "imagos." These internalized part-objects are fantastically distorted images of the real (external) objects upon which they are based. Distortion occurs because of unconscious fantasy and the relative isolation of these imagos from accurate perception. Much unconscious fantasy is of a sadistic, persecutory nature. Innate sadistic tendencies are reinforced by the inevitable frustrations of the feeding process. Attempts to diminish the sense of inner threat by projecting sadistic impulses to external objects merely shifts the locus of threat. Coexisting with the persecutory internal objects are "good" internal objects, again innate and acquired. All objects at this stage tend to be split into separate good and bad representations. This splitting process is the prototype of ambivalence. It partly safeguards good objects and permits greater reliance on them. Continuous favorable experience with the real world, especially the mother, gradually ameliorates the ego's persecutory anxiety and diminishes the good-bad splitting process. The infant recurrently experiences anxiety lest his ego and its good objects be overwhelmed and annihilated by his bad objects and by id impulses.

An adaptive aspect of these anxieties is the incentive provided to

> ... observe and make sure about the external object-world, from which the inner world springs, and by these means to understand the internal one better. The visible mother thus provides continuous proofs of what the 'internal' mother is like, whether she is loving or angry, helpful or revengeful. The extent to which external reality is able to disprove anxieties and sorrow relating to internal reality varies with each individual, but could be taken as one of the criteria for normality" [1940, p. 313].

The earliest defense against paranoid anxiety is "scotomization" or the denial of psychic reality; this defense can generalize to external reality as well, thus providing the groundwork for the most regressive psychotic disturbances. However, the principal defenses of the ego in the paranoid phase are the attempted destruction, and projection or expulsion, of persecutory objects. Obsessional defenses derive from efforts to keep good and bad objects separated lest the former be overwhelmed by the latter.

The superego evolves during the first year of life. Its earliest progenitor is the feeling of bad conscience experienced by the ego in relation to the persecutory bad objects. The ego feels prey to "contradictory and impossible claims within." These claims include: persecution by internalized objects, assaults of bad objects on each other and on good objects; the compelling need to protect good objects and to comply with their strict, moralistic demands; and the resultant dread of instinctual demands that offend the good objects. The ego's need to separate good and bad, real and fantastic objects results in

> ... a conception of extremely bad and *extremely perfect* objects, that is to say, its loved objects are in many ways intensely moral and exacting. ... As the infant cannot fully keep his good and bad objects apart in his mind, some of the cruelty of the bad objects and of the id becomes attached to the good objects and thus increases the severity of their demands. These strict demands serve the purpose of supporting the ego in its fight against its uncontrollable hatred and its bad attacking objects, with whom the ego is partly identified [1934, pp. 288–289].

The ego's prime anxiety during the paranoid phase relates to its preservation from persecutory objects. As the ego's capacity to introject and identify with whole objects increases, its prime anxiety shifts to the preservation of its identification with a whole good object. In the paranoid phase, the ego is too fragmented and too subject to persecutory doubts and suspicions even of internalized good objects to sustain a positive identification. An adaptive aspect of this persecutory phase is strengthened observation of the external world in order to avert threat. However, the objectivity of observation is inversely related to the strength of persecutory anxiety. Initially, the ego's defenses are inadequate to cope with such demands.

The transition from the paranoid to the depressive position occurs at about 4–5 months of age. At this point, both weaning and growing oedipal concerns occur. Minor frustrations, such as temporary unavailability of the feeding breast, elicit rage and anxiety lest the ego's uncontrollable greed and hatred have destroyed the desired object. Initially, the ego's fantasies provide a similar explanation for the loss of the breast during the weaning process, and these fantasies evoke acute anxiety lest the same fate befall the loved parents. As the ego becomes more differentiated and integrated, real objects are increasingly discriminated from the unreal; internal objects from external ones; good and bad components of objects are tolerated with less splitting; hostility is more appropriately directed toward hostile objects and love toward loving objects. The ego increasingly identifies with, and seeks to preserve, its internalized representation of the good mothering object; the better the real mother the more accurate the internal representation. But the ego's increased awareness of its persecutory objects and sadistic impulses, which are at their peak, generates profound anxiety lest the good object be destroyed. The projective defense of the paranoid position is less effective because of the fear that good objects may be expelled as well as bad ones. The ego seeks not only to preserve but to placate and to make reparations or amends to the good object for its hostile tendencies. Reparation may occur in a variety of ways; much of it in the realm of fantasy:

> ...the infant is impelled to undo the effect of his sadistic impulses by...feelings of love. For instance urine and feces represent agents of destruction when the child hates and gifts when he loves...the 'good' excrements of his mind become the means by which he can cure the damage done by his 'dangerous' excrements....The desire to give and receive libidinal gratification is thus enhanced by the drive for reparation [1945, pp. 380–381].

But much reparative work also takes place in the form of increased control over destructive impulses and more constructive behavior. Enhanced reparative capabilities are complicated because they entail more effective interaction with and control over the parents. Triumphs in this sphere readily become sadistically tinged, transforming the parents into persecutors. That is, success against the parents may be too closely associated with wishes to harm and humiliate them, which triggers retributive fears.

Anxiety-provoking or frustrating events promptly obliterate the ego's increasingly refined discriminatory processes. The generalizing effects of such disruptive events impede the ego's ability to profit from such experience by increased foresight, i.e., anticipation of consequences. Because the infant's introjective processes still have a strong oral sadistic quality, even intense love is dangerous lest the loved object be destroyed while incorporating it. Even if successfully introjected, the good object is then exposed to the assaults of persecutory objects. The extraordinary tie of the infant to the mother is not merely a function of dependence on her for nurturance, but of identification with her. The vicissitudes of relations with external objects are reflected, however fantastically, by their internalized counterparts; that is, anxiety and guilt are experienced both in relation to the real mother and the internalized mother. The ego simultaneously perceives the internalized good mother as a source of protection against persecutory objects, and fears for its preservation. In the earlier phase of the depressive position the ego is somewhat distrustful of the good object because of its repeated experience of good objects merging with bad ones and becoming sadistically tinged. If the real mother is actually not a very good mother, the ego's dilemma is compounded because the shortcomings of both the real and internalized mother are attributed to its own destructive impulses. Belief in a good protective mother is essential regardless of the reality distortion needed to achieve it.

The so-called "primal depression" of the infant stems from its chronic insecurity and guilt relating to preservation of the good object. That is, it fears that its badness and ineffectualness in controlling id impulses may jeopardize the good object; sadness and despair inevitably result:

> ... the ego comes to a realization of its love for a good object, a whole object and in addition a real object, together with an overwhelming feeling of guilt towards it. Full identification with the object based on the libidinal attachment, first to the breast, then to the whole person, goes hand in hand with anxiety for it (of its disintegration), with guilt and remorse, with a sense of responsibility for preserving it intact against persecutors and the id, and with sadness relating to expectations of the impending loss of it [1934, p. 290].

The chronic ambivalence, doubting, and indecision of the depressive is ascribed to the ego's doubt of both its own goodness and the goodness of the identified-with object; of its ability to love, or its worthiness to be loved.

Introjective-identification with the good object, and reparation to it, are the prime defenses of the depressive position. To the extent that such reparative efforts fail, omnipotent manic and obsessional defenses are brought into play. Manic omnipotent fantasies take multiple forms. They deny destructive attacks on the good object; or anxiety about them; magically resurrect destroyed good objects; devalue the worth of good objects so that past and current sadistic threats are not so critical. Simultaneous hunger for taking in objects and detachment about their significance is common. Thus the ego assures itself that bountiful objects are available even if many are sadistically violated, to which the ego feigns indifference anyway. The purity and power of both internal and external good objects may be vastly magnified by their overidealization. Excessive use of this defense in relation to external objects may result in profound and enduring dependency on external objects. The latter outcome is increased by projective identification in which good internal objects are projected onto the mother to insure their preservation; as a result, all goodness is perceived as coming from without. Obsessional personality features result from striving to isolate the good and bad objects. Such coercive efforts may miscarry because sadistic manipulation of good objects inevitably generates guilt. Reversion to the more primitive paranoid defense of destroying and projecting rather than merely controlling bad objects may then ensue. Because of the inherent weakness of the depressive ego, manic and obsessional defenses are invariably relied upon to an appreciable extent. They constitute what Klein terms the infantile neurosis. As the ego matures, it progressively abandons utilization of such measures. These manic-obsessive defenses, if not excessive, can alleviate enough stress to permit the development of more realistic reparative-constructive adaptations.

Klein does not contend that infants experience psychoses identical with their adult counterparts. Rather the paranoid and depressive positions are epigenetically predetermined developmental phases. Klein regards the successful resolution of the depressive position as the most critical determinant of subsequent maturation. Reactivation of the depressive position is regarded as an inevitable concomitant to loss of any significant love relation in adulthood. But psychotic depressive or inappropriate grief reactions are much more likely in those who have never successfully internalized stable good parental objects.

It is difficult to compare Klein's contribution with other psychodynamic theorists owing to her emphasis on introjection, projection, and aggression, to the virtual exclusion of narcissism which figures so prominently in other psychodynamic formulations (Zetzel, 1953). While Klein may have unduly emphasized conflict and torment during infantile existence, other theorists have probably overstressed the blissfulness of the early passive-dependent phase. It seems likely that acute conflict would result from the infant's profound dependency and susceptibility to severe frustration. Klein also pinpointed the paradox in traditional psychodynamic theory of ascribing the resolution of oedipal conflicts to superego development, yet attempting to account for much of depressive phenomena in terms of an overly-strict, orally-fixated sadistic superego. The oral phase of development, of course, precedes the oedipal phase in traditional psychodynamic theory. As noted, Klein contends that both superego development and oedipal conflicts occur much earlier than do most other theorists.

EGO-ANALYTIC CONTRIBUTIONS

Edith Jacobson (1946; 1953; 1954; 1957; 1966; 1971)[16] is one of the most influential contemporary psychodynamic theoreticians on depressive states.

---

[16] Because of space limitations it is impossible to illustrate Jacobson's concepts with clinical examples. As a result, they may appear to be even more reified and abstruse than they are.

Jacobson (1953) views psychotic depression as a mental and psychosomatic disorder. She classifies any depression with cognitive and motoric inhibition as psychotic, regardless of whether a thought disturbance is apparent. In support of her contention that psychotic depressions reflect an endogenous, psychosomatic process, she underscores the experiential, physiological, and psychosomatic differences between psychotic and neurotic depressions. In psychotic depression, retardation tends to have a fairly discrete onset; to be experienced with some detachment as ego-alien; insomnia, anorexia, amenorrhea, weight loss, and metabolic disturbances are frequent concomitants, as are gastrointestinal and cardiovascular psychosomatic symptoms. However, she admits that it is frequently difficult to discriminate neurotic from psychotic depressions. Her espousal of an unknown psychosomatic etiological factor in psychotic depression is avowedly a strategic one. Having made her obeisance to psychosomatics, she focuses on the structural rather than the instinctual psychodynamic facets of depression. She regards the instinctual aspects of extreme regression, notably cannibalistic incorporation and anal-sadistic ejection fantasies, as common to all psychoses. These fantasies accompany the decompensatory dissolution of object and self-representations and their restitutive partial fusions. Her focus is on the structural locus of these fusions. Hence her concentration on self-representations, depressive identification, libidinal and cathetic fluctuations between self and object representations, and fusions between these representations.

Loss of self-esteem (or the breakdown of "secondary narcissism") is seen as the crucial psychological problem in depressions. Her sensitive distinctions between schizophrenic, borderline, and psychotic depressive states (1954, 1966) are beyond the scope of this work.

According to Jacobson's framework, the system ego consists of self-representations, object-representations (of other persons and of things), and associated ego functions. These representations evolve from early images related to experience. Reality demands in the form of frustration, prohibition, and demands, plus rewards (especially parental love) and maturation foster increasingly realistic stable and differentiated images. Early self and object images are often fused and confused. These images or representations are gradually invested with libidinal, aggressive, and neutralized psychic energy. Narcissistic libido is that part of the ego's libido which is invested in the self-representations.

> Since the self-representations are only partly the product of our self-cognizant functions, they will never be strictly 'conceptual' but remain under the influence of our subjective emotional experiences even more than the object-representations [1953, p. 56].

Early self and love-object images provide the core of the system superego as well as the system ego. The superego consists of the ego-ideal, which is libidinally cathected, and of the critical superego, which controls libidinal and aggressive drives used to cathect the ego's self-representations.

Each infantile developmental stage is characterized by a particular fear which reflects the stage's predominant value. The step which is most relevant to depressive vulnerability occurs when the child becomes aware of its helplessness and dependency.

> The loss of belief in his own omnipotence will teach him to prefer security to pleasure and, hence, to accept a strong love-object that gives him security, though it may deprive him of pleasure [1953, p. 58].

Self-judgment is predominantly a cognitive superego function, which assesses the relation of ego-ideal and self-representation. If the discrepancy is small, the critical superego libidinally cathects the self-representations resulting in high self-esteem, whereas if the discrepancy is large it aggressively cathects them, resulting in low self-esteem. "Self-esteem is the emotional expression of self-evaluation and of the corresponding libidinous or aggressive cathexis of the self-representations [1953, p. 59]."

Common to all psychoses is a severe instinctual and structural regression. This vulnerability is attributed to insufficient neutralization of aggressive and libidinal energies, which in turn forestalls the development of firm, bounded self vs. object representations and ego vs. superego differentiation. Structures too readily dissolve, split, fuse, deteriorate into primitive images, or become externalized by projection.

> The onset of the psychosis proper is characterized by a dangerous, irresistible ... deneutralization of instincts, which unleashes a furious struggle for supremacy between the libidinous and the destructive forces [1953, p. 62].

Drive defusion may result from an underlying psychosomatic process which depletes libidinal resources, thereby disrupting the balance with aggressive drive. This process may be triggered

> ... by a reactivation of infantile conflicts ... which the defective ego is unable to master with the help of neurotic defenses. It resorts to attempts at a conflict solution by shifts, first of the libidinous, then of the aggressive cathexis from the object to the self-representations, by renewed efforts to recathect the objects and finally by increasing fusions of both [1953, p. 63].

Because psychotic depressives are more differentiated than schizophrenics, regression is not as severe, and the process is more reversible. Whereas the schizophrenic actually experiences feelings of dissolution and loss of identity, the psychotic depressive feels only threatened by such possibilities.

Jacobson (1953) contends that nonpsychotic cyclothymics tend to be warm, companionable, sexually mature, "richly sublimated," etc., but with a specific ego weakness. This weakness consists in their "remarkable vulnerability, their intolerance toward frustration, hurt, and disappointment [p. 66]." This vulnerability is more pronounced in psychotic cyclothymics.

> Manic-depressives manifest a particular kind of infantile narcissistic dependency on their love-object. What they require is a constant supply of love and moral support

from a highly valued love-object, which need not be a person, but may be represented by a powerful symbol, a religious, political or scientific cause, or an organization . . . as long as their 'belief' in this object lasts, they will be able to work with enthusiasm and high efficiency [p. 67].

The cyclothymic views the love object in extraordinarily idealized and powerful terms, whereas the self is viewed as weak and dependent on the object. This makes for highly unstable cathectic conditions. The love-object is libidinally hypercathected or overvalued; the self-representations aggressively hypercathected or devalued. Since this is a relatively intolerable state of affairs, libido is repeatedly "refluxed" between self- and object-representations. Massive use of defensive denial is essential to maintaining psychological balance. That is, the weaknesses of the real love-object must be ignored, as well as the chronic over- or underestimation of self. Severe disappointments may strengthen the use of denial, whereupon mania may ensue. Or disappointments may disrupt the effectiveness of denial, whereupon the love-object is severely depreciated (aggressively hypercathected) and the self-representation (or self-image, if regression occurs) is correspondingly inflated (libidinally hypercathected). Successes, too, may have the same effect as disappointments unless they are attributed to the beneficence of the love object. If success is construed as the result of aggressive self-assertion, which runs counter to the prevailing self-concept as helpless and dependent, deflation of the love object follows which is intolerable. The cyclothymic's

... fear of a 'loss of the object' is fear of a destructive absorption of the 'good, powerful' object-image by the self-image. Here is a situation that induces an immediate and intense need to retrieve his old position. He will be overperceptive of any flaw in his achievements and use it to confirm his own weakness and to reinstate the strength and value of the object . . . rapid reversal, undoing, and denial of the previous situation (ensue) [p. 76].

This reversal, that is libidinal recathexsis of the love-object, may be unsuccessful for reasons unspecified other than overly depleted libido. Under these conditions both self and love-object are aggressively devalued. According to Jacobson, this represents the "primary depressive disturbance" as distinguished from secondary defensive and restitutive efforts to relibidinize the love-object, thus reinstating the initial unstable balance with the self-representations. The primary depressive disturbance is characteristic of many chronic simple depressives and depressed children:

They manifest a general pessimism, disillusionment, and lack of interest in life and in themselves. Everything has become worthless, unpleasurable, or empty. They maintain a continuous denial of the world's and their own value [1953, p. 77].

Since the devalued love-object has failed to arouse a libidinal investment, the cyclothymic may seek to attach his ideal object-image to another external object in the hope of restimulating his libidinal urges. He attributes limitless love and indestructible power to the substitute object, but his demands and expectancies of love and protection are insatiable. If the probable failure ensues, he then abandons the expectancy of love and accentuates the omnipotent sadistic aspects of the object. A punitive love-object is preferred to none at all. If the latter resort fails to sustain a relationship, the cyclothymic withdraws from reality, the conflict is internalized, and psychosis follows.

With the onset of psychosis, the object-representations revert to more primitive split object-images. The love-object representation is rent into an inflated punitive image and a weak, devalued love image. The former is absorbed by the superego; the latter fuses with the self-representations. The punitive superego cathects the self-image, thus deflating or destroying it. Cyclothymics' complaints and self-accusations are denials and confessions of guilt. The love-object is not destroyed but merged with the superego. However, its representation in the system-ego has dissolved.

Fast (1967) provides a lucid synthesis and extension of the earlier classical position with those of Klein and Jacobson. These theorists generally agree that the critically predisposing events to depression occur during the second six months of life. During this period, a critical shift in the self-boundaries of the infant is underway. Unsuccessful accomplishment of this shift leaves the infant vulnerable to depressive episodes. According to this formulation, the earliest self-boundary is between all memory traces of good experience, which are experienced as self, and all bad experiences, which are experienced as nonself and ego-alien. Distinctions between real self, others, and nonhumans are negligible. Fragmentary perceptions of each fuse and split continuously. Feeling states are pervasively good or bad.

It is the next stage in self-boundary development which the predepressive fails to master. This involves awareness that the self includes good and bad aspects and that other humans and nonhuman objects distinct from the self likewise have good and bad aspects. Good-bad distinctions must be attenuated, while self-other distinctions are sharpened. This second phase is a maturational byproduct of increased capacity for perceiving continuity of objects in space and time. Inevitably good and bad aspects of the same object become apparent, and separation anxiety over anticipated loss of a good object or experiential state occurs. Objects (self, others, and nonhumans) become increasingly integrated and stable wholes. Likewise, experiential states are less pervasive and less subject to massive shifts in response to isolated precipitants. Progression through the second phase of self-boundary establishment is enhanced by good, reliable mothering that includes the mother's capacity to receive from the infant as well as to give to it. The infant flourishes on feeling that it is good and has good things to offer.

Usually because of inadequate mothering, the predepressive fails to master the tasks inherent in the second stage of self-boundary development. His self-object boundaries are infirm, still susceptible to splits and fusions on the basis of good-bad evaluations; his self and other representations are not only unstable but their benign character is untrustworthy; there is insufficient confidence in the self's ability to overcome bad states. Bad states are easily evoked by any component (guilt, rage, contempt, etc.) of previous bad states. Such mood shifts involve a partial reversion toward good-self vs. bad nonself experiencing in which the self is experienced essentially as bad, nonself, and ego-alien. Regulation of experiencing state remains excessively dependent on relations with mother; if she is gratifying all is well; if not all is bad.

According to Fast this formulation helps to clarify the frequent observation that depressives do not act as though they were genuinely guilty, but rather as though they had been unfairly rejected by powers beyond their control, which powers, if sufficiently placated, could reinstate good feelings. Furthermore, depressive bad feelings are generalized well beyond feeling of immorality to those of inferiority and inadequacy—that is to say a global, undifferentiated feeling of badness prevails. The indiscriminate self-recriminations of severe depressives are more comprehensible as a multitude of unstable object-representations criticizing and being criticized than as the more systematic criticisms of an introjected corpus of parental ideals.

Depressives fear closeness, lest loss of ego boundaries occur, yet are frightened of individuation, lest lonely alienation result. They vacillate between fears of excessive dependency and abandonment, between impoverishment if they give love and abandonment if they do not. In describing similar conflicts in schizophrenics, others have aptly termed these conflicts "the need-fear dilemma" (Burnham, Gladstone, & Gibson, 1969).

Bibring's (1953) noteworthy contribution to a theory of depression has a considerably different emphasis from other psychodynamic theorists'. According to Bibring, the basic mechanism of depression is "... the ego's shocking awareness of its helplessness in regard to its aspirations [p. 39]."

Bibring rejects the notion that oral fixations are a necessary precursor of depressive reactions. He attributes this misconception to several sources. Most importantly, the infant's recurrent experience of frustrated helplessness and ensuing depression provides a prototypical reaction pattern that is reactivated by subsequent similar events. That is, Bibring emphasizes the infant's shocklike experience of, and fixation to, feelings of helplessness rather than to oral fixation per se. He agrees, however, that depressives are typically orally dependent personality-types who are excessively dependent on external "narcissistic supplies" of love, care, and support.

Bibring posits a developmental sequence of phase-specific narcissistic aspirations; narcissistic in the sense that goal attainment is essential to the maintenance of self-esteem. The realization of powerlessness and helplessness to achieve these aspirations deflates self-esteem and evokes depression. The cognitive and behavioral inhibition commonly seen in depressives reflects their sense of the futility of continued striving for unattainable and unrelinquishable goals. Narcissistic aspirations specific to the oral phase are: the need to get affection, to be loved, to be taken care of, or the opposite defensive needs to be independent and self-supporting. Needs of the anal phase are to master one's body, drives, and objects, to be loving and clean; not to be weak or evil; during the phallic phase aspirations are directed toward being a successful competitor, admired and strong, and toward not being overly vulnerable or fearful. In brief, narcissistic aspirations relate chiefly to being loved, loving, competent, and secure. But, "... in general, one may say that everything that lowers or paralyzes the ego's self-esteem without changing the narcissistically important aims represents a condition of depression [1953, p. 42]." Clinical improvement in depressives is frequently associated with modification, attainment, or relinquishing of narcissistic aspirations with a resultant diminished sense of helplessness.

Bibring differs somewhat from other psychodynamic writers in several respects. He views depression as primarily an intrasystemic ego state rather than an intersystemic (superego vs. ego) conflict. Self-aggression and the use of oral mechanisms like incorporation are secondary restitutive[17] complications related to the collapse of self-esteem, regression to an ego state of helplessness, and submission of the ego to punishment by the superego. They are not intrinsic aspects of depression per se. As Bibring (1953) observes, "... there are depressions which are not accompanied by any self-aggression and there are cases of angry self-hatred which do not show any manifest signs of depression.... [p. 54]." He acknowledges the significance of possible secondary gains from manipulating others into providing narcissistic supplies or rationalizing aggressive behavior, but does not elaborate on their role. As noted, he attributes the inhibition of ego functions in depressives to their striving for unattainable goals rather than to the more classical explanations of exhaustion due to intersystemic (ego vs. superego) conflict or precaution lest guilt or anxiety-arousing impulses be expressed. For example, individuals may defy their conscience successfully so long as outcomes are narcissistically gratifying, but if these rewards wane, guilt and self-reproach may ensue.

Susceptibility to a reactivated state of ego helplessness is a function of several factors: constitutional tolerance for persistent frustration; the severity and duration of helplessness experienced during infancy; subsequent developmental factors that tend to modulate or magnify the intensity and ease of activation of helpless states; and the type and severity of the event precipitating the present state of helplessness.

Fixation on helplessness and excessively high narcissistic aspiration apparently develop from an insufficiency of adequate "narcissistic supplies," that is love and approval. Proper availability of such nutriment in later developmental stages can partially attenuate the damage of earlier deficiencies.

Fluctuations in self-esteem are conceived as alerting signals of impending states of helplessness whose adaptive function is to initiate preventive measures.

---

[17]When psychodynamic writers use the term restitution, they generally refer to a reinvestment of previously withdrawn energy (or libidinal cathexes) in mental representations of objects, rather than making amends to an external object.

Aggression against the self results from a perceived helplessness to direct it outwardly.

Bibring viewed his conceptualization of the depressive mechanism as applicable to all normal and neurotic depressions and "probably" psychotic ones as well.

Sandler & Joffe (1965) attempt to bridge some of the discrepancies between Bibring's position and the more traditional psychodynamic one. Their focus is on depressions of childhood. While depressive affective reactions are common in childhood, depressive syndromes or illnesses are relatively rare (Cytryn & McKnew, 1972). The core qualities of most depressive reactions are felt helplessness, passively resigned behavior, and inhibitions of functions. Spitz's (1945, 1946) so-called anaclitic depressive syndrome during infancy is regarded as a basic psychophysiological reaction to deprivation of any variety: psychological and/or physiological. Depression is accorded the same conceptual status as anxiety, that is, as a basic psychobiological affective response. Depressive affect ostensibly occurs in response to a specific form of threat: the feeling of being unable to do anything about a loss, or the inability to acquire something essential to one's "narcissistic integrity"; it is a state of "deprivation-resignation." Emphasis is placed on threat to a sense of well-being rather than to loss of a valued object per se. This formulation has much in common with Bibring, except that more of the traditional stress on aggression is retained. Also, the depressive reaction is linked to the basic biological nature of pain as a state of ill-feeling in preference to Bibring's more complex psychological construct of self-esteem. Even when object-relations are more advanced developmentally, loss of an object may be responded to more in terms of loss of a sense of psychological and biological well-being than genuine grief for the lost object per se. Hence it is not surprising that anger complicates many normal grief reactions to loss, much less pathological depressive reactions (Lindemann, 1944). Mental pain is conceptualized as the discrepancy between one's actual and ideal state of well-being. It is hypothesized that mental pain normally elicits an aggressive response designed to reduce the discrepancy by affecting its perceived source. However, aggression thus mobilized may remain unexpressed out of fear of internal or external sanctions. Conscience may repress aggressive impulses or turn them against the self; or fear of external retaliation may lead to suppression of aggression with resultant deprecation of the self. That is, aggression may readily be turned against the self without necessarily invoking a pathognomic introjection and identification.

Healthy developmental progression entails successive "de-idealization" of infantile aims and their replacement with reality-adapted ideals. The more rigid the adherence to unrealistic ideals, the more susceptible the individual is to depression.

Zetzel (1953, 1965) maintains that psychological maturity is partly contingent on the ability to recognize, tolerate, and master affective states. Susceptibility to depression as an ego state usually begins toward the end of the first year of life. At this age, separation anxiety is acute, because the child is still very dependent on others for his sense of well-being. Self-object differentiation has been achieved, and object-relations are emergent. But self-identity, trust, and self-esteem are fragile and vulnerable. Separation anxiety, an especially acute threat, readily elicits rage, anxiety, helplessness, and depression. Children try to defend against such aversive affects by reliance on feelings of omnipotence or the "illusion of self-sufficiency." At this early stage of depression mastery, the critical developmental task is to be able to recognize, and to tolerate passively, an affect, without resorting to reality distorting denial or fantasies of omnipotence. That is, the realistic limitations of oneself and of others must be increasingly acknowledged and accepted without negating the existence of the frustrated wishes or the disappointment at their unfulfillment. This degree of objectivity can only be sustained when object-relations are sufficiently stabilized to avert regression to splitting objects into wholly good or wholly bad representations or the loss of self-other differentiation.

The subsequent developmental task in the mastery of depressive affect is the development of a disposition to mobilize adaptive efforts for modifying the sources of felt helplessness. These efforts could include such methods as altering one's perceptions, acquiring needed skills, or developing substitutive gratifications. There is, of course, considerable chronological overlap in these stages of depression mastery, the second phase reputedly extending up to the onset of the oedipal phase. The second phase of depression mastery complements rather than supersedes the earlier one. The Scylla and Charybdis of this critical development task are overpassivity on the one hand and underestimation of reality limitations on the other. An overpreponderance of either orientation may result in an overtly satisfactory social adjustment, but one that is vulnerable to depression. Because of an interaction of social and biological factors, males and females tend to have different susceptibilities to feelings of helplessness and resultant depression. Males are prone to overaccentuate their capabilities and to minimize even essentially unalterable reality limitations that must be passively endured, whereas females are more likely to experience depression due to overpassivity.

Zetzel contends that moderately severe early experiences of anxiety and depression have considerable prophylactic value. Both are apt to acquire a signal function that alerts the ego to impending danger and permits appropriate defensive and adaptive operations before the situation assumes traumatic proportions. Such aversive signal affects tend to be quite situation-specific and transient.

Chronic or characterological depression occur when basic trust and positive ego-identification are weak. Self-esteem tends to be low, the anticipation of failure and rejection high; hence the sense of futility associated with striving to diminish helplessness. This personality pattern tends to result from considerable aversive experience preceding structural differentiation. Self-other differentiation and object relations are achieved, but aversive affects are highly generalized with negligible signal quality. Characterological and psychotic depressives differ in that the former remain object related, that is, interested in and hungry for interpersonal relations, while the latter are more regressed, hence relatively uninvested in such relations. Psychotic depressives retain more omnipotent fantasies (Pao, 1968); have unrealistic expectations of themselves and others, and thus are more susceptible to feeling frustrated, rejected, enraged, guilty, and helpless. Zetzel's observations on the adaptive significance of tolerating awareness of depressive affect are in close accord with Lindemann's (1944) on adaptive versus pathological grief reactions to traumatic losses.

NEOANALYTIC VIEWPOINTS

Cohen et al. (1954) intensively studied a dozen manic-depressives from a Sullivanian, interpersonal orientation. Whereas Freudians emphasize intrapsychic and instinctual constructs, Sullivanians stress interpersonal and sociocultural constructs. Many heuristic distinctions can be drawn between the two approaches (Thompson, 1950), but recent elaborations of both psychodynamic approaches have attenuated these differences. Indeed, Cohen et al. concluded that many of their findings accord especially well with Melanie Klein's position. As noted before, Klein is regarded as a Freudian extremist even by her sympathetic critics (e.g., Zetzel, 1953). The Sullivanians and Klein dissent from the classical analytic contention of an initial, largely self-sufficient, narcissistic developmental phase. Both regard the infant as partially object-related from birth.

According to Cohen et al., manic-depressives typically are reared by mothers who are intensely concerned with elevating the family's social status, which they perceive as marginal. Marginal status may involve ethnic, religious, or health factors, but almost always includes the father's failure to attain the mother's standards of success. These mothers are described as unusually ambitious, aggressive, martyred, and blaming, but dependable; their husbands regard them as cold and contemptuous. The fathers tend to be weak, dependent, self-depreciating, but more lovable than their wives. The mothers' behavioral standards tend to be strict, conventional, and impersonal. Since social acceptance is critically valued, the children are constantly enjoined in terms of "what would the neighbors think." Reliance on such vague external models suggests that the parents' own values are poorly conceptualized and internalized. Often multiple and/or transient authority figures coexist in the home. Despite intrafamilial strains, the need to cling together against a threatening world is stressed.

Mothers of manic-depressives appear to enjoy and indulge their infants' dependency, but they severely punish their rebellious, assertive, autonomous strivings. The latter behaviors are increasingly evident toward the end of the first year of life. Crucially important alterations in interpersonal closeness and object relations accompany the infant's growing independence. The infant is less close to its mother because it is less totally dependent on her, yet the infant is increasingly aware of its dependence on its mother and its vulnerability to her influence. Furthermore, at this stage the infant is just progressing from relating by identification with partial aspects of others toward synthesizing the good and bad aspects of others into whole separate persons. Progress in this synthesizing task is facilitated by maternal warmth and consistency. But mothers of manic-depressives shift abruptly toward harsh punitiveness at this critical juncture when the infant begins to rebel and assert his independence. Much of the manic-depressive's subsequent ambivalence is attributed to maternal reinforcement for dependency and conformity and to punishment for assertiveness and autonomy. As a result,

> an important authority is regarded as the source of all good things, provided he is pleased; but he is thought of as a tyrannical and punishing figure unless he is placated by good behavior (Cohen et al., 1954, p. 117).

The critical interpersonal traumas of manic-depressives occur developmentally later than those of schizophrenics. This assumption derives from the manic-depressive's retention of his self-identity even when acutely psychotic, whereas the schizophrenic frequently loses his. Presumably this loss reflects regression to a more primitive developmental state.

Since not all siblings of manic-depressives are so afflicted, the question arises as to what special influences may have affected the patient-to-be. Cohen et al. hypothesize that the premanic-depressive child is singled out by the mother as the most potentially effective elevator of family prestige. Expectancies of good behavior, approval-gaining, and successful accomplishment are highest for this child. In addition, he may be given early, heavy responsibilities. His special status among his siblings inevitably engenders intrafamilial rivalry and envy. Such thoughts and feelings tend to be denied awareness by all participants, since they are incompatible with clinging together and with conventionally acceptable behavior. The need to deny important segments of intrafamilial transactions lays the groundwork for subsequent cognitive and communicative defects. Sensitivity to interpersonal relations is subordinated to obsessionally sticking together. Premanic-depressives often attempt to defend themselves against envy and competitiveness by underselling their abilities and accomplishments and by excessive helpfulness. As the premanic-depressive matures, his conflictual aspirations and defenses severely complicate his effectiveness and security. The perception of oneself as highly successful, independent, and universally admired, without awareness of others' envy, competitiveness, and resentment is apt to require considerable reality distortion. The manic-depressive evolves what Arieti (1959) has aptly designated an "outer-directed" personality. In Reisman's (1950) terms, the manic-depressive has neither the exquisite radar-like interpersonal sensitivity of the "other-directed," nor the stable, gyroscope-like internalized guidance of the "inner-directed" (Becker, Spielberger, & Parker, 1962).

Superficially the manic-depressive may appear to be adequately adjusted, but close scrutiny of his social relations suggests highly stereotypic patterns of relating to others. He tends to have numerous acquaintances, but only one or two intensely dependent relations. In these dependent relations the manic-depressive tends to be extremely demanding, though unwittingly so. This demandingness inevitably alienates the needed other, which elicits frustrated rage, depression, and increased demandingness in the manic-depressive. The depressive's sense of injustice at the estrangement is rooted in his perception of having made multiple sacrifices on the object's behalf. This perception can be viewed as a defense against awareness of how little the manic-depressive actually has given.

In the occupational realm the manic-depressive again feels inferior and needful of support. The sources of his anxieties about self and others' envy and competitiveness are largely out of awareness. Since direct striving for success might arouse these unacceptable impulses, devious manipulations are often resorted to, such as attempting to ingratiate himself with his boss. Underselling himself may result in underachievement, and if his self-proclaimed devaluation is accepted by colleagues, they incur his hatred.

Cohen et al. (1954) summarized their conception of the adult manic-depressive's personality as follows:

> . . . a person apparently well adjusted between attacks . . . conventional, well-behaved and frequently successful . . . hardworking and conscientious . . . typically involved in one or more relationships of extreme dependence in which he . . . seeks to control the other person in the sense of swallowing him up. . . . He is extremely stereotyped in his attitudes and opinions, tending to take over the opinions of the person in his environment whom he regards as an important authority. . . . His principal source of anxiety is the fear of abandonment . . . the anxiety is handled by overlooking the emotional give-and-take between himself and others, so that he is unaware of the person's feelings toward himself or of his feelings toward the other . . . [p. 120].

The hypothesized relations between adult character and infantile development are as follows:

> . . . interpersonal relations have been arrested . . . at the point where the child recognizes himself as being separate from others, but does not yet see others as being full-sized human beings; rather he sees them as entities who are now good, now bad, and must be manipulated . . . the adult's poorness of discrimination is understandable. His life and welfare depend upon the other's goodness . . . [p. 121].

He is unable to recognize that his own and others' behavior may oscillate between acceptance and rejection. The conventional stereotypes emphasized in the early home environment contribute to the manic-depressive's interpersonal insensitivity. Thus, what begins as a developmental defect becomes an anxiety-avoiding defense. The dependent manic-depressive cannot integrate good and bad aspects, but must screen out the bad; hence his interactions are stereotyped and flattened.

Cohen et al. differ from most other psychodynamic theorists on depression by attaching considerably less importance to hostility and guilt. Hostility is viewed as secondary to the frustration of his manipulative attempts, or to the miscarriage of efforts to restore dependent relations by manifesting needfulness. Guilt-like expressions do not convey genuine contrition and intent to change. Rather suffering is a means toward regaining approval; the patient despairing of better relations "... merely resorts to the magic of uttering guilty cries to placate authority [p. 125]."

Other ego-analytic, transactional and interpersonal concepts of depressive mechanisms owe much to Alfred Adler (1959). Kurt Adler (1961) and Bonime (1966) have recently summarized and extended these ideas. Adler's theory of Individual Psychology is a neo-Freudian "culturalist" one that essentially rejects energy distribution and instinctual concepts as well as the overdetermining role of early experience on subsequent personality development. The latter is viewed as a continuously evolving, future-oriented process largely derived from repetitive patterns of social interaction.

Nonetheless, according to the Adlerian view, the psychogenesis of depression is rooted in an "unrealized childhood." The parents of depressives reputedly provide a model of manipulativeness, often under the guise of oversolicitude. Basically, the parents deprive the child of spontaneous and genuine regard. Appropriate expectancies of the child are ignored or rebuffed. As a result,

> the discouraged child who finds that he can tyrannize best by tears will be a cry-baby; and a direct line of development leads from the cry-baby to the adult (depressed) patient (Adler, 1959, p. 288).

In general, the predepressive feels cheated of what was rightfully his, and determined to exact recompense or revenge. His inevitable feelings of inferiority and worthlessness lead to compensatory fantasies and affectations of superiority. His impaired capacity for reciprocally rewarding relations handicaps their establishment, and his excessive needfulness and demandingness often result in his depreciating their value. To a considerable extent, this depreciation of others' affection and concern stems from the predepressive's inability to experience such overtures in terms other than attempted manipulations of himself. Because of an earlier history of manipulative exploitation, the depressive has an "allergic sensitivity" to being influenced. Responsibility as well as mutuality are eschewed for similar reasons.

While depressive behavior is construed as largely a manipulative attempt to gratify insatiable emotional demands for compliance, sympathy, and help, the genuineness of suffering is not questioned. But whereas traditional psychodynamic theory views much of this suffering as unconsciously sought atonement for destructive impulses, the Adlerians view the suffering as an inevitable and unwelcome consequence of a life style. Because of the way he lives, the depressive inevitably experiences disappointment, loneliness, and resultant anger at his frustration. Much of the depressive's anxiety, traditionally ascribed to guilt, is attributed to chronic concern about how much others can be manipulated without permanently alienating them. Apparent guilt operates simply as another manipulatory device. The manipulative power struggle becomes an end in itself, functionally autonomous as it were. The concern with who will control whom overrides the articulation of adaptive interpersonal and intellectual capabilities.

Depressive symptoms are regarded as fairly direct manipulative operations, so that anorexia serves to reduce energy; self-depreciation to mask resources; psychomotor retardation to prevent grasping problems; indecisiveness to suspend action; and perfectionism to exaggerate task difficulties.

> In such a condition then, social relations, and with it, all obligations, are safely excluded, and the patient's proof of sickness, irresponsibility, and need for those who will serve him are firmly established . . . this, then, is the relentless effort of the depressive: to prevail with his will over others, to extort from them sacrifices, to frustrate all of their efforts to help him, to blame them—overtly or secretly—for his plight, and to be free of all social obligations and cooperations, by certifying to his sickness (Adler, 1961, p. 59).

However, according to such writers, depressives are largely unaware of their demandingness, manipulativeness, and hostility.

As usual very scant data are presented in support of these Adlerian-culturalist formulations. In terms of their range of applicability, Bonime (1966) contends they are germane to ". . . the whole span of depression from moping to psychotic withdrawal [p. 240]."

Chodoff (1970), another transactional theorist, identifies two subtypes of depressives: the extractive and obsessional. Both types share the core depressive characteristics of low self-esteem, hopelessness and helplessness, unresolved dependency needs, and ambivalent interpersonal relations, but their defensive styles in coping with these difficulties are distinctive. The extractive type is more akin to Bonomine's manipulative depressive, who decompensates if he cannot exact sufficient gratifications from others. The obsessional type is somewhat more like Bibring's (1953) and Arieti's (1959) characterizations. Obsessionals deny their dependency needs and reactively establish overexacting, perfectionistic standards; they become depressed when they despair at the fulfillment of their goals.

Like most psychodynamic writers, Chodoff accepts the possible etiological role of biological factors and contends that depressives are largely unaware of their ambivalent dependency needs; hence the experience of becoming depressed requires a rationale for the self: guilty protestations often reflect these self-explanatory attempts as well as having manipulative pay-off initially.

> Existentially guilt, not only in clinical depressions but more generally, may represent a longing for order or meaning in a capricious, acausal world. To blame oneself for an untoward happening is to imply that punishment is deserved and can be expiated with resultant lifting of the evil. In this sense guilt also serves to deny the unbearable responsibility imposed by a world without absolute standards or extra-human ordering (Chodoff, 1970, p. 59).

Also within a transactional framework, Salzman (1970) pursues the attempt to distinguish normal grief reactions from depressive reactions. In rejecting the notion of depression as a disease, he suggests that psychological factors may play a crucial role in the metabolic anomalies of some depressives. He cites the reversibility of potentially fatal adrenal insufficiencies in voodoo victims when given the proper "word" from the chief. According to Salzman (1970), depressives respond neurotically to the loss of narcissistic supplies by refusing to accept the loss and by attempting to coerce its restoration. Normals, on the other hand, accommodate to vital losses by accepting them if inevitable and by seeking adequate substitutes. But, "It is the rare, truly mature individual with solid self-esteem who does not have periodic depressed reactions" [p. 113].

Like other transactionalists, he views the traditional role of hostility turned against the self in depression as greatly overrated. Most depressive hostility results from the frustration of dependency needs. The traditional Freudian hydraulic model which asserts that the quantity of hostility expressed is inversely related to the quantity of hostility suppressed or repressed is regarded as clinically untenable.

Given the imprecision of much psychodynamic terminology plus the dearth of systematic empirical data provided in support of its constructions, it is not surprising that previous reviewers of the depression literature agreed poorly on its internal consistency. Rosenfeld (1959) states:

> It must have become clear from the facts collected in this paper that there are only very few points where we can talk about a real controversy and disagreement concerning the psychopathology of depression [p. 126].

Whereas Mendelson (1960) asserts, ". . . there is but limited consensus among writers on depression. Disagreement is acute on numerous issues . . . [p. 137]."

Suffice it to say that the overwhelming bulk of systematic research on depression today is biological in nature. Psychodynamic speculations have stimulated very limited research effort, as will be evident in Chapters 7 and 8. The scarcity of such research may reflect an unsympathetic research climate, at least with regard to the intrinsic difficulty in deriving testable hypotheses. Most biological research on depression is being done on relatively pure endogenous depressives, who constitute only about 15% of diagnosed depressives. The need for psychological investigations on the range of depressive disorders requires no belaboring.

Some trends in psychodynamic thinking are apparent. Depression is increasingly accorded an equal theoretical status with anxiety as a basic affect rather than as a defense. The old mechanistic hydraulic conception of depression as a partial manifestation of aggression turned inward is now being questioned. Conceptualizations of depression are progressively more compatible with a general systems approach (Engel, 1971). Elements of such an approach have been evident since Abraham's first paper, but the biological substrate and environmental surround of the intrapsychic system and their interactions were relatively neglected. Regrettably, psychodynamic family studies, which have done much to illuminate aspects of schizophrenic functioning, are still a rarity with depressives.

6
COGNITIVE AND BEHAVIORAL THEORIES OF DEPRESSION

It is memory that gives us the power of foresight: We push into the future with images in which we fixed the past. Full consciousness therefore looks both ways, and its most important look . . . is into the future. All biological processes are directed toward the future, but man is distinguished by being consciously directed — his consciousness includes the future (Bronowski, 1966, p. 80)[18]

Contributions from general behavioral theory to depressive theory have been fragmentary. Several factors have probably contributed to this neglect. Anxiety has served almost as a generic term for any dysphoric affects. Since anxiety is frequently associated with other dysphoric affects, this is not surprising. Nonetheless, psychologists are probably confounding independent constructs. Clarification of this issue urgently requires systematic comparison between the antecedents, correlates, and consequents of trait and state depression and anxiety. As indicated in the previous chapter, it seems feasible to obtain independent measures of these constructs (Costello & Comrey, 1967).

Psychologists may also have neglected depression because of the relatively high suicide risk and indifferent success of conventional psychotherapeutic methods. As a result, a high proportion of depressives are treated in psychiatric facilities with somatic methods such as electroconvulsive therapy (ECT) and antidepressant drugs.

COGNITIVE APPROACHES

Most psychopathologists would readily agree that deviant personality functioning is a joint determinant of predispositional (genetic endowment plus

---

[18]The direct source of this quotation was Melges & Bowlby (1969).

early experience) and situational factors. In general, psychodynamic explanations of psychopathology weight early experience factors more heavily, whereas behavioral explanations stress current situational determinants more heavily. Cognitive approaches to psychopathology may prove to be useful integrators of these disparities. Many psychodynamic concepts may prove translatable into cognitive concepts which are embedded in somewhat more systematic and rigorous general psychological theory and research. For example, notions like good and bad objects warring with each other, being introjected, projected, assimilated, annihilated, etc., are apt to be intensely alien to behavioral scientists. The observational bases for such notions are all too likely to be dismissed out-of-hand. But the same observations formulated in terms of cognitive patterns or schemas may prove more acceptable. Few would argue that the infant tends to form vague concepts about various aspects of his experience, and that experience tends to invest these concepts with varying affective associations. These schemas may be veridical or fantastically distorted; compatible or mutually exclusive; readily available to awareness or virtually inaccessible, etc. With maturation, some concepts are strengthened, some are weakened; increasing differentiation and hierarchization occurs. In short, the following cognitive approaches to depressive phenomena may not be as radical departures from the preceding psychodynamic approaches as they first appear.

Depression as a Thought Disorder

According to Beck (1967), all psychogenic disorders are primarily thought disorders. His main explanatory construct is the schema. Schemas (Harvey, Hunt, & Schroder, 1961; Miller, Galanter, & Pribram, 1960) are mediating cognitive structures between stimulus inputs (internal or external) and personality responses. They consist of organized clusters of attitudes, beliefs, and assumptions related to objects, events, or relations. Schemas act as stimulus scanners, filters, decoders, information processors, interpreters, and response encoders. They vary in abstractness, differentiation, availability to awareness, and hierarchical level. Supraordinate schemas influence subordinate schemas. Hence the referent of a simple lower-order schema might relate to cognitions about a specific person, while a higher-order one relates to mankind. Beck contends that all personality disorders share the same kinds of formal and logical cognitive distortion. But the characteristic schemas of each disorder have a systematic bias or "idiosyncratic ideational content" to which content appropriate affects are associated. During exacerbations of personality disturbances, these biased schemas become prepotently activated, resulting in selective misperceptions of reality.

The supraordinate schemas most implicated in depression are those pertaining to the self, the outer world, and the future. Powerful constellations of negative evaluative attitudes are associated with all three concepts, which are termed the "depressive cognitive triad." The most significant systematic bias or error in depressive cognition is a negative evaluation of the self. Depressives view themselves as worthless because they feel personally responsible for irreversible, critical deficiencies. They are beset with self-coercive injunctions such as 'should' and 'must' and plagued with the constant feeling that no matter what they do, it is insufficient. They experience the environment as overdemanding, blocking, depriving, or depreciating, and despairingly anticipate more of the same.

Depressives acquire their biases and vulnerabilities as a result of prior experience, perhaps especially from perceived appraisals by significant socializing agents (usually the parents) and their identification with such agents. That is, if the predepressive child perceives his parent(s) as disparaging his worth, he is highly likely to internalize such evaluations. Furthermore, if one or both parents were quite self-disparaging, and the predepressive child identifies with them, he will also tend to internalize their self-disparaging tendencies.

Depressive affect is triggered by events that evoke negative cognitions. Such events tend to have cue properties similar to those responsible for the initial acquisition of negative attitudes, although overwhelming nonspecific stresses or prolonged psychological strain may also precipitate depressive episodes. While the link between negative cognitions and depressive affect is not fully understood, Schachter's studies (1964) suggest that affective experience is a joint product of cognitive labeling and physiological arousal. Beck (1970c) illustrates the causal role of cognitions as affect determinants by pointing to such commonplace occurrences as good news inducing happy affects or terminating sad ones. He posits a feedback effect between cognitions and affect such that affects stimulate congruent cognitions and vice versa. Once a relevant cue has triggered the negative set, illogical and automatic data processing proceeds. The commonest reality distortions are as follows:

> *Arbitrary inference* is the process of drawing a conclusion in the absence of evidence to support the conclusion or when the evidence is contrary to the conclusion.
>
> *Selective abstraction* refers to the process of focusing on a detail taken out of context, ignoring other more salient features of the situation, and conceptualizing the whole experience on the basis of this element.
>
> *Overgeneralization* refers to the pattern of drawing a general conclusion on the basis of a single incident.
>
> *Magnification and minimization* refer to errors in evaluation that are so gross as to constitute distortion.
>
> *Personalization* refers to the patient's proclivity to relate external events to himself when there is no basis for making such a connection [pp. 51–52].

Arbitrary inferences tend to be highly automatic, involuntary, plausible, and perseverative, which makes them difficult to modify. Subjectively, they make good sense and therefore are difficult to prevent or terminate.[19] Plausibility and

---

[19] But for an excellent discussion of recent therapeutic innovations designed to effect these goals, see Beck (1970a); for their relation to conventional behavioral therapy, see Beck (1970b).

degree of affective involvement seem to have a strong positive correlation and an inverse relation to modifiability.

Beck regards distorted cognition as the causal or independent variable in depression; the affective, motivational, and physical accompaniments are secondary derivatives. While this is not a typical position, it is not unique (Kelly, 1955; Harvey, Hunt, & Schroder, 1961; Ellis, 1962). According to Beck, variations in depressive feelings like sadness, shame, boredom, loneliness, frustration stem from variations in cognitive emphases.

Likewise the specific motivational deficits in depression, such as indecisiveness and volitional paralysis, strong escape and avoidance tendencies including suicide, and heightened dependency, are linked to specific negative cognitions. If the depressive feels that coping efforts are totally futile, paralysis results; if he can still at least envisage the possibility of better things, escape, avoidant, or dependent behaviors occur.

Physical symptoms such as retardation, fatigue, and agitation are similarly linked to the nature and intensity of prevailing cognitions. For example, retarded stupors may be associated with the delusion of death. Even physical symptoms like fatigue are subjectively more than physiologically valid. Despite common feelings of exhaustion, hospitalized depressives perform quite adequately in a multiplicity of standardized test situations (Friedman, 1964).

Beck's position is a stimulating and provocative one, unusually well tied to clinical data, and capable of generating testable hypotheses, as demonstrated in the subsequent chapter on psychological research.

Using Festinger's (1957) theory of cognitive dissonance, Averill (1968) postulates that many of the depressive's guilty cognitions may be attempts to make sense of the biologically determined grief which inevitably accompanies significant object loss. Indirectly, this formulation touches on one of the most central issues related to depression: whether depression is primarily an emotional or mood disorder or a disease with a necessary and sufficient biological etiology. Averill acknowledges the validity of Engel's (1961) contention that emotions and diseases have strong resemblances (a patterned etiology, expression, and course), but notes that emotions, unlike diseases, imply social relations and judgments. In short, are depressive cognitions mere epiphenomena of a disease or prime etiological agents? This issue is not idle conjecture. For example, the catecholamine hypothesis was largely stimulated by observations that reserpine activates depressive states, including typically depressive cognitions in nondepressed humans (Schildkraut, 1965).

Goal Attainment

Stotland (1969, p. 34) argues that depression results when important goals are strongly devaluated. He postulates that the greater the importance of a goal, and the lesser its probability of attainment, the higher the level of anxiety. Decreasing the importance of the goal alleviates anxiety. But since the motivation to act derives largely from the perceived probability of attaining important goals, diminishing the importance of goals lessens motivation. Thus the reaction to lowered goals is depression, apathy, and withdrawal. This formulation may account more adequately for apathy than for depression. As Mowrer (1960, p. 197) notes, the "miserable and tortured" inactivity of the depressive reflects not a lack of motivation, but a sense of utter futility about the utility of action. In this respect Mowrer's position is similar to Bibring's (1953).[20] After goal deflation, reality changes that even slightly increase hopefulness may substantially reinflate the value of the previously devalued goals. A resultant shift toward higher aspirations with limited hopefulness may increase the amount of anxiety relative to depression. As an example, Stotland cites findings on World War II pilots who were required to complete 30 combat missions before obtaining military leave (Grinker & Spiegel, 1945). Since mortality rates were high, many pilots despaired of completing the required tour of duty and displayed depressive attitudes about the meaninglessness of life. But as completion of their tour approached, hopes for survival increased somewhat, while the value of survival increased greatly. Intense anxiety often accompanied this shift.

The schema concept occupies a central role in Stotland's theorizing as well as Beck's. Stotland contends that schemas derive primarily from experience, communication, and observation. The strength of a schema is determined by the frequency with which its assumptions or propositions are confirmed and the importance of the person from whom it derives. Higher order schemas are relatively insusceptible to change; nonconfirmatory inputs tend to motivate alterations in perception designed to minimize discrepancies. Schemas are modified by the consequences of activity, but activity is significantly affected by motivation. Powerful higher-order schemas to the effect that one is a failure and hopeless, the world frustrating, arbitrary, and demanding, are apt to diminish the motivation needed to generate performances that might refute or modify such schemas. Thus higher-order schemas tend to be self-perpetuating. Stotland also thinks that activated higher-order schemas probably play a significant role in mood and self-esteem regulation (1969, p. 80). The generality and abstractness of higher-order schemas contribute to the difficulty in pinpointing their instigators, which in turn complicates efforts to counteract their influence. The variegated manifestations of depression may be due to the simultaneous activation of several powerful and strongly associated higher-order schemas or to differences in associated lower-order ones. Conceivably, agitated depressions may be associated with despair of attaining goals rigidly adhered to, as Bibring suggests, whereas retarded depression may conform to Stotland's notion of deflated aspirations with a correlative feeling that goal striving is meaningless. Or, to speculate further within Stotland's framework, depressive inhibition may

---

[20] However, goal directedness is a peripheral aspect of Mowrer's theory of depression (1961). As indicated before, he attributes depression to real guilt over unacknowledged and unexpiated moral and social transgressions.

be related to the socialization paradigm adduced by Cohen et al. (1954). The latter suggest that the mother of the predepressive enjoys the dependent relation and is intolerant of assertiveness, rebelliousness, or striving toward autonomy, although she invokes conventional success as a desirable goal. The schemas and drives aroused by a history of being punished or ignored for assertive efforts, while being exhorted that conventional success is the only meaningful goal in a competitive society, would be intensely conflictual. Stotland indicates that anxiety or depression related to goal attainment are particularly apt to occur when goals become important in areas of limited competence. Perhaps this partially explains the high incidence of depression among married females in their forties. Pressures for autonomous functioning are apt to be markedly heightened by the departure of their grown children and the immersion of their husbands in occupational pursuits. Likewise, Stotland's association of deflated goals with depression may provide a useful hypothesis for understanding the apparent rise in youthful depressions. Traditional goal striving is increasingly challenged by youth. Those unable to engage meaningful alternative goals may succumb to a sense of futility. Intense interdependencies seem characteristic of many alienated youths; rather than manifesting independence, many appear to conform rigidly to their subcultural norms. To continue with possible parallels between Cohen et al.'s depressive socialization hypotheses and Stotland's ideas about goal attainment, the former emphasize the lack of well internalized standards in the parents of depressives. This lack results in their admonishing their children to do 'what the neighbors would approve of.' Such parents may thus provide fairly clear, if unrealistic, conventional standards about good grades, moral conduct, economic success, and social status, but they are less likely to provide much in the way of instrumental response training or role modeling on how to attain such ends. Stotland implies that the greater the ambiguity about desirable goals, or about the means to attain them, the greater the vulnerability to hopelessness. To further complicate matters, almost any activity tends to alleviate hopelessness. Hence behaviors which have been adaptive in the past may persist despite their irrelevance to present objectives. If dependence, conformity, demandingness, and suffering have paid off in the past, they are apt to be resorted to again as measures to alleviate hopelessness. However, just as aggression against the self may be largely a function of powerlessness to direct it against others, so may dependency be the result of an inadequate instrumental response repertoire. Indeed, it may be the strongest response in the depressive's goal frustration response hierarchy.

Stotland heavily stresses the acquisition of schemas by observation, especially of others of high status or of strong perceived similarity. The potency of familial figures in early schema acquisition is self-evident. Investigations of the incidence of depression in parents of depressed patients during the predepressive's childhood should be fruitful, although positive findings would be subject to genogenic interpretations. Hopefulness is substantially mediated by the perceived availability of support from important others. Jacobson's (1956) and

Lewinsohn & Shaffer's (1971) reports suggest that spouses of depressives are not uncommonly hostile, rejecting, and destructive.

As Tolman noted (1951), supports are essential to goal attainment. Loss of support is functionally equivalent to an external or internal obstacle, according to Bull & Strongin (1956). The latter contend that any threatening goal obstacle initially arouses strong attack or escape responses; the individual's preoccupation with his negative subjective state increases. With persistent frustration and a mounting sense of inability to recover goal directedness, depression may ensue. Depression is defined as occurring when the

> organism having lost its goal, becomes fixated on some aspect of its own entanglement and consequent discomfort, while it perseverates in a display of helplessness and protest, designed, like screaming in a baby, to call attention to its plight (p. 533).

The crying pattern is considered the prototype of all depressive reactions. Depressive inhibition becomes an internal obstacle to goal attainment. The symptomatic manifestations of the depressive are construed as a mixture of attack and escape reaction to his internal obstacle, plus an appeal for succor.

Lichtenberg (1957) has a more differentiated theory of frustrated goal attainment and depressive subtype. Like Bibring, he attributes depression to felt helplessness about attaining goals when the failure is ascribed to personal defects. The obverse of depression is hope, which is a function of the perceived probability of attaining crucial goals. Hope of goal attainment is determined by the availability of appropriate action patterns, sufficient time, and adequate environmental supports, physical and interpersonal. This model evolved from observations of depressives' work habits and from depression-inducing research on cooperative behavior in normal subjects (Lichtenberg, 1956). Depressives are described as loath to initiate tasks, as preferring either simple repetitive tasks or large unrealistic ventures. They constantly seek to avoid responsibility and to elicit help and attention.

Lichtenberg postulates a three phase ontogenetic development of expectancies about goal attainment. Variations in depressive manifestations depend on which of these expectancy orientations are chiefly implicated in failing to fulfill crucial aspirations. The earliest expectancy orientation is a highly generalized one akin to Erikson's (1950) concept of basic trust. It pertains to hopefulness about environmental gratification of needs regardless of behavior. The degree of hopefulness depends on the relative balance of perceived need gratification and frustration. In the second stage, there is growing awareness that behavioral style is related to goal attainment; hope depends on the perceived adequacy of behavioral style to goal attainment. In the final stage, the child realizes that behavior style must be accommodated to particular situations. There is greater differentiation of style and circumstance and recognition of the need to reconcile the two.

Associated with helplessness about particular situations, behavioral styles, and generalized goals are specific forms of depression: neurotic, agitated, and retarded, respectively. Explicit, potentially testable predictions are made about the impact of particular expectancy orientations on a wide range of reactions: for example, time perspective, availability of supports, and assessment of potential secondary gains and losses. The logical consistency between the theoretical model and predictions is not always self-evident, but many of the hypothesized relations are provocatively interesting. An attempt to validate these relations empirically would seem well worthwhile. Meanwhile, Melges & Bowlby (1969) have provided a speculative but testable analysis of hopelessness and goal expectancy differences in depressives and psychopaths.

Role Loss

E. Becker (1962) also ascribes depression to a loss of meaningful instigators to activity. He argues that ego integrity, identity, and self-esteem are rooted in a symbolically mediated attachment to reality. Among the most vital attachments are those which involve social role enactment with significant others (or objects). Object loss tends to be disastrous for the depressive because of his limited range of roles and objects. The depressive has little capacity for substituting roles or objects when losses or frustrations occur. Participation in role or game activity with objects is the prime motivation for activity; lack of motivation to participate results in depressive inhibition. Much of the depressive's self-abusive cognition stems from an effort to make sense of what he experiences. His rationales are highly colored by his parents' extensive use of guilt-inducing socialization practices. But they also reflect the dependence of self-esteem on an accurate labeling of ego states. When there is no meaning in activity, self-esteem declines, blame is attributed, and the self is a likely candidate for such blame. Becker's central point is that loss of meaningful role activity is at least as crucial an etiologic factor in depression as loss of an object per se.

Role and Task Adaptation in Stress and Crisis

Davis (1970) views depression as a maladaptive response to social crises. As he notes, the peak incidence of depressive episodes occurs in females between 45–54. A typical female at that age has recently lost her father and is about to lose her mother; is in the process of losing her children; and has just gone through menopause. A fair proportion, about 7%, are already widowed. In short, women during this age span are typically faced with a number of major role adaptations. Depression can result if previously rewarded behavioral patterns, which are no longer functional, persist in the absence of new adaptations which require appropriate means and reinforcers. Experimental extinction or habituation of major behavioral systems may ensue. He supports this argument by the equal sex incidence of depression after age 65, when men must adapt to retirement. Davis derives his formulation from Caplan's crisis theory (1964) and his own experimental investigations of extinction (1952) and perceptual processes (1964). Caplan contends that psychiatric illnesses reflect failures to cope with critically important changes in life situations. Davis draws an analogy between such life crises and laboratory situations in which highly motivated subjects are confronted with insoluble tasks. He reports that a reliably observable sequence of response patterns occurs under such frustrating conditions. His apparatus was the "Cambridge Cockpit," which simulated a pilot's task. The apparatus was adjusted so that subjects could not attain their goals. Subjects initially responded with overactivity and aggressive expressions; as frustration and anxiety mounted, responses became increasingly disorganized; perceptual disorganization of the field with perseverative focusing on limited aspects of the task demands followed; finally, ignoring of limited aspects of the task was generalized to the entire task; responses became slow and weak. At this stage, variously referred to as inertia, habituation, and experimental extinction, subjects became self-disparaging. In sum, they displayed many characteristics of retarded depression. The same response sequence occurred with a much simpler, but inherently frustrating, motor task (Caplan, 1964). In a visual perception task requiring identification of a gradually more illuminated image, depressed patients developed perseverative hypotheses that poorly integrated the available information. Davis speculates that depressive reactions may result from continuous confrontation with demands that cannot be met or ignored. This formulation is similar to current behavioristic speculations about the relation between depression and deprivation of positive reinforcers. Despite the depressives' impoverished apperceptive acuity, they often display an excellent recall of past painful experiences. Davis observes that contemporary events do not seem to elicit focused, sustained attention in depressives. Several psychodynamic (Federn, 1926, Weiss, 1944) and existential psychiatrists (Ellenberger, 1958) have commented on the depressive's dulled experience of reality. It is as though the prepotent negative schema (Beck, 1967) largely preempts awareness. Under these conditions, available positive reinforcers may not be perceived and a state of mild stimulus deprivation with resultant facilitation of autistic processes may occur.

Passive Avoidance

Averill (1968) notes interesting analogies in the combined behavioral depression, physiological activation, and dysphoric affect that occur in grief, depression, and passive avoidance (Mowrer, 1960, pp. 31–33). As indicated earlier, Averill conjectures that grief serves the biologically adaptive function of motivating socially oriented animals to avoid separation. He notes Hamburg's (1963) observation that threats to critical social relations may elicit as much psychophysiological stress as a predatory attack. The early distress during grief and depressive reactions presumably reflects a mixture of stress and reparative efforts. If the latter are continuously frustrated, the depressive may shift to passive avoidance of goal directed activity as a means of lessening distress.

Learned Helplessness

Seligman (1971) speculates that the experimental results of administering unpredictable and uncontrollable aversive events to infrahumans may provide a useful model for conceptualizing reactive depression in humans. As Seligman notes, an optimal laboratory model must extend beyond descriptive behavioral analogies to similarities in etiology, pathophysiology, psychopharmacology, cure, and prevention. His evidence for such parallels between his model and reactive depression is admittedly tentative.

To appreciate Seligman's notions it is essential to be familiar with his basic experimental paradigm and the effects it produces.

Naive dogs were randomly assigned to an experimental or control group. All training and test trials occurred in a shuttle box. This box contained an entry shock chamber which is separated by an adjustable barrier from a nonshock escape-avoidance chamber. Both experimental and control dogs underwent a series of signalized escape-avoidance training trials in the shuttle box.

Prior to the signalized training, the experimental dogs were subjected to a pretraining series of inescapable electric shocks. During these pretraining trials, the experimental dogs were strapped into a hammock inside the entry chamber of the shuttle box. There they received 64 inescapable electric shocks of 5″ each and of 6.0ma intensity which were randomly distributed temporally. On the following day the experimental dogs received the same standard signalized escape-avoidance training in the shuttle box as the control dogs. In the standardized training trials, the unrestrained dog was placed in the entry half of the shuttle box; a *CS* (dimmed illumination) started the trial, and after 10″ the *US*, a "severe pulsating" 4.5ma shock, went on. If the dog leaped the barrier to the exit portion of the box, the CS and US were automatically terminated, and the dog escaped from the shock or trauma. If the dog failed to leap the barrier, the CS and UCS continued for 50″.

Dogs in the control group received only the standard signalized escape-avoidance learning, without the pretraining exposure to inescapable shock.

The difference in the response of the experimental and control dogs to the standard signalized escape-avoidance trials was striking. Ninety-five percent of the control dogs (who were not previously exposed to unavoidable shock) rapidly and reliably learned to leap the shuttle barrier to safety. They then progressively shifted from escaping the shock after its onset to avoiding it by responding to the CS as a signal of impending shock.

In marked contrast, two-thirds of the experimental dogs (earlier subjected to unavoidable shock) failed to learn to escape or avoid shock on the standard training trials. The experimental dogs tended to manifest two behavioral deficits. First, they attempted few adaptive responses, and second, even when they displayed an adaptive response, they failed to learn from it. For example, once a control dog leaped or stumbled over the barrier, thus terminating the shock, he tended to repeat the action consistently on successive trials with progressively reduced latencies. But experimental dogs who surmounted the barrier by chance or design did not tend to repeat the response. They typically reverted to the passive acceptance of 50″ of severe pulsating shock. The latter behavioral phenomenon has been termed learned helplessness by Seligman and his associates.

The consequences of unavoidable trauma on subsequent adaptiveness are broadly generalizable to multiple species and types of trauma. Neither the clinical nor experimental literature suggests that traumas per se have adverse consequences on subsequent adaptiveness. More specifically, it is unpredictable and uncontrollable trauma that tends to be associated with passive resignation and defective learning.

The etiology of learned helplessness has been conceptualized thusly: organisms (Os) continuously and simultaneously learn about the probabilities that reinforcers will occur as a result of either emitting or not emitting particular responses. So long as these probabilities are not equal, the O may be said to have some control over the consequences of his behavior. But when the consequences of responding or not responding are approximately equal or independent, the organism lacks control over the consequences of his behavior. It is under these conditions that learned helplessness is most likely to occur. During the pretraining phase of inescapable shock, the termination of shock is in no way contingent on anything the animal does. Presumably, in the subsequent signalized escape-avoidance training, shock mediates the generalization of the initial learned helplessness. In other words, if an organism is exposed to fairly massive and/or sustained inescapable trauma he is likely to respond with passivity. The more subsequent traumatic experiences resemble the conditions under which passivity was acquired, the greater the likelihood that passivity will generalize as a response to the subsequent trauma, even though the latter may not actually be inescapable.

In sum, learning that response and the onset and/or termination of trauma are independent has both motivational and cognitive effects. Motivation to respond is largely contingent on an incentive to respond in order to achieve desirable consequences. In the absence of such incentive the organism is unmotivated to seek relief. Furthermore, acquisition of the cognitive expectancy that activity and relief are independent inhibits the acquisition of knowledge to the contrary. Thus even if by chance the organism succeeds in preventing or terminating the traumatic conditions, the response contingent relief is less likely to result in an associative link that increases the probability of a subsequent adaptive response. Numerous alternative hypotheses such as adaptation (increased shock), sensitization (mild shock), acquisition of a competing response (curare), etc., have been tested in a series of ingenious experiments and found wanting. Several are briefly discussed. One experiment tested the hypothesis that trauma per se rather than inability to control trauma accounted for learned helplessness. There were two experimental groups, respectively designated as the "escape" and "yoked" groups, and a control group. Only the experimental groups received pretraining. Dogs in both groups were as usual confined in the hammock, but dogs in the escape group could terminate shock by touching a panel with their nose or head. Dogs in the yoked group received exactly the same amount of shock as dogs in the escape group but could do nothing to terminate shock. All three groups were then run in the standard signalized escape-avoidance procedure. The escape group and the naive control group readily learned escape-avoidance; the yoked group (6 of 8) manifested typical learned helplessness.

Many learning theorists have been highly skeptical of cognitive explanations of behavior. They could argue that in the pretraining phase experimental dogs acquired a passive response as a result of its association with shock termination. And that it is this passive response, which is antagonistic to learned barrier jumping, that accounts for learned helplessness rather than a cognitive negative expectancy set. To test this alternative hypothesis an experiment was designed with two experimental groups, respectively designated as the "passive-escape" and "yoked" group, and a control group. The experimental groups had pretraining and then all three groups went through the standard signalized escape-avoidance procedure. In the pre-training phase, the passive-escape group could terminate shock only by remaining absolutely passive. The yoked group received exactly the same amount of shock as the passive escape group but could do nothing to control the shock. The prediction for the noncognitive position (response-learning) would be that dogs in both experimental groups would respond passively in the standard trials, whereas cognitive protagonists would predict that animals in the passive-escape group who had learned that shock could be controlled by passivity would adopt an active problem-solving set toward the standard situation. The latter prediction was supported. Initially dogs in the passive-escape group did seek for a "still" solution for the trauma, but when this was unsuccessful they shifted to an active, appropriate barrier-leaping response. As would be expected, the yoked group failed to display adaptive behavior. In short, learning that passivity reliably controls trauma does not interfere appreciably with learning to abandon passive responding and to shift to active responding when the reinforcement contingencies have changed.

Turning to the etiology of clinical depression, Seligman draws on concepts derived from Bibring's (1953) classical ego-analytic paper *The Mechanism of Depression.* Bibring argued that depression is a basic ego state reflecting felt helplessness about the possibility of fulfilling aspirations critical to the maintenance of self-esteem. Passivity or inhibition results from the feeling that striving is meaningless. Most speculations on the precipitants to depression emphasize losses of a critically important person, relationship, possession, value, that is, the onset or cumulation of uncontrollable aversive events. Furthermore, Bibring contends that many depressions occur in individuals predisposed by previous shocklike encounters with the ego's helplessness in coping with disturbances in the acquisition of essential narcissistic supplies. Most depressions are viewed as reactivations of this ego state of despair rather than as regressions to orally fixated defenses and object relations. However, even if it is accepted that uncontrollable losses frequently precede depression, there remains the problem of the lack of specificity of such a relation to depression. A host of organic and psychosomatic disorders also seem to be preceded by significant losses.

Seligman's third criterion for an adequate animal-derived model of depression is a similarity in physiology and psychopharmacology. Here Seligman's evidence is self-admittedly weak and tentative. As noted, he contends that learned helplessness is analogous to reactive depression rather than to endogenous depression, which he views as more likely biologically determined. Nonetheless, the factors he cites as common to learned helplessness and depression are more characteristically associated with endogenous depression. His data are based primarily on rats subjected to inescapable shock. They manifest more anorexia, weight loss, and norepinephrine depletion than rats subjected to controllable shock. Preliminary evidence suggests that the commonly used antidepressant tricyclic drug imipramine, or tofranil, which appears to increase the amount of norepinephrine at central adrenergic receptor sites, disrupts learned helplessness in dogs.

As for commonalities in the treatment of learned helplessness and depression, these too are presently tenuous and suggestive only. Multiple efforts to disrupt learned helplessness in dogs were unsuccessful. Experimenters removed the barrier to the safe chamber and tried to call the dog to it, or to lure it with food; they kicked the shock chamber, all to no avail. That is, efforts to mobilize animals to initiate an adaptive response were futile. Only tying a leash to the dogs' harness and repeatedly dragging them (20 to 50 trials) to the safe chamber was effective. The multiple forced passages required and the strength of initial resistance buttress the contention that learned helplessness results in low motivation to initiate responses (if not actual resistance) and diminished ability to learn response-relief contingencies.

There are no direct parallels to forced exposure to previously traumatic conditions in the treatment of depressives, but many behavioral approaches seek to foster the conditions which Bibring specified as related to recovery from depression. He maintained that when critical aspirations again become attainable in modified or unmodified form, self-esteem is restored and the depression lifts. Seligman without undue violence reconstrues this position within his framework. Thus, a restored sense of dependency between response-relief contingencies alleviates helplessness and depression.

As for prevention, Seligman notes that initial exposure of dogs to the signalized escape-avoidance procedure is a highly effective prophylactic for learned helplessness when these animals are subsequently exposed to inescapable shock and then again to avoidable shock. Furthermore, cage-reared dogs are much more susceptible to learned helplessness than naturally reared dogs. One-third of the latter never succumbed to learned helplessness and those that did succumb typically required double the number of inescapable shock sessions as their cage-reared counterparts.

BEHAVIORISTIC FORMULATIONS

Theory, treatment, and research are closely meshed within the "behavioristic" approach to depression (Liberman & Raskin, 1971). Behavioral modification approaches as usually construed include operant, desensitization, aversive, and role modeling procedures (Bandura, 1969).

Although depression is among the commonest forms of personality disturbance, behaviorists have had relatively little to say or do about it. Lazarus (1968) attributes this dearth to difficulties in operationally defining and measuring depression, Wolpe (1971) to reactive depression's being largely secondary to anxiety.

In Ferster's (1965) operant analysis of depression, he contends that the core feature is "... a reduced frequency of emission of positively reinforced behavior [p. 24]." Large segments of behavior can be under the restricted control of very limited aspects of the environment. In such situations, abrupt shifts in the controlling environment may result in a failure to elicit many performances within the person's behavioral repertoire. As an illustration, he cites the classical clinical example of two spinster sisters who live in seclusion until one dies, whereupon the survivor becomes psychotically depressed. Presumably, most of the reinforcers essential to the maintenance of the depressed person's behavioral repertoire are no longer forthcoming. This form of analysis is applicable to the effects of any abrupt shift in reinforcement contingencies that entail a major loss of positive reinforcers. Assumption of adolescent, adult, or retirement roles which do not positively reinforce sizable segments of the extant behavioral repertoire may greatly reduce the emission of hitherto positively reinforced behavior. Deficient ability and skill in discriminating and acquiring potentially rewarding behaviors may enhance and prolong the depressing effects of such events.

According to Skinnerians, behaviors are ultimately sustained by positive reinforcers. But varying amounts of behavior are controlled by negative reinforcers which facilitate escape or avoidance from aversive stimuli. To the extent that behavior is controlled by negative reinforcers, less behavior is emitted that could result in positive reinforcement. Therefore, a low ratio of positive reinforcement occurs and the behaviors sustained by it are weakened. Clinical accounts of the familial environment of depressives (e.g. Cohen et al., 1954; Jacobson, 1956) strongly suggest the operation of excessive aversive control. Low ratios of positive reinforcement may have effects akin to those of high fixed-ratio reinforcement schedules which require great amounts of effort to obtain positive reinforcement. Low operant emission is especially pronounced immediately following receipt of reinforcement on such schedules. Skinner (1953) likens such behavior to abulia or loss of will, a very common manifestation in depressions. A possible explanation for the high recurrence rate of depression is that relatively weak behavior is more readily suppressed or disrupted by aversive environments. By contiguity, many previously neutral stimuli associated with aversive ones acquire aversive properties; hence many apparently innocuous cues tend to suppress or disrupt behavioral chains which might yield positive reinforcement if carried to completion. The assumption, of course, is that depressives have weak behavioral repertoires for eliciting positive reinforcers.

Ferster is quite aware that the same factors which account for lack of adaptive behaviors are abundantly present in other forms of personality disturbances, but he does not address himself at length to the particulars of depression. Nor does he or any other behaviorist attempt to explain how a disorder based on extinction tends to be self-limited in duration.

Lewinsohn's group have conducted a series of interrelated laboratory and treatment studies which test assumptions about depressive behavior within a social learning framework (Lewinsohn, 1972). Their guiding assumption has been that depressives evoke a low rate of positive reinforcement (such as attention, affection, interest, etc.) from others. The depressive's weak evocative capacity is chiefly ascribed to his poor social skill at emitting positive elicitors and inhibiting negative elicitors. Also, environmental changes (e.g., separation, accidents, misfortune) may have deprived the depressive of previously higher rates of reward. Low positive reinforcement schedules tend to evoke depressive behavior (e.g., guilt, fatigue, self-depreciation) which is jointly determined by intrinsic reactions to extinction schedules and by the sympathetic responses of others to such behaviors. These supportive responses from others may decrease with time as the depressive behaviors acquire an increasingly aversive quality. The depressive's principal therapeutic need is for increased positive reinforcement of nondepressive behaviors. Effecting this increase is complicated by the depressive's poor social skills and restricted range of friends and interests. Hostility in depressives is accorded secondary importance. Accruing evidence which indicates that an abrupt, substantial lowering of positive reinforcement schedules initially elicits aggressive behavior is cited (e.g., Azrin, Hutchinson, & Hake, 1966). Lewinsohn et al. conjecture that since expression of hostile behavior would tend to diminish the rate of positive reinforcement even further, the depressive probably tries to suppress such behavior.

Note that in the Lewinsohn et al. formulation of depression the chief antecedent condition tends to be lack of social skill. This must be carefully borne in mind in weighing the supporting experimental and clinical evidence reported to date. The experimental studies have been done with college students designated as depressed on the basis of psychometric test scores, such as MMPI T scores: $L < 60$, $D < 70$, $Hy < 70$ and Pt (K-corrected) $< D$ (Byrne, 1961) and Lubin's Depressed Adjective Check List (1965). As compared with clients seeking outpatient treatment for depression, these students would fall within the mildly depressed range. Most of Lewinsohn et al.'s treatment studies seem to be with persons having clinical depression of moderate severity.

Whether depressive behaviors are etiological factors or secondary to the depressive state is unclear. Logically, the etiological link makes sense, inasmuch as resistance to extinction is directly related to the strength of a response and is inversely related to its effortfulness (Millenson, 1967). If premorbid social behavior has been weak and labored for the depressive, it should be relatively susceptible to impairment. The kind of reinforcement regimen that generated a vulnerability to such impairment might also account for the nature of Beck's cognitive triad (pessimism about self, world, and future), as well as the behavioral passivity. In turn, these cognitive biases may exaggerate the self-perceived extent of deprivation and inadequacy.

Even assuming that social skill deficiency is related to depression, a progressive sharpening of the hypothesis is necessary. For example, on a priori grounds one would assume that schizoid individuals are at least as unskilled socially as depressives. Lewinsohn et al. display a commendable awareness of the theoretical and empirical status of such crucial constructs as positive reinforcement and a noteworthy eschewal of futile polemics. They explicitly avow, e.g., the probable importance of cognitive factors in depression, although this is not their current focus.

Wolpe (1971) asserts that normal depression is an adaptive response to loss which motivates the search for alternative gratifying objects. He notes the frequent concurrence of neurotic anxiety and reactive depression and compares the experimental analogs for generating the two states. The chief distinction in the respective experimental paradigms is the frequency of unavoidable shock administered. With a limited frequency, anxiety and active avoidance responding occur; with greater frequency, as in Seligman's work, passivity or learned helplessness results. Wolpe prefers a conditioning explanation of learned helplessness to Seligman's cognitive explanation. Wolpe argues that Seligman's dogs in the inescapable shock situation exhaust their repertoire of adaptive shock responses: "... when the whole repertoire has been extinguished motor responding ceases [p. 364]." He prefers this rationale for the frequently observed sequence of high, sustained anxiety followed by depression over the Pavlovian (1941) alternative of protective inhibition in response to excessive autonomic excitation. Wolpe cites the failure of Seligman's dogs and of reactive depressives to 'catch on' to favorably changed circumstances as evidence against the adequacy of cognitive or insight explanations but does not attempt to deal directly with the definitional problem of what constitutes insight. Somewhat indirectly, he provides a useful hypothesis for why "insights" may not be acted upon constructively. Such actions may be inhibited by the effects of conditioned anxiety. The person may know quite well what is a desirable course of action, but be too anxious to pursue it, feel unable to control the situation, and so despairs and becomes depressed. Quite plausibly he suggests treating such conditions by desensitizing the inhibitory anxiety; or by using in vivo desensitization, which involves the successful completion of a series of tasks of graded difficulty; or by assertiveness training.

Lazarus (1968) is somewhat more specific regarding the antecedents of depression. He reaffirms his earlier contention (Wolpe & Lazarus, 1966, p. 162) that neurotic depressions are consequences of severe and/or prolonged anxiety, but argues that the antecedents of anxiety and depression are distinguishable. Anxiety is viewed as a response to noxious or threatening stimuli, whereas depression is a reaction to an actual or anticipated reduction in positive reinforcers of such magnitude as to weaken seriously the behavioral repertoire. Reduction in positive reinforcers may be associated with factors ranging in subtlety from money to inactivation of major motivational systems as a result of success.

Lazarus subscribes to a dichotomy between depressions which are psychogenic, or reactive-neurotic, and those which are endogenous, or physiologically rooted. Both varieties tend to share many physiological and psychological characteristics such as weeping, weight loss, motor retardation, sleep difficulties, and unresponsiveness to many stimuli. Even family histories of depressive occurrences may differ negligibly. Lazarus provides "one pragmatic rule" for distinguishing psychogenic and endogenous depression: in the former, depressive complaints focus upon distressing emotional experiences, whereas in the latter complaints are more formless and global. The chief contributions of behavioristic approaches to endogenous depressions have been to increase diagnostic accuracy and to prevent secondary psychogenic depression maintained by the consequences of behaviors manifested during the primary endogenous depression. Lazarus' behavioristic treatment approach to psychogenic depression, while sketchily presented, appears quite ingenious, economical, and promising. He expresses considerable skepticism about Freud's conceptual distinction between normal grief and depression, and especially takes issue with Freud's injunction that the "normal" grief processes should not be interfered with therapeutically.

It is too early to assess the contribution of behavioral approaches to depression, but their emphasis on systematic, testable, formulations must inevitably sharpen conceptualizations and expand the essential data base for adequate theory building and rational treatment programs.

7
PSYCHOSOCIAL RESEARCH ON DEPRESSION

Psychotic depression is the welt left by the whiplash of conscience; in those social-structural situations in which there is strong group sense of belonging, the group is as much a part of the censoring mechanism of the conscience as are the abstract ideas of right and wrong and good and evil which are implanted by the socializing agents (Cohen, 1961, pp. 483–484).

Little psychological research was done with depressives until recently. Variabilities in subject sampling, the scarcity of replications, and dearth of logically interrelated studies do not yet provide a firm base for empirical generalization or theoretical clarification.

PREMORBID LIFE HISTORY[21]

Parental deprivation during childhood has received major emphasis in research on relations between early life events, premorbid personality, and adult susceptibility to depression.

Parental Deprivation

Parental deprivation studies were instigated by reports of depressive-like states among infants separated from their mothers (Bowlby, 1969; Spitz, 1945). Paradoxically, the existence of depression during childhood is strongly disputed (Poznanski & Zrull, 1970; Rie, 1966). Of nine studies comparing the incidence of childhood parental loss in depressives and controls, only three showed a

[21] See Granville-Grossman (1968) for a detailed substantive review and methodological critique of this problem area.

significantly higher incidence of loss in depressives (Granville-Grossman, 1968). There were no differences between groups in the other studies. As Granville-Grossman (1968) notes, clarification of the discrepant findings is complicated by differences between studies in such factors as subject criteria for selecting depressives and controls, social class (which is related to parental mortality rates), and ages of patients and parents. The average age of parental mortality has risen progressively in recent decades.

Angst (1966) and Perris (1966) compared European unipolar depressives, bipolar depressives, and the general population for incidence of broken homes during childhood and found no differences. However, unipolars became clinically depressed earlier if reared in broken homes. American bipolars have a much higher incidence of broken homes during childhood than unipolars (Keith, Brodie, & Leff, 1971). Half of the parents lost by male bipolars were fathers and half mothers, while all of the parents lost by female bipolars were fathers. The latter finding may have implications for the unsuccessful marriages of most father-deprived bipolar females. Keith et al. also replicated Leonhard, Korff, & Schulz's (1962) finding that a higher proportion of suicides occur among parents of bipolar patients than among unipolars. Another frequently but inconsistently reported trend is toward a positive relation between severity of depression and the probability of parental, especially maternal, loss (Birtchnell, 1970).

In short, there is no consistent, substantial evidence for a relation between early parental loss per se and either predisposition to depression or severity of depressive episode. It is quite possible however, that as yet unexplicated pathological and moderating factors associated with parental deprivation account for the variable findings. A promising start at looking beyond early bereavement to quality of parent-child relations during the childhood of depressives is provided by Abrahams & Whitlock (1969). These investigators compared groups of hospitalized bipolars, endogenous unipolars, mixed depressives, reactive depressives, and nonpsychiatric controls on bereavement and quality of family relation during childhood. The groups did not differ in frequency of bereavement but differed significantly in their family relations. The latter were assessed by the Bene-Anthony Family Relations Scale (Anthony, Bene, & Bene, 1957) and a clinical interview. Relations were classified as good, unsatisfactory, or bad. Reactive and mixed (endogenous plus reactive symptoms) depressives had significantly poorer relations than the control, bipolar, and endogenous depressive groups, which did not differ among themselves. Incidence of bereavement was significantly related to severity of depression. The family relations scale was readministered 18 months after the initial interview to determine whether the depressive state had influenced responses.[22] There were

---

[22] A systematic comparison of observer versus patient self-ratings on psychopathology scales during and after depressive episodes indicates that the remitted ratings are much more reliable (Prusoff, Klerman, & Paykel, 1972).

no appreciable changes. This study is among the best designed in the problem area.

Birth Order

Birth order has also been studied as a possible antecedent factor in depression. This variable seems to have important implications for the development of personality patterns (Schachter, 1959), and personality disorders may be associated with personality types (Eysenck, 1964).[23] Firstborns, for example, become more dependent when stressed; hence, the ratio of firstborns among depressives might be expected to exceed chance. Significant differences from chance expectancy, and from nondepressed controls, have been reported in several studies of sibship position within families of depressives, but again the nature of these differences is not consistent across studies. Unfortunately, as Granville-Grossman (1968) points out, these data have not been analyzed separately by sex, which is differentially related to birth order among schizophrenics.

In sum, there are no consistent findings to support the argument that early environmental events predispose individuals to depression. However, only a limited number of variables have been examined, and they may have been selected more because they are easy to measure than because they have critical relevance to theoretical issues. The complexities of data gathering and interpretation even with the variables used are formidable. For example, as Granville-Grossman suggests, a high incidence of parental suicide in the premorbid life of the depressive could be variously construed as evidence for: (1) a significant environmental predisposer; (2) a genetic manifestation of the same illness in parent and patient; or (3) an interaction of the two.

Family and Cultural Background

The sociocultural-interpersonal formulations of manic-depressive personality (Arieti, 1959; Cohen et al., 1954; Fromm-Reichmann, 1949) have stimulated a number of studies. This investigative follow-through is probably due to the Sullivanian tradition of tying theoretical constructs closely to relatively objectifiable interpersonal events and phenotypic personality attributes.

Several investigators (Finley & Wilson, 1951; Wilson, 1951) studied a dozen families with manic-depressives from the southeastern United States, where the prevalence of this disorder is relatively high. Interviews, rating scales, and hospital records were used. Manic-depressives were selected essentially by

---

[23] Foulds (1965) contends that this is an unwarranted assumption which contributes to diagnostic unreliability. He is somewhat supported by the failure of Hagnell's (1966) prospective study to find relations between premorbid personality and subsequent psychiatric diagnosis.

Kallman's (1954)[24] criteria, so that most probands would probably be regarded as bipolars. Controls were sketchily described, but consisted largely of college students.

Finley and Wilson accept the high probability of a hereditary component in manic-depressive disorders, but argue that clinical reports plus wide variations in incidence and prevalence rates justify the exploration of intrafamilial environmental factors. These investigators concur with English's (1949) and Fromm-Reichmann's (1949) observations on the "rigid," "one-track," "impenetrable shell" thinking and communicating of manic-depressives regardless of their clinical state. Much of this quality is attributed to their attachment to geographically and culturally static families dominated by a central theme (such as social or financial success) which brooks no deviations from familial patterns. Family members feel 'walled in,' frustrated, and guilty about rebellious tendencies. Alcoholism and coronary disorders are frequent among such family members whether or not they conform, rebel, or have affective disorders. Regrettably, this interesting pilot work has not been pursued more systematiclly.

Gibson (1958) attempted to replicate the Cohen et al. (1954) findings on manic-depressives and to determine their discriminant validity from schizophrenic controls. A questionnaire with five subscales covering (1) Relation to Community, (2) Envy, (3) Role of Parents, (4) Authority in the Home, and (5) Conventionality was devised. The subscale items deal with the family background and early experience factors which Cohen et al. posited as predisposing factors in the rearing of manic-depressives.

Gibson rated the original Cohen et al. criterion group on his rationally derived scales and compared these ratings with those made on comparison groups of 27 heterogeneous manic-depressives and 17 schizophrenics at St. Elizabeth's hospital. The latter is a federally supported psychiatric hospital for the District of Columbia, roughly corresponding to a state mental hospital. Ratings were based on interviews with collateral informants and on hospital records. Each subscale had 3 items and each item could be rated low, moderate, or high. Items were so worded that high scores conformed with the observations of Cohen et al. Reasonably good inter-rater and intra-rater reliabilities were obtained. The criterion group of manic-depressives obtained the highest scores on Gibson's questionnaire; the St. Elizabeth's manic-depressives scored intermediately and were essentially no different from their criterion counterparts. The major differences between manic-depressives and schizophrenics occurred on the scales for Relation to Community, Envy, and Conventionality.

On the bases of his findings, Gibson proposed some modifications in the Cohen et al. formulation. He found no quantitative support for the marginal

---

[24] Kallman's criteria (1954) are: "...cyclic cases which showed periodicity of acute, self-limited mood swings before the fifth decade of life and no progressive or residual personality disintegration..." [p. 9].

status of the family in the community and therefore questioned this as a source for the prestige-seeking pressure exerted on the premanic-depressive. Nor did he find that family members, especially siblings, were unaware of envy and competitiveness within the family. Unfortunately, Gibson reported nothing on the socioeconomic status of his subjects. It has been repeatedly demonstrated that schizophrenics tend to be of lower social class than manic-depressives, and perusal of Gibson's items suggests the strong possibility that scores may have been confounded by socioeconomic class factors.

A series of studies at Duke University (Parker, Spielberger, Wallace, & Becker, 1959) also investigated aspects of the Cohen et al.-Arieti sociocultural assumptions about manic-depressives. The first survey study involved interviews with patients and family members of 62 manic-depressives, 100 schizophrenics, and 100 psychoneurotic depressives. All patients were hospitalized male Caucasians, most of them patients at the Durham Veterans Administration Hospital. The incidence of manic-depressive disorder among the parents of the manic-depressive probands was 22%, which is remarkably similar to Kallman's (1954) finding of 23.4% for the parents of his proband sample. Also, as in Kallman's data, schizophrenia rarely occurred in proband's families. But diagnoses of family members were inferred by Parker et al. chiefly from proband and sibling descriptions. Given the relative unreliability of interrater psychiatric diagnoses (Zubin, 1967), even with direct access to the clinical source, it is difficult to assess whether such uniformity arises from the stability of the phenomenon or the operation of unwitting biases.

Educational attainment among all three psychiatric groups in the Parker et al. study was higher than the state's (North Carolina) average. Within the psychiatric groups, the manic-depressives had more schooling than the other two groups. Socioeconomic data per se were obtained only for manic-depressives. But from the educational attainment and religious affiliation it could be inferred that the manic-depressives came from higher socioeconomic backgrounds than their psychiatric controls.

Congruent with Cohen et al.'s report of frequent minority group membership among manic-depressives, Parker et al. found that manic-depressive religious affiliation was disproportionately high in the state's diminuitive Presbyterian, Episcopalian, and Catholic membership and low in the predominant Baptist sect. Also, as indicated in the Cohen et al. report, maternal dominance occurred frequently in the families of manic-depressives (53.2% maternally dominated, 29.1% paternally dominated, 17.7% equalitarian or indeterminate), but no comparative data were presented for the other psychiatric group. A review of psychosomatic conditions among the manic-depressive probands indicated an unuaually high incidence of peptic ulcer. The occurrence of such ulcers has been linked with conflicts about overly dependent personality dispositions (Lidz & Rubinstein, 1959).

Another paper in the Duke series dealt with Arieti's (1959) contention that there is a lower incidence of manic-depressive psychosis within geographic areas that have an other-directed characterological orientation (Riesman, 1950). Arieti supports this contention with several lines of evidence, such as (1) cross-cultural data, which indicated a higher incidence of manic-depressive psychosis relative to schizophrenia within presumably more inner-directed cultures; (2) a lowered incidence of manic-depressive psychosis in New York City (down two-thirds in 20 years from 13.5% of first psychiatric hospital admissions in 1928 to 3.8% by 1947); and (3) a much higher incidence (4.33:1) of manic-depressive psychosis than schizophrenia within American Hutterite communities, which Arieti termed as typically inner-directed.

In response to Arieti's position, Becker, Spielberger, & Parker (1962) argued that the core conflicts of manic-depressives as described by Cohen et al. were more akin to those ascribed by Riesman to cultures in transition from inner to other-direction than to those that have already changed. The socialization pressure within a transitional culture requires the individual to " . . . rechannel the competitive drive for achievement, as demanded by the parent, into his need for approval from his peers (Riesman, 1950, p. 103)." Becker et al. (1962) agreed with the potential utility of linking psychopathological character types to ones derived from sociopsychological investigations. They urged the merits of using the achievement concepts of McClelland (DeCharms, Morrison, Reitman, & McClelland, 1955) and the authoritarian personality construct of Adorno, Frenkel-Brunswick, Levinson, & Sanford (1950) as a framework for evaluating the personality characteristics of manic-depressives. These conceptual systems are more empirically derived and systematically developed than Riesman's character types.

Kendell (1970) contends that it is difficult to test the psychodynamic theory that depression involves aggression turned against the self because of its intrinsic circularity. Observed changes in patient functioning are ascribed to " . . . intrapsychic events which cannot be observed, only inferred on the basis of the same behavioral changes that they were adduced to explain" [p. 308]. A reformulation of the hypothesis testable by variations in operationally definable variables more than compensates for any alteration in the scope of the original hypothesis, he contends. His modified proposition is that most depression, " . . . both as a mood and as a syndrome, is caused by the inhibition of aggressive responses to frustration" [p. 308]. He predicted therefore that a high incidence of depression would occur in contexts that involve a high instigation to frustration-engendered aggression with limited opportunity for its overt expression, and a low incidence would occur in contexts with either low instigation to such aggression or with many opportunities for expressing it. Epidemiological data are used to explore the validity of these propositions, although with full acknowledgment that " . . . the comparisons involved are beset with methodological pitfalls, and few of the relevant facts are established" [p. 316]. He predicted that the incidence of depression should be relatively low in the lower class, among combat troops, in younger males, and in less cohesive cultures with low population densities; incidence should be relatively high in the upper classes, among prisoners, in females, and in cohesive, densely populated urban subcultures, especially among threatened minority groups; suicide and homicide rates should be inversely related; and the ratio of manic to depressive episodes should be higher in cultural contexts that have a lower incidence of aggression. As Kendell notes, the evidence for his hypothesis, while largely equivocal, is generally favorable and without serious contraindications. As more adequate epidemiological data become available, this method of testing the hostility-depression hypothesis merits periodic reassessment. Even if the initial trends are sustained, however, critical tests for ruling out alternative genetic and cultural explanations must be devised.

Social Attainment

Educational and occupational achievements are related to premorbid history, although they are attained only in part during the premorbid era. Earlier studies of differences in the socioeconomic status of various psychopathological groups consistently yielded differences in distribution between schizophrenia and depression. The former is associated with lower socioeconomic status, whereas the latter is more evenly distributed or associated with higher socioeconomic status. The conflicting results in the latter regard are briefly summarized in several recent studies which compare the educational and occupational achievement of unipolar and bipolar depressives (Woodruff, Robins, Winokur, & Reich, in press; Woodruff, Robins, Winokur, & Walbran, 1968).

Woodruff et al. compared hospitalized bipolar probands, their well brothers, and their affectively ill brothers with corresponding groups of unipolars and first degree relatives. Bipolar probands did not differ on education or occupation from either their well or sick brothers. Nor did unipolar probands differ from theirs on educational level; a small, but significant, difference was obtained in occupational level. In contrast, differences between bipolar and unipolar patients and family members on educational attainment were strikingly in favor of the bipolars: for probands only, the differences were significant at $p < .005$ and, for all bipolar family members versus all unipolar family members, at $p < .0002$.

Group differences were much less pronounced for occupational attainment. Bipolar and unipolar probands did not differ between themselves, although, with all bipolar family members pooled and compared with all unipolars, the former had a somewhat higher level of achievement. These differences held when achievemement levels were corrected for the greater youth and education of bipolars. In comparison with local and national educational norms, unipolar occupational achievement was average and bipolar achievement above average. Discrepancies in earlier studies on the socioeconomic distribution of depressives may have resulted from differing proportions of bipolars and unipolars in the survey samples. As Woodruff et al. (in press) note, any social advantage that may exist initially in bipolar families appears to weaken with time.

Keith et al. (1971) also examined achievement orientation in their sample of bipolars and unipolars. Their findings are consistent with those of Woodruff et al. (in press), in that 50% of well siblings of bipolars reported parental emphasis on achievement as a means of enhancing familial prestige, versus only 16% of the well sibs of unipolars. These findings may be inconsistent with Cohen et al.'s (1954) contention that premanic-depressives are uniquely singled out because of special talents as the family's "standard bearer."

In a related "nonreactive" study of premorbid achievement in depressives, Burns & Offord (1972) compared the scholastic achievement of depressives, their siblings, and matched controls. All depressives had had severe episodes, which included hospitalization and improvement from ECT; about 80% were unipolars and 20% bipolars. The groups did not differ in school administered group I.Q. tests, academic grades, grades completed, or grades failed. The social mobility of depressives and their siblings was also examined. Both groups had attained a higher social class status than their family or origin, but they were not compared with controls on this variable. Since the proportional distribution of occupations within the county studied had not changed from 1940 to 1960, the authors argue for upward mobility within depressive families. However, age distribution within occupational categories was not determined. Since younger people tend to be better educated, it is quite possible that depressive probands and siblings would not have differed in social mobility from matched controls.

Personality Traits

Numerous clinical papers have asserted a relation between the premorbid personality of depressives, age of onset of depression, and symptom manifestations (e.g. Hopkinson, 1964). Some clinical writers (e.g. Abraham, 1916, 1924) have especially stressed the obsessional aspects of depressives premorbidly and during their depressive episodes. Most writers agree that so called involutional depressives (depressions ostensibly due to biological changes during the involutional phase) have markedly obsessional premorbid personalities, but bipolars have frequently been described as extroverted and many unipolars as hysteroid. Research on these propositions has inferred premorbid personality from the test performance of depressives during clinical remission.

Snaith, McGuire, & Fox (1971) divided 50 unipolar primary depressives into early and late onset groups (onset pre and post age 45). Patients were assessed for presence and severity of retardation, agitation, guilt, irritability, hypochondriasis, obsessionalism, and phobias during their depression. The occurrence of the latter two symptoms was also evaluated prior to onset and following remission. Four months after remission patients were administered a battery of personality tests which included the Maudsley Personality Inventory and two measures of obsessionalism. No relations were obtained between premorbid personality traits (as inferred from the personality tests during remission) and age of onset or pattern of symptomatology while depressed. The investigators concluded, "the closer and more rigorously personality traits are studied in depressed patients, the less do they appear to have relevance to any of the features of the illness" [p. 244].

Kendell & Discipio (1970) used the recently developed Leyton Obsessional Inventory (Cooper, 1970) to investigate obsessionalism during and after depressive episodes. The Leyton Inventory has four subscales which measure obsessional traits, symptoms, resistance to obsessional thought and behavior, and interference with activities from such thoughts and behaviors. The first two scales in a sense assess extent of obsessional concern and the latter two their severity. Cooper's norms for normals, "houseproud wives," and obsessional neurotics were compared with data from 92 hospitalized primary depressives. As in the Snaith et al. study, test performance during remission was assumed to reflect premorbid personality functioning.

Neurotic depressives were more obsessional premorbidly than psychotic depressives. During the depressive episode, there was no group difference in scores; hence psychotic depressives develop more new obsessional symptomatology than neurotic depressives when depressed. Efforts to test manics were " ... foiled by a combination of distractibility, irritability, and facetious jollity" [p. 71].

The premorbid obsessional scores of the depressives were twice as high as Cooper's normals although less than his obsessional neurotics. Thus the contention that depressives have stronger than average obsessional tendencies was supported. As the investigators note, however, Cooper's normals may not be a representative sample, and one small study of obsessionalism in depressives that had a well-matched non-psychiatric control group failed to obtain differences.

There is patently little substantiated knowledge about any typical patterning in the premorbid personality of depressives.

Marital Status

A follow-up study of depressed women suggests that maturity of heterosexual relations may be the best prognostic indicator (Burke, Deykin, Jacobson, & Haley, 1967), as with male schizophrenics. Overall (1971) has found that categorizing psychiatric patients into three groups: never married; once married (whether divorced or not); and multiply married yields more meaningful correlates than the usual breakdown into never married versus ever married. The incidence of depression was much higher in once married patients. Overall conjectures that such patients may be more "culturally bounded" and "semi-socialized" than multiply married patients who are more sociable and aggressive.

Bipolar males are less apt to marry than bipolar females or unipolars of either sex. Except for bipolar males, marriage and fertility rates for depressives do not differ from those of the general population (Perris, 1969). The divorce rate

(Keith et al., 1971) for bipolars (57%), especially after the onset of the first manic episode, is much higher $(p < .01)$ than for unipolars (8%).[25]

Probably the best hope for clarifying the role of early environmental predisposers to depression would come from longitudinal studies of high risk families similar to Mednick & McNeil's (1968) work with schizophrenics. Children of depressed parents and the recently bereaved hold promise as high risk groups. As to what to look for in such populations, many psychopathologists believe that functional psychopathology reflects the disruption of a premorbid personality with relatively specific vulnerabilities by relatively specific stresses. If this assumption is valid, then the identification of distinctive depressive precipitants, pre- and intra-morbid personality deviations, and effective therapeutic modalities might illuminate the nature of these vulnerabilities and suggest fertile hypotheses regarding their source. To date, such research is almost as scant and inconsistent as that on the premorbid personality (Metcalfe, 1968).

PRECIPITANTS OF DEPRESSION

Stressors and Crisis Theory

The differential incidence and severity of clear precipitating events in depression and schizophrenia supports the likelihood that they are discrete disorders (Beck & Worthen, 1972). Consecutive inpatient admissions to a comprehensive community mental health center were repeatedly interviewed to determine the incidence and hazardousness of stressors prior to hospitalization. Almost all of the depressives reported clear precipitants, while only half the schizophrenics did so. Furthermore, the depressives' precipitants were rated as much more hazardous than the schizophrenics' precipitants by psychiatric outpatients and by the Holmes and Rahe Social Readjustment Rating Scale. Most depressive precipitants were losses or exits (Paykel et al., 1969). The investigators contend that crisis theory (Caplan, 1964) is poorly suited for the conceptualizing or handling of these inpatient cases. Crisis theory is best suited to treating well-functioning normals confronted with acute, hazardous stress. Virtually all cases in this sample displayed serious character pathology before exposure to precipitants.

Stressors in Unipolars and Bipolars

The role of precipitants in the onset of affective disorders was discussed earlier in relation to the endogenous-reactive controversy. The traditional notion that bipolar manic-depressive disorders are endogenous receives limited support

---

[25] For some graphic notions of the vicissitudes of living with a bipolar spouse see Janowsky, Leff, & Epstein (1970).

in several studies that compare bipolar and unipolar depressives. Keith et al. (1971) report that about 85% of unipolars underwent serious environmental stress within six months of their initial and subsequent hospitalizations. About the same percentage of bipolars encountered such stress before their first hospitalization, but this drops to about 54% for subsequent episodes. Perris (1969) reports a similar pattern for unipolars and bipolars although the percentages rated as significantly stressed are substantially lower than for Keith et al. (1971). The latter are quite candid about the subjective nature of such judgments, describing them as "often vague and ill defined" [p. 1089].

Bereavement

Adult bereavement is often implicated as a precipitant of depression. Parkes (1964) presents interesting data which support the notion that the intensity of social interaction with the deceased is probably a determining factor in the severity of depressive response. In two university affiliated London hospitals the percentage of psychiatric patients admitted during a two-year span who had lost a parent did not depart from chance expectancy for the general population. But the rate of admission for patients who had lost a spouse within six months was six times chance expectancy. The proportion of bereaved female patients to all bereaved patients was higher than that of nonbereaved female patients to all nonbereaved patients ($p < .02$). A higher incidence of affective disorders (65%) was diagnosed among bereaved patients than among nonbereaved ones (47%, $p < .01$). The subcategory of reactive depression discriminated most clearly between bereaved and nonbereaved patients (28% vs. 15%, $p < .01$). Females were more susceptible to adult bereavement as a precipitor of severe personality disturbance than males, and bereavement reactions were more likely than chance to eventuate in affective disorders, but not overwhelmingly so: 72% of bereaved patients received diagnoses other than reactive depression.

Parkes (1965) also compared a sample of psychiatric bereavement reactions with Marris' (1958) nonpsychiatric bereaved widows. The two groups differed chiefly in that psychiatric patients had greater difficulty in accepting the reality of loss and expressed more self-blame or guilt toward the deceased spouse. Retarded depressions, which usually include many endogenous symptoms, rarely occur in grief reactions, nor does mania. The impressive amount of reality distortion even in nonpathological grief reactions is graphically borne out in Parkes' recent (1970) longitudinal study of nonhospitalized London widows.

Huston (1971), citing the inevitable problems with retrospective studies which attempt to link bereavement and depression, urges the initiation of prospective studies. On the basis of Maddison's (1968) investigation of factors affecting widows' health during grief, Huston predicts that the adequacy of coping mechanisms available to the bereaved will be the chief determinant of whether depression ensues. Maddison found that "bad outcome" widows lacked emotional support for airing their thoughts and feelings about their deceased husbands. These widows felt that others responded to such activity with hostility or excessive efforts at distraction. Huston properly cautions against an undue tendency to explain heightened morbidity and mortality in the bereaved on the basis of depression alone.

8
PERSONALITY FUNCTIONING IN DEPRESSIVES

Clinical experiences indicated that the expression of overt anger (in depressives) was not impaired but that the direct communication of needs, wishes, or feelings was. The anger described by Bibring was secondary to a frustrated wish to be cared for or to an impasse in a close relationship (Weissman, Klerman, & Paykel, 1971).

COGNITIVE FUNCTIONING

Subjective State and Performance

Severe depressives frequently complain of their inability to perform intellectually because of poor concentration and perseverance. But there is limited objective data on the functional capabilities of depressives. Friedman (1964) compared the cognitive functioning and self-perceptions of severe depressives and matched nonpsychiatric controls. His hospitalized depressives are described as homogeneous, but included psychotic and borderline depressives, depressed manic-depressives, agitated depressives, and involutional depressives. Three independent psychiatric raters regarded each patient's primary diagnosis as a 'pure' form of severe depression. The Lewis & Piotrowski (1954) signs were used as an additional safeguard for screening out schizophrenics.[26] Depressive and control subjects were matched on age, sex, education, vocabulary score, ethnicity, and employment status. However, about two-thirds of the Ss in both samples were Jewish, which complicates the interpretation of results. Studies

[26] These signs discriminate patients whose initial and subsequent diagnoses have been manic-depressive from patients initially diagnosed manic-depressive but ultimately rediagnosed as schizophrenic.

have repeatedly shown that Jews tend to be strong need achievers (McClelland, 1961, pp. 364–367); that is, they tend to strive indiscriminately to attain high internalized standards of excellence. Such needs may well have confounded Friedman's findings. Depressives were tested within the first week of hospitalization, but no mention is made of what clinical treatment they were undergoing. Presumably most were receiving antidepressant drugs rather than electroconvulsive therapy. If this surmise is correct, their psychometric performance was probably not affected much by treatment (Baker, 1968). Controls who were quite depressed on the day of testing were apparently excluded; the controls were drawn from a State Employment Office.

Subjects were administered 33 cognitive, perceptual, vigilance, and psychomotor tasks, plus the Clyde Mood Scale (Clyde, 1960). The performance of depressives was significantly poorer than controls on only 9 of the 82 measures. The depressives had more 'scatter' or inconsistency in their intra-test performances and larger standard deviations. The large variance between depressive subjects suggests possible subtype heterogeneity within the depressive sample. The depressives' moderate performance decrements reflected impairments in: short-term memory or sustained concentration; psycho-motor speed and visual-motor coordination; and flexibility in 'shifting' set and orienting behavior. On tasks involving series of trials, depressives tended to do more poorly on later than earlier trials, but the experimental design did not provide a basis for inferring whether such decrements were a function of reactive inhibition, conditioned inhibition, or lack of motivation.

Whereas performance differences between groups on the psychometric tasks were neither strikingly large nor clearly patterned, differences between groups on the Clyde Mood Scale were highly significant. Differences ($p < .01$) were obtained on 82% of the items, most of them in the predicted direction. Depressives, for example, described themselves as more withdrawn, lonely, and helpless and as less cheerful, satisfied, energetic, and relaxed than controls.

The spontaneous comments of the depressives in the testing situation corroborated their self-rating scale responses. While they frequently complained of extreme fatigue and helplessness, only one depressive was untestable. Furthermore, no significant correlation was found between a composite rating of severity of depression within the depressive sample and their test performance. (The constricted sample range of depression may have attenuated these relations.) Likewise, depressives' self-ratings of the quality of their task performances were unrelated to their actual performance.

In sum, depressives performed about as well as nondepressives in this structured situation, despite their severe feelings of incapacity. Friedman interprets his empirical findings as most in accord with Bibring's (1953) theoretical conception of depression as an ego phenomenon, involving lowered self-esteem and subjective feelings of helplessness and hopelessness.

Overinclusiveness

In a study of overinclusive thought Payne & Hewlett (1960) compared schizophrenics, endogenous depressives, neurotics, and nonpsychiatric controls. In an effort to match groups on age, vocabulary level, socioeconomic status, and educational attainment, a nonrepresentative sample of younger depressives was used.

Payne & Hewlett (1960) were investigating whether overinclusive thought is specific to schizophrenia or is characteristic of psychotics generally, as suggested by Eysenck (1952a). Eysenck had compared nonpsychiatric, schizophrenic, and manic-depressive soldiers on a large and varied psychometric battery. Only one factor, "psychoticism," differentiated Eysenck's groups: normals were least psychotic and depressives were most psychotic. No factor was identified that distinguished schizophrenics from depressives. In subsequent studies Eysenck (1952b) and his associates (Eysenck, Granger, & Brenglemann, 1957) have pooled schizophrenics and depressives, labeling them as psychotics.

Payne and Hewlett's battery of 60 measures assessed intellectual speed, motor speed, concreteness, overinclusiveness, and psychoticism. The general findings were that neurotics (subdivided into 'dysthymics,' who were mostly reactive depressives, and 'hysterics') did not show any more signs of thought disorder than the nonpsychiatric controls. Schizophrenics were more overinclusive than any other group at all levels of task complexity. Psychotic depressives and schizophrenics displayed more retardation than normals and neurotics, but did not differ between themselves. Contrary to Eysenck's findings, schizophrenics scored higher on a factor of psychoticism than psychotic depressives, and psychotic depressives, except for being slower, tested much like the nonpsychotics. In sum, while a thought disturbance may be present in depression, as Beck contends, it was not reflected in these measures of overinclusiveness.[27]

Psychomotor Retardation in Depression

Whether retardation in depressives is a general characteristic, situationally specific, or subtype specific is controversial. Colbert & Harrow (1968) compared retardation within recently state hospitalized female depressives and schizophrenics. Three sets of observations were obtained: (1) patients' responses to interview questions regarding manifestations of retardation during the week prior to hospitalization; (2) psychiatrists' and psychologists' ratings during the first week of hospitalization; and (3) patients' reaction and response times to the Bender-Gestalt Test. Depressive patients reported significantly more retardation prior to hospitalization than schizophrenics (p < .001), but only 23% of depressives were rated as retarded by staff, and there were no group differences

---

[27] The notion that overinclusiveness most effectively accounts for thought disturbance phenomena in schizophrenia is also highly questionable (Chapman, Chapman, & Miller, 1964).

in test performance. The investigators suggest that the stimulation of the new hospital environment and the test demands may have counteracted much of their retardation. Alternatively, the investigators acknowledge the possibility that depressives were not more retarded than schizophrenics prior to admission, but only perceived themselves to be. Furthermore, in the absence of a nonpsychiatric control group, or an independent measure of retardation, it is possible that the lack of obtained differences reflects retardation in both groups.

Degree of retardation among depressives was unrelated to subtype (manic-depressive, reactive depressive, and involutional). In common with earlier studies that have used various measures of psychomotor response time, speed of performance on the Bender-Gestalt was negatively related to age in depressives but unrelated to age in schizophrenics.

However, King's (1969) review of psychomotility in psychopathology strongly suggests that psychomotor responses are much more sensitive indicators of pathology than simple neuromotor or complex perceptual motor tasks. Colbert & Harrow (1966) assessed perceptual motor performances, primarily.

Depression and Apparent Organic Brain Damage

A differential diagnosis between depression and organicity is sometimes very difficult (Colbert & Harrow, 1966). Teasdale & Beaumont (1971) report several cases in which high state depression scores were positively related to organic like test performance. This relation held even for repeated testings over diurnal variations within the same patient within a single week ($r = -0.89$). Norms for most tests of organicity are based on the performance of nonpsychiatric controls versus organically brain damaged patients. This paper indicates a definite need for systematically investigating the effects of mood disturbance on tests for brain damage, since differential diagnosis is frequently the reason for test referral.

CONDITIONABILITY

Pavlov's speculations on the relevance of his neurophysiological concepts to clinical psychopathology (1941; 1960) have stimulated several studies of conditionability in depressives (Astrup, 1965; Ban, 1964). Unfortunately, most of these papers are published in Soviet journals, whose contents are sometimes difficult to evaluate because of their sketchily presented methodology and data analysis (Hartman, 1965, p. 63). Faddeyeva, Ivanov-Smolensky, and Protopopov have been the principal Russian investigators. Many of their papers discuss conditioning phenomena in manic-depressives, but it is not always clear whether the subject criteria require bipolar depressives or not. Sample sizes tend to be very small. They report that simple motor conditioning in manics is quick and strong, whereas in depressives it is slow and weak; the orienting response in manics is strong and persistent; in depressives, weak and unreliable.

The above results are attributed to excessive cortical inhibition in depressives and excessive cortical excitation in manics. Melancholics, who presumably correspond to unipolar depressives, are regarded as constitutional inhibitory types, hence more akin to schizophrenics than to manic-depressives. Reactive depression results from marked life changes which require shifts to new dynamic stereotypes (neurally integrated patterns of perception, cognition, and action). Such shifts produce inhibitory strains in persons predisposed toward inhibitory responses. In such persons, conditioned responses associated with older dynamic stereotypes may be almost unmodifiable and nonextinguishable. Prolonged strain results in neural exhaustion, which in turn prevents the transmission of neural excitation. Pavlov (1941) described his inhibitory type dogs as timid and cowardly, to whom, like the melancholic, "every event of life becomes an inhibitory agent" [p. 377]. While it is difficult to establish positive conditioned responses in such organisms, once established they are highly reliable. But the susceptibility of such responses to weakening distractive disinhibition is much greater than for negative, inhibitory conditioned responses.

Ban, Choi, Lehmann, & Adamo (1966) compared neurotic depressives, endogenous depressives, schizo-affectives (depressed) and normals (7 each) in a conditioning reflex procedure which they assert enabled them "... to reveal and measure [their] characteristic differences" [p. 103]. The experimental procedure involved an intense auditory stimulus as the UCS, white and yellow light as the CS, and GSR as the response measure. Orientation responses and discrimination learning were compared as well as UCRs and simple CRs.

Representative findings were as follows: normals and neurotic depressives differed most clearly from endogenous depressives and schizophrenics in orienting response (OR) and disinhibition. The mean amplitude of the OR for normals was higher than for any other group, and for neurotics, lower. Qualitatively, both normals and neurotics had smooth habituation response curves to repeated administrations of the light stimuli, whereas endogenous depressives and schizophrenics had uneven curves. Likewise normals' UCRs had the greatest amplitude and tended toward the shortest latencies. Among the patient groups, schizo-affectives had higher UCR amplitudes than the other patient groups.

Disinhibition of the OR was measured by response to the first pairing of the UCS with the 8th and last stimulus in the initial light stimuli sequence. Orienting response habituation is attributed to internal inhibition; thus the observation of interest is the extent to which this inhibition is disrupted by the initial pairing of the CS (light) and UCS (tone). Normals showed significantly greater disinhibition than all other groups and endogenous depressives and schizophrenics least; indeed, most of the latter Ss showed *no* disinhibition.

Normals condition more quickly, reliably, and with higher amplitudes than any other group. Endogenous depressives had the longest response latencies and required more trials to condition, but once conditioned were very stable, consistent responders.

In regard to the two basic Pavlovian neural processes of excitation and inhibition, Ban et al. conclude that neurotic depressives differ from normals only quantitatively, whereas endogenous depressives also differ qualitatively. Endogenous depressives and schizo-affectives have a much more dominant inhibitory process. Ban et al. venture some potentially testable neurophysiological hypotheses which may account for the observed differences. Decreased thalamic and brain stem reticular nuclei functions are implicated in the quantitative differences and neocortical functions in the qualitative ones. They properly stress their lack of nondepressive neurotic and psychotic controls, which seriously limits the generality-specificity of their conclusions. It is nonetheless surprising that such relatively clear-cut differences emerged, given the small sample sizes. Patently this line of investigation merits replication and extension if the initial findings are reliable. The results may stem from the "prototypical" nature of cases used and their careful matching on age, sex, recent admission, and no medication. However, caution is especially needed in evaluating these results, since others have reported negligible differences in conditionability between schizophrenics and manic-depressives, especially Stern, McClure, Jr., & Costello (1970) and Stewart, Winokur, Stern, Guze, Pfeiffer, & Hornung (1959).

EFFECTS OF SUCCESS AND FAILURE

Beck and his colleagues have examined the effects of experimentally manipulated success and failure experiences on various aspects of depressive cognitive performance. In these studies, psychiatric patients scoring high and low on the Beck Depression Inventory were compared, regardless of their diagnostic classification. Since previous studies in this series had indicated strong self-punitive tendencies in depressives, it was predicted that self-ratings of mood, self-confidence, and perception of others would be more adversely affected by failure experience in depressives than in nondepressives. In the first study (Loeb, Feshbach, Beck, & Wolf, 1964), both depressed and nondepressed hospitalized subjects who "succeeded" on the experimentally manipulated task showed increased self-confidence and happiness and perceived others as happier than did the "failure" groups; the latter groups did not differ between themselves. "Successful" depressives predicted that they would perform better on a word production task than any of the other groups, whereas "failure" depressives predicted the poorest performance. However, the latter's prediction did not differ significantly from the predictions of the nondepressive groups.

A second, related study (Loeb, Beck, & Diggory, 1971) tested the hypothesis that self-evaluation and expectancies are more affected by success or failure experiences in depressives than in nondepressives. Psychiatric outpatients were grouped according to their Beck Inventory score and randomly assigned to initial experimentally manipulated success or failure conditions. Depressives and nondepressives initially had similar levels of aspiration, but depressives expected to perform less well and rated their performance less favorably than nondepressives. After the initial manipulated success task was completed, a second performance task was administered to determine the effects of prior experience on work efficiency and performance expectancy. Speed of performance on both work tasks was clearly unrelated to depression, which replicates an earlier finding of Botwinick & Thompson (1967). A marginally significant interaction ($p < .10$) suggests that prior success enhances depressives' work performance, whereas prior failure enhances nondepressives' performance. These results suggest that the alleged self-punitive tendencies of depressives do not preclude at least short-term increases in optimism and productivity as a result of successful experience.

Lewinsohn & Flippo (1969) failed to demonstrate a hypothesized interaction between failure and self-esteem in depressives and controls. Depressive and nondepressive college students, selected on the basis of MMPI and interview rating criteria, were subjected to one of three intrinsic failure conditions (i.e., 25%, 50%, or 75% of the puzzles to be solved were insoluble). The self-esteem ratings of both depressives and nondepressives diminished significantly with either 50% or 75% failure conditions; as indicated, there were no differences in effects between groups.

In sum, there is negligible experimental evidence that depressives' self-esteem is appreciably more vulnerable to failure than nondepressives', despite a widespread clinical impression to the contrary. Whether there is in fact no difference, or response measures have been too insensitive, or the stimuli too potent, unambiguous, or irrelevant, remains to be determined. None of the experimental studies to date take cognizance of the reactive-endogenous dimension among depressives. One might expect greater variability in the response of heterogeneous depressives to failure because of their alleged differences in responsiveness to environmental events. Such results were obtained by Rosenzweig (1959) when he compared the self-esteem reactions to failure of hospitalized depressives and medical patients.

ACHIEVEMENT ORIENTATION

Investigations of manic-depressive personality within McClelland's framework were stimulated by apparent differences between interpersonally oriented theorists (Arieti, 1959; Cohen et al., 1954) in the motivational basis for high levels of aspiration which they ascribed to manic-depressives. McClelland and his associates have described two types of achievement orientation: need-achievement and value-achievement. The "high need Achiever" is concerned with living up to high internalized standards of excellence. Such individuals prefer moderate risk taking, strive hard for achievement in fantasy and actuality, and tend to be independent of social influence and low in authoritarianism. McClelland (1955) has linked the high need Achiever with Riesman's inner-directed character. And Arieti (1959), in describing the adult manic-depressive's personality, states that, "In many cases we find a self-conscious individual, always motivated by duty, of the type of personality Riesman has called 'inner-directed' " [p. 434].

In contrast with the high need Achiever, the high value Achiever overtly avows a high standard of achievement which is unrelated to fantasied or actual performance and positively related to authoritarianism and susceptibility to social influence (DeCharms, et al., 1955). McClelland, Atkinson, Clark, & Lowell (1953) speculate that persons with strong value Achievement have developed a defensive orientation in response to ". . . authoritarian pressure from their parents to be ambitious and the resultant motive which has originated in external sources shows itself primarily as a fear of being unsuccessful" [p. 419]. Value Achievement correlates appear similar to attributes ascribed by Cohen et al. to manic-depressives. Value Achievers and manic-depressives may share a common defensive pattern of outwardly adopting the values of others in order to placate and gain approval from them. Both value achievers and manic-depressives are reportedly authoritarian, imperceptive of self and others, intolerant of ambiguity, and highly conventionalized in behavior and attitudes.

Becker (1960) sought to clarify the relations between manic-depressive personality and achievement orientation. He compared remitted male, bipolar manic-depressives with nonpsychiatric controls. Remitted manic-depressives were used in order to avoid the possible confounding effects of severe personality disturbance and treatment regimens (e.g. drugs or ECT). Over 90% of the former patients who were contacted by letter agreed to participate without remuneration.

Multiple patient selection criteria were employed to ensure a relatively pure sample of remitted manic-depressives. These criteria required hospitalization for at least one manic and one depressive episode. Subjects with more than one questionable Lewis & Piotrowski sign (1954) were not included.

As an additional safeguard, prospective subjects were rated on a five point Certainty of Diagnosis Scale by a senior psychiatrist. Patients with a "certainty" rating of less than 3 ("probable") were excluded. As a check on the patient's remitted status, the patient filled out a self-report mood scale, Hildreth's Battery of Feeling and Attitude Scales for Clinical Use (1946).

The control group[28] in Becker's initial study (1960) had no history of serious psychiatric disturbance or psychosomatic illness. It was originally intended to draw all of the controls from the medical and surgical wards of the same hospital that provided the remitted psychiatric patients. This was impractical because numerous prospective controls failed to meet either the sixth grade literacy or medical/psychiatric requirements. Therefore, only half of the controls came from intramural sources and half from miscellaneous extramural sources.

---

[28]The problem of adequate controls for psychiatric samples is formidable, and only compromise solutions are possible. See Mednick & McNeil (1968) for an excellent discussion of the intrinsic difficulties.

The response measures used in Becker's study were designed to discriminate between need and value Achievers. These measures included McClelland's TAT measure of need Achievement (1955), DeCharms' Likert-type value Achievement attitude scale (1958), the California Fascism Scale (F scale) Adorno, et al., 1950), the Traditional Ideology Scale (TFI) (Levinson & Huffman, 1955), and two work performance tasks: Xs-in-Circles (Atkinson & Reitman, 1956), given with task oriented instructions, and an Additions task (Williams, 1955), given with achievement oriented instructions.

If manic-depressives performed like value Achievers[29] on this array of tasks, they would score higher on value Achievement and not differ from controls on need Achievement. They would also score higher on the F and TFI scales than the controls, but would not differ on the work tasks. If, on the other hand, manic-depressives performed like need Achievers, they would score higher on need Achievement but not on value Achievement, lower on the F and TFI scales, and higher on at least one of the work tasks.[30]

The results of Becker's (1960) study supported the hypothesis that manic-depressives perform like value Achievers. There were no differences between groups in need Achievement scores. The manic-depressives scored higher than controls on value Achievement, the F scale, and the TFI scale, and the groups did not differ on the performance tasks.

In a follow-up study, Becker's manic-depressives and nonpsychiatric controls were compared with schizophrenics and neurotic depressives (Becker et al., 1963). The manic-depressives scored highest on all scales (vAch, F, TFI) and the nonpsychiatric controls lowest; all differences between these two groups were significant. But manic-depressives were not significantly different from the other psychiatric groups. The pooled psychiatric groups scored higher than the controls on all scales, which suggests that conventionalized authoritarian attitudes are somewhat common within all psychiatric groups, but especially so among manic-depressives.

Further analyses of the attitude scale scores examined their relations to the concomitant variables of age, education, literacy score, and mood state. These correlational data are interesting in several respects. In both psychotic groups (manic-depressives and schizophrenics) conventionalized authoritarian attitudes are relatively uninfluenced by educational level, whereas in neurotic depressives and normals there is an inverse relation. In both depressives and normals, authoritarian defensiveness increases with age, whereas in schizophrenia it tends

---

[29] The analog between the personalities of manic-depressives and value achievers relates to limited characteristics, not an identity of character types. They may differ in many other regards.

[30] "Task" and "Achievement" oriented instructions were used because of inconsistencies in the literature as to which set most effectively discriminates high and low need Achievers. Task oriented instructions may fail to engage the achievement motive, whereas achievement oriented instructions may arouse the motive so strongly and generally that individual differences are obscured.

to decrease. Wolff (1959) conjectured that authoritarian ego defenses tend to be more intensively used as the capacity for realistic adjustment diminishes with age.

An additional study of remitted bipolar female manic-depressives (Becker & Altrocchi, 1968) obtained no differences between the bipolars and non-psychiatric controls on any of the personality measures previously discussed (need Achievement, value Achievement, need Affiliation, F Scale, TFI scale, or performance tasks).

THE CONTINUITY ASSUMPTION IN MOOD LABILE NORMALS

Becker & Nichols (1964) examined the so-called continuity assumption. This disputed assumption asserts that similar personality attributes are associated with a broad range of cyclothymic tendency (Fenichel, 1945). Cyclothymics display extremes of euphoric-depressive variability in terms of frequency and intensity of mood change. From the Cohen et al. (1954) position plus convergent findings by Finley & Wilson (1951), Gibson (1958), and Becker (1960), it was hypothesized that nonpsychiatric but cyclothymic college students would manifest value achievant, conforming orientations.

A paper by Groesbeck (1958) on the personality correlates of various need Achievement-need Affiliation configurations led to the inclusion of a measure of need Affiliation in the cyclothymic study. The personality correlates ascribed by Groesbeck to persons high in need Achievement and low in need Affiliation (concern with initiating and maintaining social relations) are impressively similar to those ascribed by Cohen et al. (1954) to manic-depressives: conforming, imperceptive of their social stimulus value, and lacking in self-insight.

The Wessman, Ricks, & Tyl (1960) self-rating scale was used to assess mood variability. This 10-item state Elation-Depression Scale has a range of scale scores from 10 for "Complete elation, rapturous joy and soaring ecstasy" to a score of 1 for "utter depression and gloom. Completely down. All is black and leaden." Each day, for 42 consecutive days, subjects indicate their (a) highest, (b) lowest, and (c) average mood for the day. Several indices of cyclothymia were derived from this measure. A priori, rationally derived cyclothymic scores were positively correlated with TFI and need Affiliation scores, negatively correlated with need Achievement, and unrelated to value Achievement and task performance. Contrary to prediction, cyclothymic scores were unrelated to F scale scores. These findings closely paralleled those of the previous study (Becker, 1960), especially for remitted male manic-depressives below the sample median age as compared with controls below the median age. Thus Becker & Nichols (1964) provided moderate support for the continuity hypothesis.

However, Wessman & Ricks (1966) reported a quite different pattern of correlates for mood variable male and female students at Harvard and Radcliffe than Becker and Nichols obtained at the University of Illinois. The personality correlates of the mood variable female students at Illinois were akin to those observed for mood stable students by Wessman and Ricks. As the latter sagely concluded;

> ... such differences indicate that variability is highly related to significant personality variables in diverse cultures, but that the correlates of variability in one culture cannot lightly be assumed to hold in another [p. 240].

In brief then, broad characterization of cyclothymics and depressives according to achievement orientation or authoritarianism appears to be unwarranted. It may yet prove fruitful to explore the validity of Bibring's (1953) contention that such persons can be grouped according to their rigidly adhered to "narcissistic aspirations." Cyclothymics and depressives may have intense achievement needs that are more goal-class specific than in nonpsychiatric high need achievers.

CONFORMITY AND ANTICONFORMITY

Several studies have investigated conformity behavior in depressives by experimental manipulation rather than as an inferred correlate of achievement behavior or of authoritarian attitudes. Katkin, Sasmore, & Tan (1966) compared the conformity tendencies of hospitalized psychotically depressed and acutely schizophrenic patients. The depressed patients were diagnosed as involutional and psychotic depressives. The investigators' rationale for extending findings on manic-depressives to psychotic depressives rests on Cohen et al.'s (1954) contention that the basic psychotic pattern in manic-depressives is depression [p. 225]. Acute schizophrenics were used to control for hospitalization, psychosis, and, to some extent, dysphoric affect. Assessment measures included the MMPI D Scale, Edwards Social Desirability Scale (Edwards, 1957), and TFI, F, and V-Ach. Scales. In a variant of the Asch-type yielding experiment (1956), Ss rated 15 Likert-type items after listening to the tape-recorded responses of three alleged patients like themselves (actually nonpsychiatric confederates of the experimenter). On the 10 noncritical items, confederate responses averaged to a neutral rating; on three critical items, the confederates verbalized extreme agreement, and on two critical items, extreme disagreement. All items were preselected on the basis of similar ratings by pilot groups of depressives and schizophrenics.

There were no differences between depressives and controls on any of the attitude measures except the Edwards Social Desirability Scale. High scores on the latter probably reflect defensive strivings for social approval (Ford, 1964; Ford & Herson, 1967). Contrary to prediction, schizophrenics scored higher ($p < .001$) than depressives on the Edwards Scale.

Consistent with Katkin et al.'s predictions, female depressives were more conforming ($p < .01$) than schizophrenics in the Asch-type yielding experiment. That is, on the five critical items, depressives changed more from their premanipulation response (after listening to the tape) toward the confederate position than the schizophrenics.

In addition, the depressives showed more variability or change ($p < .02$) from pre- to post-test on the 10 noncritical items (i.e., those items on which the confederates lacked consensus) than schizophrenics. Willis (1965) has conjectured that variability reflects self-anticonformity and a motivation to avoid responding.

... as if making a particular response has the effect of causing it to be negatively evaluated. Such might be the case if the individual's self-esteem is so low as actually to be negative [p. 382].

Diminished self-esteem is, of course, a prominent feature of depression.

Katkin et al. (1966) conjecture that for depressives,

... verbalizing attitudes which conform with those of others is secondarily reinforcing, since perceived conformity may have been associated previously with security and acceptance [p.411].

In a study similar to Katkin et al.'s, Becker & Altrocchi (1968) compared 16 remitted bipolar manic-depressive females with 16 nonpsychiatric control females. Subject selection criteria for the remitted patients were identical with those previously used by Becker (1960). Patient and control groups did not differ significantly in age, educational attainment, literacy level, or self-reported mood state when tested. An experimental conformity manipulation followed a blood sampling and the same personality and performance measures that were previously used with male bipolars (Becker, 1960).

Becker & Altrocchi's (1968) experimental conformity procedure differed somewhat from Katkin et al.'s, which may partly account for their discrepant findings. A prerecorded tape of attitude item judgments by confederates was used in both studies, based on Crutchfield's (1955) finding that physical presence or absence of confederates made a negligible difference. Becker et al. used 12 TFI items, four of which were predesignated as critical items. On the latter items, pilot testing had indicated that ratings clustered around the neutral point; the remaining eight TFI buffer items were randomly selected from the residual pool of 35 items. In recording the tape, conferates were instructed to register extreme agreement with two designated critical items and extreme disagreement with the other two. On the buffer items, they were told to express their real opinions. When S was alone in the experimental situation, she first heard E read an item; next she heard the confederates successively verbalize their recorded points of view; and then S verbalized and marked her opinion rating on a scale. Subjects were told that they were listening to the "live" voices of other women in similar rooms.

Post hoc analyses of the confederate ratings of the eight buffer items indicated high spontaneous confederate agreement on individual items. Mean transformed confederate ratings of the buffer items (1 = extreme disagreement, 7 = extreme agreement) had an overall mean of 2.52; therefore these items were grouped as a third experimental condition reflecting moderate confederate disagreement.

Means and variances of the patients' and controls' initial ratings did not differ for any of the 12 TFI items used in the experimental conformity phase. A 2×2 repeated measures analysis of variance was used to compare the conformity scores of patients and controls under the three conditions of extreme confederate agreement, extreme confederate disagreement, and moderate confederate disagreement.

Contrary to prediction the remitted female manic-depressives were significantly less conforming than nonpsychiatric controls. This overall group difference ($p < .01$) was significant in the extreme agreement and extreme disagreement conditions. In the agreement condition, the patients showed marked anticonformity; that is, when confederates showed extreme agreement with the two TFI critical items, the patients moved toward greater disagreement with the item. Remitted patients were unaffected by the confederates' extreme disagreement with items and slightly conforming in response to their moderate disagreement. By contrast, controls moved toward conformity with confederates in all three conditions.

Although Katkin et al. (1966) and Becker & Altrocchi (1968) used similar experimental paradigms, it is difficult to compare their discrepant findings of greater and lesser conformity respectively in female depressives. Different depressive (psychotic and involutional vs. manic-depressive) and control groups (schizophrenic vs. nonpsychiatric) were used and psychiatric status varied (acute state vs. remitted), as did item content and method of analysis.

Speculatively, Becker & Altrocchi's findings suggest that under anonymous conditions of strong peer pressure, remitted female manic-depressives become rigidly constricted and/or negativistic, whereas under moderate, somewhat inconsistent pressure, they become more conforming like normals.

Several dissertation studies at the University of Washington (Lamont, 1969; Miranda, 1971; Wallace, 1969) sought to clarify various facets of depressive susceptibility to social influence, such as its magnitude, direction, and governing conditions. The social-personality literature on persuasibility and self-esteem provided much of the conceptual background. The hypothesized antecedents of low persuasibility (Ableson & Lesser, 1959), low self-esteem (Coopersmith, 1967), and depression (Bonime, 1966) have much in common. Regrettably, systematic research on their antecedents is sparse and the findings variable.

Lamont (1969) contended that the depressive's excessive vulnerability to influence (Fast, 1967) may lead to resistance to influence when he feels threatened or pressured. He cites Brehm's (1966) reactance theory and research as evidence that resistance is a normal response to the perception of infringed autonomy. According to transactional theorists, depressives have a low threshold for perceiving others as coercive or manipulative and a strong 'content-free' predisposition to respond to such perception with resistance. Since low self-esteem is a salient feature of depression, experimental correlates of low self-esteem may be quite relevant to depression. For example, Lamont noted the Tippett & Silber (1966) study of the effects of 'expert' comment on self-judgments of high and low self-esteem Ss in support of his contention.

Subjects first rated themselves on a 30-item self-esteem scale; they were then informed that expert informants who had examined their psychological tests thought that they had rated themselves too highly on 10 critical items; subjects then rerated themselves on all 30 items. Low self-esteem subjects did not alter their judgments on the 10 critical items but lowered their ratings on the other 20, whereas high self-esteem subjects did the opposite. In short, low self-esteem Ss resisted direct influence attempts but were vulnerable to its indirect effects, whereas high self-esteem Ss modified their position in the face of what appeared to be valid, relevant information, but did not inappropriately generalize the negative input.

Essentially, Lamont (1969) tested Bonime's contention that depressives are "allergic to social influence." Subjects were 48 psychiatric inpatients (24 with heterogeneous depressive diagnoses and 24 with diagnoses other than depression) and 24 nonpsychiatric, unhospitalized controls. Groups did not differ in socioeconomic class. Subjects first listened to tape-recorded personality descriptions of two adolescent boys, Bill and Larry. The traits of the former corresponded to Bonime's (1966) description of a neurotic depressive, and the traits of the latter to a normal, healthy stereotype. Subjects then listened to a recorded series of appeals by a high school principal who urged the boys to study harder. Four types of appeals at weak and strong intensities were used: (a) to be like others or to conform; (b) to be considerate of others; (c) a cheerful positive approach; and (d) a flattering, manipulative approach. After hearing each appeal the subject rated how he thought Bill or Larry would respond. As predicted from Bonime's position, depressed subjects projected significantly more resistance to influence than either of the control groups, and the manipulative, flattering appeal best differentiated the depressives from the other groups. Contrary to prediction, strength of appeal elicited no differences within or between groups.

Wallace (1969) used the Willis-Hollander conformity model and experimental paradigm (Hollander & Willis, 1967). She investigated susceptibility to social influence in college females grouped according to Beck Depression Inventory scores. The Willis-Hollander two-dimensional model is designed to avoid the shortcomings of more typical unidimensional conformity models, which allow scores for conformity or independence only. The two-dimensional model permits the derivation of anticonformity and sheer variability scores as well. Apparently valid reservations have been raised about the variability aspect of this model (Stricker, Messick, & Jackson, 1970), but overall it seems to reflect a definite advance in the theoretical conceptualization and operational definition of conformity concepts.

Wallace used the Willis-Hollander binary judgment task. In the initial phase, the subject was presented with a series of stimuli, each of which depicted a line and an indicated length (e.g. $1''$) beneath it. The subject's task was to judge whether the line was longer or shorter than the indicated length. In all instances the line was exactly as long as the length indicated. In the second phase of the experiment the subject viewed the same series, but before making a second judgment, his initial judgment and bogus, or preprogrammed, judgments of confederates were displayed. Response latencies were also obtained. A $2 \times 2 \times 2$ factorial design with two levels of depression, self-esteem, and confederate pressure was used. Data were analyzed by multiple linear regression with linear contrasts (Lunneborg, 1967), which allows for correlated predictor variables (depression and self-esteem, r = .39, $p < .005$). High depressives responded to the social influence manipulation with more variability ($p < .025$) and anticonformity ($p < .005$) than low depressives. Self-esteem and depression scores independently predicted response equally well and were more effective combined than either alone. Level of conformity pressure (1 or 2 confederates) had no effect, and response latency times were nondiscriminating.

Miranda (1971) examined the effects of confederate social support versus confederate competence on the conformity behavior of depressives. In his pilot work with small numbers of psychotically depressed patients and controls he obtained virtually no overlap between groups. Depressives were highly conforming with strong social support and unaffected or anticonforming with confederate competence only, whereas nonpsychiatric controls performed in an opposite manner. However, for Miranda's dissertation (1971), Ss were college students divided into high and low groups with the Beck Depression Inventory and a self-esteem measure. The highly depressed group mean corresponded to Beck's norms for a psychiatric outpatient group. With these samples, group differences were markedly attenuated as compared with the pilot data. Depression scores did not predict conformity behavior, and self-esteem scores did so at marginally significant levels.

The performance of depressives on personality measures ostensibly related to dependent and conforming behavior have not differed appreciably from nondepressives. Koran & Maxim (1972) found no difference in field dependence scores between bipolar patients and normals regardless of whether the patients were manic, depressed, or remitted. Field dependence scores were unaffected by affective state. Abramowitz (1969) reported a moderate relation between perceived external locus of control and depression in college students, but adjustment of the scores for social desirability attenuated the correlation to a marginally significant level.

Even speculations, much less generalizations, about susceptibility to social influence among depressives appear to be as premature as for the much more extensively studied relations between persuasibility and self-esteem (McGuire, 1968). The earlier global notion that depressives are indiscriminately more conforming than psychiatric or nonpsychiatric controls is patently untenable. Conditions under which social influence is exerted appear to be critically important. But other factors as well, such as severity and subtype of depression, sex of patient, conceptual model of social influence and its related experimental paradigm, also probably affect the susceptibility of depressives to social influence.

HOSTILITY

The classic psychodynamic postulate that severity of depression is related to the amount of aggression turned against the self has probably stimulated more research than any other psychological hypothesis. In part this may be due to the proposition's relative specificity to depression, and in part to its seductive (but elusive) susceptibility to objective evaluation. As indicated in the section on theories of depression, the role of aggression in depression is strongly disputed. Classical psychodynamic formulations emphasize the turning of aggression against the self following the loss and pathognomonic introjection of an ambivalently and narcissistically cathected object (e.g. Freud, 1917). The turning inward of aggression was chiefly inferred from the guilty, self-depreciating, and self-injurious behavior of depressives (Fenichel, 1945). Bibring (1953) and Cohen et al. (1954) among others have challenged the centrality and/or universality of aggression turned against the self in depression on theoretical grounds. Recent empirical findings support the necessity for modifying the classical position. Numerous investigators have identified depressive subtypes with strong outwardly directed hostility.[31]

Hostility as a Function of Clinical Status

In the Raskin et al. (1970) drug study of depressives previously discussed, a revised Buss-Durkee Inventory of hostile-aggressive tendencies was administered weekly. Friedman (1970) gave this scale to 98 nondepressed controls, group matched with 190 depressives from the Raskin et al. study on age, education, sex, and religion. The Inventory yields seven subtypes of hostile-aggressive behavior: assault, indirect aggression, negativism, verbal hostility, resentment, suspicion, and internalization of anger. If traditional interpretations of psychodynamic theory are correct, inverse relations between subscale scores for expressed anger and internalization would be predicted. And, as clinical improvement occurs, diminished internalization and an increased expression of anger would be predicted. Neither prediction was supported. All measures of hostility were positively correlated with each other and negatively correlated with clinical improvement. The chief differences between depressives and controls were that depressives reported less verbal hostility ($p < .01$) and more resentment ($p < .001$) than controls. However, these scores had a strong positive correlation with each other among depressives. Thus, hostility is apt to be expressed in multiple, simultaneous ways: overtly covertly, outwardly, and inwardly. Likewise, it is apt to occur in a wide range of contexts and role performances (Paykel, Weissman, Prusoff, & Tonks, 1971), but is apt to be most intense toward those closest to the depressive (Weissman, Paykel, Siegel, & Klerman, 1971), especially their children (Weissman, Klerman, & Paykel, 1971).

---

[31] The definition and assessment of aggression or hostility is a complex matter beyond the scope of this volume. Gottschalk, Gleser, & Springer (1963) and Berkowitz (1965) ably discuss these issues.

Hostility in Obsessional versus Hysteroid Depressives

Gershon, Cramer, & Klerman (1968) investigated whether depressive affect is: (a) positively correlated with inwardly directed hostility; (b) negatively correlated with outwardly directed hostility; or (c) variably patterned among patients. Although the miniscule sample size (6) virtually precluded anything but suggestive results, the results were interesting and the methodology should be emulated.

Depression was assessed by periodic clinical interviews using the Depressive Symptom Scale (DSS). This scale, which measures psychological symptoms only, is a factor analytically derived modification of the Hamilton Depression Scale (1967). Direction and intensity of hostility were evaluated by analyzing repeatedly obtained speech samples from depressive inpatients with a modification of Gottschalk et al.'s (1963) Hostility Scales. These Scales include Hostility-Out, Hostility-In, and Ambivalent Hostility. The first two scales respectively assess externally and internally directed critical-destructive statements; the third assesses hostility perceived as directed against the self by external influences.

The first prediction of a positive relation between amount of depression and inwardly directly hostility was affirmed ($r = .43$, $p < .01$), while the second prediction of a negative relation between amount of depression and outwardly directed hostility was negated ($r = .03$). The first result is consistent, and the second inconsistent, with derivations from the classical concept of relations between depression and direction of hostility. Both results are consistent with previous empirical findings (Gottschalk et al., 1963; Wessman et al., 1960).

The third hypothesis was tested in post hoc fashion. On the basis of previous work (Grinker et al., 1961; Harrow et al., 1966; Lazare & Klerman, 1968), Gershon et al. (1968) distinguished two subgroups of depressives: one with hysterical, the other with obsessional symptom patterns. The two groups did not differ in severity of depression on the DSS or on the relation of Hostility-In to DSS scores. But whereas DSS is unrelated to Hostility-Out in the obsessional subgroup, it is positively related to Hostility-Out in the hysterical subgroup. In addition, on an Affect-In Scale tapping verbalization of depressive affect, lowered self-esteem, and personal loss, the hysterical subgroup scored significantly lower than the obsessional group.

In interpreting their results, Gershon et al. point out that the classical psychodynamic notions of the relation between depression and hostility date from early Freudian theory, when hostility was still equated with a feeling state. This conceptualization preceded Freud's dual instinct theory of aggression and libido. Relations between hostility, instinctual aggression, and depression have not been explicated within psychodynamic theory (Mendelson, 1960, p. 101). Gershon et al. (1968) construe their overall findings as most nearly consistent with Bibring's theoretical position. They conclude that "... each type of hostility ("in" and "out") may have separate mechanisms both for its initiation and for its defensive alterations [p. 235]."

Antidepressant Drug Response and Hostility

In a subsequent study Klerman & Gershon (1970) investigated the longitudinal effects of an antidepressant drug, imipramine, on the direction of hostility in depressives. Previous clinical observations had suggested that imipramine mobilizes the expression of hostility outwardly, thus turning it away from the self. They found no support for this hypothesis. Patients improved clinically on imipramine, but there were no differences in the magnitude or direction of their hostility scores, at least as measured by Gottschalk et al.'s (1963) verbal sampling method. Klerman & Gershon's 1970 paper contains a worthwhile discussion of research design problems in this investigative area.

Self-regard, Blame, and Depression

Laxer (1964a) compared the real and ideal self-concepts of hospitalized depressives and various other psychiatric patients upon admission and discharge. Using the semantic differential, he found that only depressives show a marked discrepancy between their real and ideal self-ratings, initially. Groups did not differ at any point in ideal-self, and at discharge did not differ in real self-ratings either. Laxer regards the depressive's initial low ratings of self as support for the psychodynamic concept of aggression against the self. A subsequent study with hospitalized neurotics (Laxer, 1964b) buttressed this assumption. Psychiatric patients responded to a Blame Assignment Scale, the semantic differential real-self rating scale, and the Wessman et al. (1966) mood rating scale. The Blame Assignment Scale was devised for measuring tendency toward self-blame versus blaming others. A highly significant interaction was obtained, which indicated that patients with low mood and self-blaming tendencies evaluate themselves negatively, whereas patients with low moods who blame others do not devaluate themselves. Clinically diagnosed depressives tended to fall in the former category.

Hostility in Melancholics versus Paranoids

Caine (1960) explored the hypothesis that paranoids attribute their hostility to others (project hostility), whereas melancholics direct their hostility against themselves (introject hostility) in the form of guilt, self-criticism, and inferiority feelings. Hospitalized paranoids and "melancholic" females group matched for age and vocabulary were compared. Caine devised a number of acting-out, projected, and introjected hostility measures designed to tap varying levels of subject awareness. In terms of decreasing overtness of the test materials, measures included rationally derived MMPI scales, sentence completions with scrambled words, TAT stories, and a tapping task. Groups did not differ on the more direct measures of acting-out hostility. In line with the basic hypothesis, paranoids consistently scored higher on projected hostility and melancholics higher on self-criticism and guilt.

Hostility in the Dreams of Depressives

Beck's initial studies of depression also investigated the frequently hypothesized relation between inverted hostility and depression. As he noted, few of the psychodynamics postulated to explain depression are even relatively specific to the disorder; but inverted hostility is an exception. Beck's clinical observations indicated that his depressed therapy patients had an unusually high incidence of 'masochistic' dreams, which he defined as dreams in which the patient suffers. Whether the suffering is self-motivated, that is, reflects a need to suffer, is unclear. Beck & Hurvich (1959) constructed a scoring manual for masochistic dreams. Dreams are scored strictly for the presence or absence of masochism, not for its intensity. Very high inter-rater scoring reliability was established. The first 20 dreams of 6 depressed and 6 nondepressed patients matched on a number of variables were scored blindly for frequency of masochistic content. Such content included themes of trying to do or to get something unsuccessfully, losing a valued object, or being personally deficient, or as Beck put it, being a 'loser.' Depressed patients reported more masochistic dreams than nondepressed patients ($p < .025$). This finding was subsequently replicated in several better designed studies with larger numbers of subjects which also assessed the incidence of masochism in early memories and thematic projection stories (Beck, 1961; Beck & Ward, 1961). Scores on the Beck Depression Inventory were used as subject criteria for classifying Ss as high or low in depression regardless of clinical diagnosis. Beck regards the diagnosis of depression as too unreliable for research purposes. Despite his successful replications, Beck decided that it was impossible to test validly the motivational aspect of the inverted hostility hypothesis. He has shifted his approach to the cognitive approach discussed earlier, in which negative concepts of self, world, and future constitute the chief independent variables explaining depressive affect, motivation, and behavior (Beck, 1969).

Miller's (1969) investigation of depressive dreams seems to clarify apparent discrepancies in earlier studies. These studies plus clinical observations had suggested two hypotheses: that psychotic depressives have bland or pleasant dreams; and that with improvement their dreams become more conflictual and display more aggression toward others. In a group of hospitalized, psychotically depressed females, the first hypothesis was supported and the second partly confirmed. Improving patients' dreams were more conflictual, but their main theme involved others coercing the patient. This finding probably provided the first research support for Bonime's (1966) atypical theoretical emphasis on coerciveness in the depressive's life style. As Miller notes, Bonime stresses the depressives' very active efforts to coerce and to resist coercion. Miller identifies the probable source of disparities in previous findings as variance in the clinical status (severity and improving or chronic) of their patient samples.

Reaction Time to Hostile Content

Bodin & Geer (1965) tested the assumption that conflict over hostile impulses is directly related to severity of depression, an assumption supported by the empirical findings of Rapaport, Gill, & Schafer (1945). A predicted interaction between level of depression and verbal reaction time to words varying in level of hostility was not obtained. As indexed by number of errors rather than response time, depressed patients were superior to nondepressed patients under repetitive, stereotypic response conditions and inferior under more varied and complex conditions. This paper is quite instructive about the complexities of method and interpretation intrinsic to an approach that initially seems very straightforward.

Hostility in Normals as a Function of Mood Fluctuation

Wessman, Ricks, & Tyl (1960) investigated the directional expression of aggression in normal college females as a function of mood fluctuation. Subjects rated their mood daily on a 10-point Depression-Elation Scale. Each night for six weeks, Ss indicated their highest, lowest, and average mood for the day. On a high and low mood day, Ss administered a Q sort of self-descriptive phrases and the Rosenzweig Picture-Frustration Test (Rosenzweig, Fleming, & Clarke, 1947) to themselves. The latter measure was used for testing the hypothesis that intropunitive responses are more frequent in depression than in elation and that extrapunitive responses are less frequent. Contrary to the psychodynamic prediction, Ss responded more extrapunitively (i.e. resentment directed against the frustrator) when depressed and less intrapunitively (i.e. resentment directed against self) when elated.

A second hypothesis, that need-persistive or problem solving efforts would be lower in depression than in elation, was supported. Wessman et al. (1960) conjectured that "... the point at which mounting hostility shifts from an outward to an inward direction may mark the transition from relatively mild depression to severe affective pathology [p. 125]." But as they noted, their Q sort data were not consistent with this speculation.

The self-administered Q sort consisted of 45 evaluative, descriptive phrases pertaining to feelings, interactions, and cognitive traits. On each of two occasions (high and low mood state), Ss sorted these phrases twice into a seven-point forced normal distribution ranging from most to least characteristic of themselves. One sort described their actual self; the other sort their ideal self. Self-descriptions were significantly more self-critical in the depressed sort than in the elated sort. If verbal self-criticism is equated with hostility against the self, as Gottschalk et al. (1963) and Gershon et al. (1968) view it, then Wessman et al.'s results from the Rosenzweig P-F and the Q sort are not congruent.

A partial replication and extension of the Wessman et al. (1960) study to 17 Harvard males (Wessman & Ricks, 1966) did not fully support their initial findings. For males, there was no relation between depression-elation and direction of aggression or need-persistence on the Rosenzweig P-F, although again Q sorts during a depressed state were more self-critical.

Inconsistencies between measures of aggression (or virtually any other personality variable) on the same Ss are not unusual (Gottschalk et al., 1963) and may be due to a host of factors ranging from the untenability of conceptualizing aggressiveness as a trait (Berkowitz, 1965) to the insensitivity of the measures employed.

When Wessman & Ricks (1966) pooled their male and female Rosenzweig data the results indicated that in depressed states behavior is more extrapunitive ($p < .025$) and less need-persistent ($p < .025$). Wessman et al.'s findings are compatible with the relatively neglected theoretical speculations (Bull & Strongin, 1956; Lichtenberg, 1957) that link depression to frustrated goal striving and with Bibring's contention that depression entails a drop in self-esteem which is orthogonal to the parameters of aggression. Not only were males and females more self-critical when depressed, but their self-ideal Q sort correlations were lower than when elated. The latter correlation is commonly (although controversially) regarded as a useful index of self-esteem.

Clearly the overall results on the relation of direction and amount of hostility to depression support the need for much more detailed and testable specification of hypothesized relations. The global notion that severity of depression is positively related to the amount of aggression turned against the self and negatively related to externally directed aggression is unsupported or invalidated depending upon how intrinsically testable the hypothesis and the adequacy of assessments are regarded.

GUILT AND CONSCIENCE

Harrow & Amdur (1971) compared the severity of guilt with self image in two large series of consecutive admissions to the Yale-New Haven Hospital inpatient service. Psychiatrists' and patients' self-ratings were obtained. Comparisons were made between pooled depressives and all other psychiatric patients and between neurotic depressives, psychotic depressives, schizophrenics, and personality disorders. Pooled depressives did not differ in amount of guilt from other patients, although neurotic depressives were somewhat guiltier than psychotic depressives and other patients. Depressives had a more negative self-image as measured by Q-sort ratings than other patients ($p < .01$), and guilt was more strongly related to negative self-image ($p < .01$) than to diagnostic category.

Harrow & Amdur venture some interesting possibilities for explaining their failure to affirm clinical stereotypes which posit more guilt in depressives (especially psychotic depressives) than in other psychiatric categories: (a) they believe that clinicians may have confounded guilt and negative self-image; (b) their measures may have been more sensitive to overt than to subtle guilt; (c) the culture probably imposes less personal responsibility and blame for psychiatric disorders than before; and (d) patients are probably treated earlier and more effectively so that less severe pathology tends to develop. An additional point that was not discussed was the unusual youthfulness and high educational attainment of their psychiatric samples. However, they did not obtain any relation between sex, age, and guilt within their sample.

In a subsequent paper, Amdur & Harrow (1972) compared strictness of conscience within patients from the second in-patient sample previously discussed. In their conceptual distinction between conscience and guilt, the former refers to " . . . a person's standards about how he should live or behave which may act as an inward monitor of his conduct," whereas guilt is

> . . . a painful, negative, psychological feeling directed toward oneself, with an accompanying belief that one has not lived up to or has violated one's own internal values or standards about how one should live or behave [p. 259].

Three scales which intercorrelated highly were used to assess strictness of conscience. Support for the construct validity of these scales was provided by the finding that nonsociopathic patients had stricter conscience scores ($p < .01$) than sociopathic patients. Between diagnostic categories, combined depressives (psychotics and neurotics) had stricter consciences than nondepressive patients, but the two depressive groups did not differ from each other. Since age is related to strict conscience ($p < .01$), the most pronounced group differences were in the younger age ranges. Sex gender and hysteroid tendencies were unrelated to conscience.

Strictness of conscience was repeatedly assessed during hospitalization. Despite very substantial clinical changes in depression, performance on the conscience scales was quite stable. Thus the investigators conjecture that a strict conscience is probably a premorbid personality trait in at least a subgroup of depressives and may, therefore, be a predisposing factor to depression. While strict conscience and guilt are related, the former was more strongly associated with a primary depressive diagnosis than the latter.

SELF-CONCEPT

Apparently the ideal and normal self-concepts of bipolars do not differ from those of nonpsychiatric controls (Platman, Plutchik, Fieve, & Lawlor, 1969). In the remitted phase, bipolars' self-descriptive ratings of their "least-liked" and "remembered depressive" states are highly related ($r = .90$), whereas their "remembered manic" state is uncorrelated with any other self-described state. Ratings were made with the Emotions Profile Index (Kellerman & Plutchik, 1968). In a further study (Platman, et al., 1969) patients' self-ratings during their psychotic episodes were compared with their "remembered" ratings of these episodes during remission; these ratings were also compared with staff ratings. The acute and remitted patient descriptions of depression agreed well with each other and with staff, but acute manic self-ratings did not agree well with patients' "remembered manic" ratings nor with the staffs'. The latter two sets of ratings agreed highly. The actively manic patient describes himself as much more sociable, trusting, unaggressive, and pleasant than the remitted manic or staff. Presumably these disparities reflect the manic's denial and poorer reality contact.

SOCIAL ROLE FUNCTIONING

In a stimulating series of exploratory papers, Klerman and his colleagues described the social role functioning of depressed females, especially as mothers (Deykin, Jacobson, Klerman, & Solomon, 1966; Jacobson & Klerman, 1966; Paykel et al., 1971; Weismann, Paykel, & Klerman[32]). Middle-aged females whose children have recently left home comprise a substantial proportion of diagnosed depressives. Their state is termed the "empty-nest" syndrome, and several variants are identified. The overt conflict type involves direct severe conflict between depressed mother and children. These mothers were usually poorly educated, constricted, traditionally-oriented, and poorly Americanized. In contrast, the latent conflict variety involves a masked conflict between depressed mother and children accompanied by ill-defined dissatisfactions. The latter situation is more likely to arise in a better educated, less traditional mother who intellectually accepts the needs of the children for autonomy, but who depends on them for emotional gratification. These investigators are attempting to develop objective methods for applying Spiegel's (1957) model for the resolution of family role conflict to depressive mother-child interaction. They present a very interesting analysis of one case (Jacobson & Klerman, 1966) with their admittedly still crude methodology. The basic notion is that compatible role expectancies between role partners are essential for a harmonious relation. When conflict arises, resolution can be attempted by mutual role modification or unilaterally manipulated induction. The former type of resolution tends to be more stable and productive. Fluctuations in the frequency of home visits and severity of depression in a hospitalized mother as a function of role conflict resolution with her daughter are illustrated.

The damage wrought by depression in mothers is unfortunately not confined to relations with late adolescents and early adults. Clinical evidence strongly suggests that a high proportion of filicides (child murders) and child battery is committed by depressed, hostile, irritable mothers. Weissman et al. (submitted for publication) used evolving concepts of stages in the life cycle of nuclear families, each with a specific sociobiological function, as a framework for comparing the maternal performance of depressives and matched normals. Depressive mothers scored significantly higher on lack of involvement, impaired communication, friction, lack of affection, guilt, and resentment. The clinical

[32] Submitted for publication.

vignettes describing the stage specific impairments in mother-child relations among the depressive sample are quite illuminating. The percentage of depressive mothers with impairments at each life cycle stage was disturbingly high. But also disturbing is the unexplained failure to provide comparable data on the normal sample.

As Paykel et al. (1971) demonstrated, the role performance deficiencies of depressed females are very numerous. The Social Adjustment Scale was given in a semistructured interview to the previously described sample of 40 depressed and 40 normal females. Items covered performance effectiveness, interpersonal behavior, friction, and feelings and satisfactions in major role areas. Factor scores indicated that depressives have poorer work performance, more friction, less communication, more dependency, and more anxious rumination than normals across a broad range of functions: marital, parental, social, leisure, and work.

As equity theory (Adams, 1965) suggests, the resentment experienced by those who feel themselves unjustly situated in an unprofitable equity position may motivate efforts to restore balance by withholding from or depriving others. This formulation is closely akin to Bonime's (1966) but perhaps the more systematized equity theory would lend itself more readily to investigating ungivingness phenomena in clinical depression.

COMMUNICATION

Grinker (1964) offers some interesting speculations on depressive communication deficits, although he provides no data. His observational base is the oft noted tendency of depressives to repeat exhausting, monotonous, and eventually anger arousing litanies about their hopelessness, helplessness, sadness, guilt, deficiencies, etc. The responses by the recipients of these messages are reputed to be largely ignored by depressives. Grinker & Spiegel (1945) observed similar phenomena in combat exhausted soldiers; only time relieved their self-derogation, questioning, demanding behavior. Grinker hypothesizes that apparent communication deficits in depressives are defensively determined. He speculates that just as the combatant's ego is exhausted by external stress, so the premorbid depressive's ego is exhausted by internal stress. The internal stress results from unresolved conflicts and inadequate problem-solving techniques. When external stresses aggravate these vulnerabilities, the ego's problem-solving capacities diminish further, its control weakens, and hopelessness and exhaustion ensue. This dysphoric state is increased by any sense of added responsibility and/or personal deficiency. By highly stereotyped perception, cognition, and behavior, the depressive defensively blocks informational inputs which he might be obliged to act upon despite his felt inability to do so. Grinker's parallel between the depressive's incessant reiterations and those of 3 to 5 year old children who ostensibly want more information but can't accept it seems more tenuous.

Reusch (1962) has been so impressed by the communicative deficits of depressives that he argues for the near futility of verbal interchanges during treatment. He contends that denotative synchronization between verbal and action systems is severly impaired.[33]

POSITIVE REINFORCEMENT AND SOCIAL SKILL

Lewinsohn (1972) and his colleagues have designed a series of investigations to test their behavioral formulation of depression. This formulation stipulates that positive reinforcement and depression are inversely related. To test this notion (Lewinsohn & Libet, 1972) daily ratings on mood level and a Pleasant Events Schedule were obtained over 30 consecutive days from three groups of college students. Students were grouped as depressed, psychiatric but nondepressed, and normal on the basis of MMPI scores and interview ratings on Grinker et al.'s (1961) Feelings and Concerns Check List. A substantial relation between mood and activity level was obtained for the combined sample of 30 students ($p < .001$). An attempt to determine by an autocorrelation method whether mood or activity had a causal relation to each other suggested strong inter-individual variation. Perhaps the most important contribution of this paper is its demonstration of a methodology for empirically developing a set of individualized activities that are functionally related to mood variation. The relation between engaging in particular activities and mood improvement was significantly stronger in both psychiatric groups than in normals.

Further, corroboration of the low level of reinforcing activity in depressives resulted from a study with largely clinical samples of depressives, nondepressives, and a normal control (Lewinsohn, 1972). Subjects were asked to rate each item of the Pleasant Events Schedule for its occurrence during the previous month and for its enjoyability. Scores were obtained for frequency, enjoyability, and the summed products of frequency x enjoyability; the scores are designed to reflect activity level, reinforcement potential, and obtained reinforcement, respectively. The depressives were significantly lower on all three scores than the psychiatric nondepressives and normals who did not differ between themselves.

In group settings, Lewinsohn's group (1972) found that depressives emitted fewer behaviors and thus elicited fewer responses from others. In these groups, emission of verbal behavior and elicitation of verbal response correlated r = .93. Also, depressives tended to emit shorter messages than nondepressives.

---

[33] For an abstruse but intriguing discussion of the function of conventionality in the verbal expression and experiencing of manic-depressives, see Smith's "The Metaphor of the Manic-depressive" (1960). Briefly, he argues that the issue of separation is the central source of anxiety in manic-depressive families. The mother of the predepressive typically handles her incapacity for emotional involvement by emotional desertion and a compensatory, defensive overemphasis on observing conventionalities.

Depressives interacted with fewer individuals within the group and tended to be more noncontingent or indiscriminate in their social reinforcement of others. In short, depressives appear to be unskilled at eliciting positive responses and avoiding behavior that elicits aversive consequences.

Home observations of interactions between depressives and their spouses support the contention that depressives are on low positive reinforcement schedules and may have poor social skills (Lewinsohn & Shaffer, 1971; Libet & Lewinsohn, in press). Observers typically rate family interactions at dinner time. Ratings are recorded at 30″ intervals for each family member (sources) on actions, quality of response elicited (positive or negative), and content of the interaction. Data are presented for a small sample of depressives and their spouses. Patients and spouses are about equally active, but patients elicit an appreciably lower ratio of positive reinforcement and a higher ratio of negative reinforcement. Alterations toward a more favorable balance were associated with clinical improvement.

Apropos of the relation of positive reinforcers to depression, it is worth noting that virtually the only environmental difference found between depressed and nondepressed recently widowed persons was the greater availability to the latter of children whom they considered emotionally close (Clayton, Halikas, & Maurice, 1972).

In summary, there are many suggestive leads in the psychological research on depression, but there has been too little replication, consistency in results, longitudinal study, and programmatic research to allow adequate evaluation of extant theories or the formulation of alternative ones. Generalized statements about depressives are not likely to be substantiated. Hypotheses will have to specify variables such as depressive subtype and clinical status much more sharply if secure underpinnings for theoretical extrapolation are to emerge.

9
BIOLOGICAL ASPECTS OF DEPRESSION: 1

Where the bond of union is between the mind and the animal fluids God Almighty alone knows, but there is no one theory better confirmed by experience than that they mutually influence one another.[34]

GENETICS[35]

Findings on the Affective Disorders, Broadly Defined

Among the functional personality disorders, schizophrenia and manic-depressive states have been most studied genetically. Recent methodological advances have yielded increasing support for a strong hereditary component in at least some forms of schizophrenia. Application of these research methods to depressive states has lagged. Therefore, the role of genetics in the etiology of depression remains highly controversial.

Case identification: dichotomous diagnoses. By definition, no specific etiology has been determined for functional disorders. Their diagnosis depends primarily on personality history and function and secondarily on biological concomitants. This diagnostic basis poses several formidable problems for genetic approaches. Phenotypic (overt) aspects of personality deviance vary considerably within and between diagnostic categories because of their

---

[34] Sanctorius of Padua, father of human metabolic studies, circa 1650 A.D. (quoted in Coppen, 1967).

[35] Appreciation is gratefully acknowledged to Dr. Gilbert S. Omenn, Department of Genetics, University of Washington, for many helpful comments on this section.

susceptibility to environmental influences. Yet most case identification in genetic and epidemiological studies is performed on a dichotomous basis; either the individual has (or has had) the disorder or he has not. But from either a genetic or environmental standpoint, disorders would be expected to manifest themselves in varying degrees (or within "spectrums") rather than on a present-absent basis. Even within disorders transmitted on a Mendelian basis by a single pathogene of high penetrance (likelihood of phenotypic expression), modifying genes or genetic-environmental interactions may considerably modify the phenotypic expression of the disorder. And most complex personality manifestations, even many relatively simple ones, are polygenically determined. That is, multiple genes contribute independently but additively to the rate and degree of trait expression. Only statistical or quantitative trait measures and analyses can detect such determinants. Dichotomous diagnostic procedures are poorly suited to their demonstration.

Consanguinity and concordance. Until recently, the genetics of psychopathology relied largely on consanguinity-concordance rates to buttress their etiological position. Given an index case, or proband, the closer the genetic relationship (consanguinity) of relatives, the higher the incidence of the disorder (concordance) should be among them. Monozygotic twins (derived from a single ovum fertilized by a single sperm) share 100% of their genes,[36] first degree relatives (parents, siblings, and children) share 50% of their genes, and second degree relatives (aunts, uncles, nieces, nephews, grandparents) share 25%. The counter argument of the environmentalist, of course, is that the greater the genetic linkage the greater the likelihood that individuals have shared the same social environment. In the absence of specific genetic indicators associated with functional disorders, this counter is difficult to refute.

Sampling and statistical biases. Furthermore, the lack of accepted, reliable, and validated case criteria enhances the probability of variable case criteria between studies and of unwitting investigator bias. The most readily accessible probands for research tend to be unrepresentative of the patient population. These are usually hospitalized patients who are more severly and chronically ill than the typical patient. Such patients are likely to come from families with a greater number and/or virulence of pathological genes. Knowledge of the diagnosis of the proband and of the hypotheses being investigated is apt to affect the investigators' diagnosis of the proband's relatives.

Furthermore, statistical predictions for the incidence of polygenic disorders are predicated on the assumption of random mating in the population, but there is growing evidence for assortative mating. That is, likes tend to marry likes: schizoids to marry schizoids, cyclothymics to marry cyclothymics, etc. Shields

---

[36] Earlier assumptions about monozygous twins are being sharply challenged (Pollin & Stabenau, 1968). The determination of zygosity is not easily made, and few studies have used definitive serological tests. Also, prenatal circulatory differences between monozygotic twins may cause marked constitutional differences.

(1968) and Gershon, Dunner, & Goodwin (1971), while acknowledging these methodological problems, concluded that the evidence for a substantial genetic factor in the transmission of affective disorder is very high.

Designs for needed genetical research. The most promising research designs for determining the probability of a genetic component in functional personality disorders are the adoptee and longitudinal studies. These approaches have only been used with schizophrenics thus far. Rosenthal (1971) identifies three types of adoptee and cross-fostering study methods. The first starts with a sample of adopted (preferably from birth) schizophrenic probands and nonschizophrenic adoptees matched for age, sex, social class, and age of adoption. The incidence of schizophrenia in the biological and adoptive parents and relatives is then determined. A higher incidence of schizophrenia among the biological relatives of the adopted schizophrenic probands than in the relatives of the nonschizophrenic children or in the adoptive parents and their relatives would support the likelihood of a genetically determined disorder. The second approach compares a sample of schizophrenic parents who have placed their children for adoption with a matched control group of nonschizophrenic parents who have also placed their children for adoption. A higher incidence of schizophrenia in the children placed for adoption by the schizophrenic biological parents would support a genetic etiology. The third method has not been attempted as yet. It would compare the incidence of schizophrenia in adoptees with normal biological parents who were reared by schizophrenic parents with the incidence of schizophrenia in adoptees of schizophrenic biological parents who were reared by normal parents. While these research designs are a decided improvement, they remain susceptible to many of the biases and problems of diagnostic unreliability discussed previously. Fool-proof designs are probably unattainable. It can only be hoped that the main effects and interactions are sufficiently powerful to attain statistical significance across studies despite a variety of random and systematic errors in any particular study.

Overview of substantive findings. In Rosenthal's (1971) review of the manic-depressive genetic data, he concluded that (a) the data strongly support a significant genetic component in manic-depressive disorder; (b) the mode of genetic transmission (e.g. dominant or recessive, autosomal vs. X-linked, single gene vs. polygenic, etc.) remains unclear; (c) the relative weight of genetic and environmental determinants is indeterminate; (d) research on the genetics of the manic-depressive disorder has been neither as "thorough or sophisticated" as that on schizophrenia; and (e) Kraepelin's distinction between schizophrenia and manic-depressive illness is supported. The present writer agrees with these conclusions, except that he is not as convinced as Rosenthal that the data provide ". . . strong evidence in favor of considering manic-depressive psychosis to be genetically influenced in good part [p. 221]."

Comparative incidence in relatives of probands and the general population. Beginning with Rosenthal's first conclusion, what would constitute evidence for the genetic transmission of a disorder? Hanna (1965) specifies several criteria, the first being a higher incidence of the disorder among relatives of the proband than among the general population. Clearly, reliable case identification is the sine qua non for valid information on familial versus population incidence of a disorder. As noted, reliable diagnosis of affective disorders leaves much to be desired. Basic requirements, such as explicit diagnostic criteria and independent diagnoses by skilled clinicians who are unaware of both the hypotheses being examined and of the diagnosis of the proband, are very rarely fulfilled. It is hardly surprising therefore, that Rosenthal (p. 204) reports morbidity risk rates for manic-depressive psychoses in the general population ranging from .07% to 7% (the median for 8 studies is .7%). Returning to Hanna's criterion of a higher morbidity rate among relatives of manic-depressives, Rosenthal presents the following ranges in morbidity rates for first-degree relatives with a "certain" diagnosis of manic-depressive psychosis: parents, 3.4% – 23.4%; siblings, 2.7% – 22.7%; and children, 6.0% – 24.1% (the respective medians are 7.6%, 8.1%, and 11.2%). Ethnic differences do not appear to account for the discrepancies, since all studies were done in Western Europe and the United States and some of the widest variations are obtained within the same nation, for example Sweden. But, wide as the variation is, the minimum percentage for each first-degree category is well above the median for the general population. Furthermore, morbidity rates for relatives sharing one-fourth rather than half the proband's genes, such as half-sibs, aunts, uncles, nephews, nieces, and grandchildren, also run at least double the population median.

Concordance rates in monozygotic vs. dizygotic twins. Hanna's second criterion for genetic transmission is that monozygotic (MZ) twins have a higher concordance rate than dyzygotic (DZ) twins. The former twins have identical genes and the latter have 50% of their genes in common, as do any set of siblings. Obtained concordance rates for MZ twins (that is, the percentage of twins of a diagnosed proband also having the disorder) range from 50% to 100% and for DZ twins from 0% to 38.5%; the concordance ratio of MZ to DZ twins within studies range from 19.2 MZ:1 DZ to 2.4 MZ:1 DZ. The consistently higher MZ concordance rate across all seven studies favors a genetic transmission. However, in addition to the possible sources of diagnostic unreliability previously cited, Rosenthal notes that many of the twins' studies relied on hospitalized samples. Such cases would tend to be more severe and thus to have a greater probability of a higher concordance rate than more benign cases would have.

Disturbance of disorder-related functions among relatives. Hanna's third criterion is that the same functional system most affected in the proband is more frequently disturbed in his relatives than in the general population. No reasonably adequate studies have sought to determine whether relatives of probands have more deviant but nonpathological mood aberrations or negatively biased thought disorders than the general population.

Typical age of onset. Hanna's final criterion for a genetic disorder is a characteristic age of onset which occurs without an identifiable precipitant. The age of risk for manic-depressive disorder in most genetic studies is 15-60, and age of onset varies widely from nation to nation, as indicated previously (Kramer, 1969). Likewise, the evidence for precipitating factors is riven with controversy. However, increasing evidence for bimodal peaks of onset is fostering speculation about several genetically distinct depressive disorders (Hopkinson & Ley, 1969; Winokur, Cadoret, Dorzab, & Baker, 1971).

Monogenic-biochemical vs. diathesis-stress explanations. In sum, two of Hanna's criteria are partially met, and evidence is unavailable or inconclusive for the other two. Support for a genetic transmission is suggestive but hardly compelling. Certainly the data reviewed thus far do not support a Mendelian pattern of inheritance, unless relatively weak penetrance is assumed. Alternative genetic explanations remain tenable, nonetheless. Hanna's criteria for a genetic etiology fit Rosenthal's description of a monogenic-biochemical theory of psychopathology better than those he terms diathesis-stress theories. According to the former theoretical approach, a specific gene or several specific genes cause a specific metabolic error, which in turn causes the disorder. A diathesis (predisposition)-stress position is more difficult to establish definitively. It implies that environmental stresses potentiate a predisposition to develop a disorder. Multiple modes of genetic transmission are possible; several examples are transmission by a single dominant gene with variable penetrance, or by multiple genes, all of which may be dominant or recessive, or a mixture of both. Variable penetrance would result from interaction of the dominant gene with other modifying genes as well as the environment. In short, then, assaying the validity of genetic theories is complicated by the existence of multiple modes of genetic transmission which vary greatly in their current testability.

A polygenic etiology can fairly readily be reconciled with the disparate findings reviewed. The very adaptability of such explanations makes for their uneasy invocation; they are all too susceptible to post hoc rationalization, given the weak data base at this time. How can the disparate findings be reconciled, assuming that they are valid estimates rather than methodological artifacts? It could be assumed that populations vary in the number and/or virulence of pathogenic genes contributing to the phenotypic expression of the disorder. However, such an assumption does not account for the discordant monozygotic twins found in all populations, nor for the widely disparate concordance rates within the same population. Conceivably the findings on discordant monozygotic twins reflect an interaction between genes and environment, while the discrepancies in morbidity rates within similar populations reflect variations in sampling practices such as diagnostic criteria and age of risk used in morbidity determination. The former contention is tentatively supported by reports that MZ twins vary considerably in constitution and personality, possibly due to differences in fetal circulation (Pollin & Stabenau, 1968).

While Rosenthal concludes that the mode of inheritance of manic-depressive psychosis remains undetermined, he cautiously inclines toward a simple polygenic theory, possibly modified to account for the higher incidence of manic-depressive psychosis in females. Because phenotypic characteristics are determined by multiple genes whose actions cumulatively determine the degree of manifest trait expression, their phenotypes tend to be normally and continuously distributed in the population. Quantitative criteria are available for determining simple polygenic inheritance (Rosenthal, 1971, pp. 111–112; Slater, 1966). Some of these criteria, like the incidence ratio of first-degree relatives to the general population, equal correlation among relatives with equal proportions of shared genes, and MZ:DZ incidence ratios, can be approximated from extant data. But other critically important criteria require currently nonexistent knowledge of what constitutes the predisposition to manic-depressive psychosis and methods for assessing the strength of such predisposing factors.

While theoretical emphasis is shifting from wholly genetic or environmentalist etiological explanations toward concern with their interaction, sharp differences persist in the degree to which heredity or environment are implicated (Rosenthal, 1968). Those who argue that functional psychoses are inherited would contend that the pathogenic genes are a necessary though probably not sufficient cause of such disorders, that the probability of clinical manifestation depends on the number and virulence of pathogenes present, and that given the presence of the pathogenic polygenes, the carrier is always at least a potential psychotic and probably exhibits subclinical manifestations of the disorder. Environmentalists virtually never discount the possible role of genetic factors but minimize their importance. Given the same genotype, noxious experience may potentiate a psychosis, or favorable experience may stimulate unusually positive attributes (Heston, 1969).

Genetic vs. environmental approaches. Despite the increased rapprochement between geneticists and environmentalists which accepts the necessity of examining the relative weights and interactive effects of genes and environment, appropriate research has lagged. An obvious prerequisite to studies of genetic-environmental interaction is an adequate conceptualization of environmental variables of presumed etiological significance. Intensive investigations of interaction within families of schizophrenics have yielded fertile hypotheses (e.g. Fontana, 1966; Lidz, Fleck, & Cornelison, 1965; Rosenthal, 1968), but much less has been done on families of depressives. Until this deficit is remedied there is little prospect of deviating from conventional genetic research designs in which environmental effects are randomized rather than systematically varied.

Schizophrenia and depression: Categorical disorders or a continuum. Returning to Rosenthal's (1971) conclusion that genetic studies support a distinction between schizophrenia and manic-depressive disorders, one again finds equivocal and even paradoxical findings. If these disorders are discrete, they should tend to breed true. That is, relatives of manic-depressive probands should have a significantly higher morbidity expectancy for the disorder than the general population, but their expectancy for schizophrenia should not differ from the general population. The obverse should, of course, obtain for schizophrenic probands. Within the limits of the usual wide variations in estimated rates, these predictions are supported with one repeated exception. Parents of manic-depressives tend to have a much higher incidence of schizophrenic children than the general population; this ranges from four to five times higher for one manic-depressive parent, to one estimate of 15 times higher for two manic-depressive parents. As Rosenthal acknowledges, whether this disparity from expected breeding patterns is due to a complex genetic transmission, misdiagnosis, environmental interaction with genes, or environmental factors alone, is uncertain. As repeatedly noted, support for the distinction between manic-depressive psychosis and schizophrenia rests on clinical observation rather than ascertained differences in etiology. Clinically, the two disorders tend to have different but overlapping courses, outcomes, and responses to treatment modalities. Schizo-affectives may have a similar genetic predisposition to manic-depressives and a developmental history like schizophrenics (Cohen, Allen, Pollin, & Hrubec, 1972).

If manic-depressive psychosis is at least in part genetically determined, its evolutionary survival poses an intriguing problem. According to Rosenthal (1971), manic-depressives have a death rate 150% greater than the general population after the onset of illness. Although as usual the data are inconsistent, six of eight studies report lower fertility rates for manic-depressives: they marry less frequently and have fewer children if married. Such factors would be expected to diminish the incidence of the disorder, progressively, but no such trends are evident. Explanatory hypotheses range from the speculation that proband siblings have higher marriage rates than the general population to postulation of a heterogeneous polygenic transmission involving allelic mutations at multiple gene loci, the mutated genes having a similar additive effect on phenotypic expression.

Unipolar versus Bipolar Genetic Findings

A currently active focus of genetic studies on affective disorders is concerned with the issue of whether similar modes of genetic transmission are found in unipolar and bipolar depressives. Most investigators apply the former term to patients who experience a single or repeated depressive episodes only and the latter to those who experience manic and depressive episodes. Others sometimes include in the bipolar group patients with manic episodes only, as well as patients who manifest repeated depressions only (Winokur, 1970), on the hypothesis that these types are bipolar gene-bearers because they have phenotypic bipolar family members. Whether depressive disorders constitute a biological unity or not is a controversy of long standing. Kraepelin grouped all varieties of depressives together on the basis of ostensible similarities in course and outcome. Supposedly, all depressions are self-limited in duration and remit without residual personality defects, but recent studies challenge these assumptions, especially in regard to bipolar depressives (Keith, Brodie, & Leff, 1971).

Perris' studies (1966; 1968; 1969) are a follow-up and extension of Leonhard's (1959) initial findings that relatives of bipolar probands tend to have bipolar affective disorders or cyclothymic personalities, whereas relatives of unipolars tend to have unipolar affective disorders or depressive personalities (Leonhard, Korff, & Schulz, 1962). Perris used relatively stringent subject criteria in order to isolate homogeneous groups of bipolar and unipolar probands. Classification as a unipolar required three hospitalizations for depressive episodes, no history of mania, and clear remissions between depressive episodes. Classification as bipolar required both clear-cut manic and depressive episodes that required hospitalization for either or both phases. His sample included approximately 150 bipolars and 150 unipolars, plus 2,400 relatives. To a remarkable and unprecedented extent, Perris reported that these disorders tend to breed true. Whereas the morbidity rate for bipolar disorder was 10.8% among first-degree relatives of bipolar probands, it was only 0.4% for relatives of unipolar probands; and whereas the rate of unipolar disorder was only 0.58% among relatives of bipolar probands, it was 7.4% for relatives of unipolar probands. A simultaneous but independently conducted study by Angst produced similar results (Angst & Perris, 1968), the corresponding percentages being 3.7%, 0.29%, 11.2%, and 9.1%. Note that Angst found a much higher incidence of unipolar disorder in relatives of bipolars than Perris. Winokur, Clayton, & Reich (1969) attribute this discrepancy to Perris' stringent subject criteria. If the latter are modified to accord with more typical criteria, the morbidity of unipolar disorder in relatives of bipolar probands rises to 8.4% for Perris' sample. Angst and Perris concluded that bipolar and unipolar disorders are genetically distinct; that penetrance and genetic loading are greater in the bipolar form, and that environmental factors play only a nonspecific etiological role. Patients with manic episodes only resembled bipolars. Perris was unable to specify a particular mode of genetic transmission for either unipolars or bipolars from his data. He contends that sex prevalence ratios (equal for bipolars, an excess of females for unipolars) and transmission by sex from parent to child (no sex linkage in bipolars and a preponderance of ill females with ill fathers for unipolars) militate against any simple dominant or recessive transmission. He argues for a polygenic inheritance, with at least one of the factors X-linked, in unipolar depression (1966). Perris' contention of two distinguishable disorders is supported by his obtained differences between samples of each in early environment, precipitants, age of onset, treatment response, psychophysiology, and suicide rate.

Further support for a meaningful distinction between unipolar and bipolar depressives was provided by Keith et al. (1971) at the National Institute of Mental Health. Probands were drawn from a pool of 200 patients with affective disorders admitted to a metabolic research ward over a five-year span. Thirty patients (bipolars) who had displayed manic and depressive episodes while hospitalized were matched for age and sex with 30 depressives (unipolars) with no previous history of depressive episodes. Subject criteria were vulnerable to some misclassification. Not all patients were beyond the age of risk for a bipolar disorder, and it is unclear whether brief hypomanic episodes after the lifting of a depression met the criteria for inclusion as a bipolar proband. Most investigators exclude such patients as bipolars unless the hypomania is prolonged and requires a change in treatment. Despite these caveats, there was substantial congruence of the findings with previous ones. Keith et al. (1971) reported that 30% of the unipolar probands had first-degree relatives with a unipolar disorder and none with a bipolar disorder, whereas 24% of the bipolar probands had unipolar relatives and 16% had bipolar relatives. Thus a tendency to breed true was reaffirmed for unipolars (Stenstedt, 1952), but not as strikingly for the bipolars as in Perris's data.

Winokur (1970) and his associates hypothesized two primary affective psychotic diseases: manic-depressive disease or bipolar psychosis and depressive disease or unipolar psychosis. By "primary" they mean a disease uncomplicated by other psychopathological conditions, and by "disease" they stated their conviction that a genetic etiology essentially determines the onset, course, and outcome of the two diseases. Bipolar psychosis is inferred from a proband history of manic episodes only, or manic and depressive episodes, or depressive episodes only within a family with a history of mania. Bipolar depressions may be clinically indistinguishable from unipolar depressions. Unipolar depression is inferred from a proband history of depression only and a family history without mania. Winokur (1970) contend ". . . that considerable genetic data exist which indicate that the two illnesses are quite distinct from each other [p. 267] ."

Much of this research has been on the families of manic probands (Winokur, Clayton, & Reich, 1969). Three groups of consecutively admitted manic probands (N = 28, 30, 31 respectively) and their first-degree relatives were studied with increasing degrees of intensity. All available first-degree relatives in group III were interviewed personally to ascertain their psychiatric history. Winokur et al. (1969) contend that their data conform reasonably well to criteria for a dominant X-linked transmission. If penetrance were complete, these criteria would include: a 2:1 ratio of afflicted females to males; no father-son transmission; all afflicted sons having afflicted mothers; all the daughters of afflicted fathers being afflicted; half the sons and half the daughters of afflicted mothers being afflicted; and a morbidity risk of 50% for parents, sibs, and children of probands. Winokur's obtained sex ratio of female to male manic probands was 1.5:1.0 (for the following percentages, all afflicted parents have an affective disorder, though not necessarily a bipolar one). One male proband had an affected father; 63% of male probands had affected mothers; the morbidity risk for fathers of female probands was only 23%; no data were given for percentage of afflicted sons and daughters of afflicted fathers and mothers, but 17 ill mother-ill daughter and 17 ill mother-ill son pairs were reported; estimated morbidity risk for parents, sibs, and children was 41%, 42%, and 50% respectively.

Instances of apparent father-son transmission are especially inconsistent with X-linked dominant transmission. But Perris (1966) reports a number of such instances. However, even within a single X-linked dominant transmission approach these anomalies can be explained either by questionable paternity or by the mother's being the actual transmitter rather than the father; if the mother is not afflicted she could be a pathogenic carrier who reflects incomplete penetrance.

Winokur et al. (1969) also found that affective disorders in relatives of probands were heterogeneous. Using data on the parents of the most intensively studied 61 manic probands, they reported eight with episodes of mania and 26 with depression only; proband siblings also displayed heterogeneous affective disorders. If the parent of the proband was also manic, 43% of the proband sibs and children were also manic. This led Winokur to postulate that while bipolar disease is transmitted by an X-linked dominant gene, the expression of mania probably depends on the transmission of a second dominant gene which is most likely autosomal (i.e. a non-sex-linked chromosome). If only the X-linked gene is transmitted, then only depression is manifested.

Winokur et al. (1969) further contend that the X-linked dominant gene is located on the short arm of the X chromosome. This is justified by relating familial prevalence of affective disorder to several X-chromosome gene markers. When gene loci are linked in coupling they are near to each other on the same chromosome and assort dependently. Trait characteristics of linked genes occur together in about 50% of family members over a few consecutive generations only. Ostensibly, the gene for proton color blindness is located on the short arm of the X-chromosome. Winokur et al. report a very high concordance rate of manic-depressive disorder and proton color blindness within two families ($p < .00025$) (Reich, Clayton, & Winokur, 1969). However, testing for such color blindness, especially within females, by the method used is not optimally reliable (Thuline, Hodgkin, Fraser, & Motulsky, 1969), and there is no indication of whether a double-blind technique was used. Moreover, the location of the gene for proton color blindness on the short arm of the X-chromosome has not been definitively established. Additional studies of linkage within families of manic probands were done with the red blood cell antigen Xg^a (Winokur & Tanna, 1969). The Xg^a gene may also be on the short arm of the X-chromosome, although this too is uncertain (Race & Sanger, 1969). Winokur speculates that the manic-depressive gene could lie between the Xg^a and color blindness genes. In three families there was suggestive evidence of a linkage between Xg^a and affective disorder. If a heterozygous Xg^a+ mother was married to an Xg^a+ father, the children tended to have affective disorders if they were positive or to be well if they were negative.

The bipolar, X-linkage hypothesis of Winokur has been challenged by independent investigators on several grounds. Dunner, Gershon, & Goodwin (1970) at the National Institute of Mental Health studied 160 bipolar and 73 unipolar patients hospitalized there for affective disorders. Twenty-three of the bipolars were male, and of these four had fathers only with affective disorders. This finding is inconsistent with X-chromosome linkage. Furthermore, a Belgian study of linkage between Xg^a and manic-depressive disorder in 66 families failed to support the hypothesized linkage (Excerpta Medica Foundation, 1971).

Winokur and his associates have recently extended their genetic investigations to unipolars (Dorzab, Baker, Cadoret, & Winokur, 1971). One hundred unipolar probands and 129 first-degree relatives were studied. As noted by others, family history for affective disorders is less positive for unipolars than for bipolars; 26% of unipolars had at least one affected parent versus 52% for bipolars. Unipolars had twice as many affected mothers as fathers. An X-linked transmission is also hypothesized for unipolars, although the possibility of unipolars being heterogeneous with one subgroup associated with alcoholism and sociopathy is broached. However, Dunner et al. (1970) report as much alcoholism in the family histories of bipolars as in unipolars. Since a criterion for unipolar proband selection was an absence of family history for mania, the repeated finding by others that unipolar disorder breeds true much more than bipolar disorder could not be evaluated.

In sum, evidence for a genetic component in affective disorders, especially for the bipolar form, appears to be increasingly substantial. However, identification of a specific mode of transmission and estimated weighting of a genetic factor continues to be elusive. Inconsistent findings are inevitable given differences in diagnostic criteria and methodological rigor, compounded by possible inherent heterogeneity within disorders and between populations. The most consistent findings seem to be an overall excess of female unipolars, a higher prevalence of affective disorder in families of bipolars, and the tendency for unipolars to breed true.

Imbalanced sex ratios are commonplace among disorders which are thought to involve a genetic predisposition but not sex linkage (e.g. thyroid diseases and lupus erythematosus). Sex hormone differences may contribute much to such imbalanced sex ratios. Winokur et al. (1969) stress the frequency of affective disorder in consecutive generations as support for a dominant mode of transmission, but vertical transmission is also found with X-linked recessives, common autosomal recessives, and with multifactorial genetic-environmental interaction. However, Winokur's formulations are ingenious; his attempt to link affective disorder with a genetic marker is particularly laudable. Such linkage would be especially compelling if the marker were a biochemical gene with probable relevance to affective disorder (e.g. MAO or tyrosine hydroxylase). Unfortunately, as Winokur acknowledges, pedigree linkage studies are highly susceptible to genetic crossovers (shifting of genes between homologous chromosomes). For example, linkage between the loci for Xg^a and red-green color blindness is reportedly loose (Renwick & Schulze, 1964).

The differential depressive behavior (Beigel & Murphy, 1971), psychopharmacological responses (Gershon et al., 1971) and neurophysiological responses (Borge, Buchsbaum, Goodwin, Murphy, & Silverman, 1971) of bipolars and unipolars are consistent with the possibility of their being distinct disorders.

Slater (1966) has devised a polygenetic computational model for comparing observed and expected distributions of secondary cases (proband's parents' sibs, grandparents and their sibs, cousins) of abnormality on paternal and maternal sides. A series of studies using this model support the likelihood that unipolar and bipolar disorders are polygenetically determined (Perris, 1971; Slater, Maxwell, & Price, 1971). Within both unipolars (Baker, Dorzab, Winokur & Cadoret, 1972) and bipolars (Mendlewicz, Fieve, Rainer, & Fleiss, 1972) multiple genetic patterns may exist, or subsets of unipolars and bipolars may be environmentally rather than genetically determined. There seems to be a higher family risk of affective disorder associated with an early onset unipolar disorder (Pollitt, 1972), as well as a strong tendency toward so-called "depressive spectrum" disorders (alcoholism and sociopathy) among the male relatives of early onset unipolars (Winokur, Cadoret, Dorzab, & Baker, 1971).

This writer inclines strongly toward Zerbin-Rudin's (1967) position that the mode of transmission for affective disorder is still undetermined. Partial sex linkage appears more likely for unipolar than bipolar disorders. Angst & Perris (1968) both found an approximately equal sex prevalence for bipolar disorder and an excess of females for unipolar disorder. Zerbin-Rudin's summary (1967) of the literature on monozygotic twins with affective disorders also found an equal sex prevalence for bipolar twins and an excess of females for unipolar twins (about 81% of monozygotic and 70% of dyzygotic twins had the same form of disorder). Perris's (1969) speculation that genetic transmission consists of a predisposition to a form of disorder and to a type of personality, both of which interact with environmental factors, seems quite plausible. With regard to probable environmental effects, Stenstedt (1952) compared the manic-depressive morbidity risk for siblings of manic-depressive probands who came from favorable or unfavorable early home environments. The morbidity risk for an unfavorable environment was triple that of a favorable one (30.9% vs. 10.2%). And Perris (1966) found that age of onset was 10 years earlier among unipolars from unfavorable family environments versus those from favorable environments. As usual, these findings for environmental effects are suggestive only. Other clinically hypothesized relations, such as that between early childhood bereavement and affective psychosis, were not borne out by Angst & Perris (1968). Clearly the time is ripe for extension of adoptive genetic research designs to affective disorders.

NEUROPHYSIOLOGY

Numerous studies indicate that depressives frequently have neurophysiological anomalies, but the specificity of these anomalies to depression or to depressive subtypes remains unclear. Grossly categorized, these studies are concerned with muscle tension, electrical activity, and metabolism. An excellent summary of this literature by Whybrow & Mendels (1969) attempts to integrate the diverse biological and clinical findings by postulating

... the existence of an unstable state of central nervous system hyperexcitability in depression, and possibly in mania, with an associated but disorganized intrinsic hyperactivity [p. 1491].

As Whybrow and Mendels noted, few of the studies undergirding their hypothesis have been replicated and among those few discrepant results are not infrequent. Nonetheless, the overall convergence of empirical findings supports their hypothesis.

Electromyography

Whatmore (1966; Whatmore & Kohli, 1968) has done most of the systematic investigation and theorizing about muscular tension in depression. His key concept is dysponesis (dys = bad, faulty, wrong; ponos = effort, work, energy), "... a physiopathological state made up of errors in energy expenditure within the nervous system [p. 103]." Dysponesis involves the motor and premotor cortical neurons that extend through the pyramidal and extrapyramidal tracts to and including the peripheral musculature. Motor efforts can be classified as (a) performing effort that involves mostly learned, observable, motor skills; (b) bracing that involves preparing for performance, especially fight or flight; (c) representing efforts that involve producing images of objects and events not present; and (d) attention efforts that involve focusing on selective sensory inputs to the exclusion of others. Dysponetic responses are covert errors in energy expenditure which are largely unobservable, unintentional, and out of awareness. These errors produce excitatory and inhibitory inputs at various points in the nervous system which affect emotional reactivity, ideation, and organ regulation. Because of the covert nature of such responses, they are most effectively detected by electromyographic studies of muscular tension. Since dysponesis is a physiological reaction to a noxious agent (e.g., events, feelings, thoughts) which leads to organic dysfunction, Whatmore considers it to be a disease. Dysponesis can occur sporadically or continuously and with or without psychological, anatomical, or biochemical pathology. Treatment of such pathological accompaniments does not affect the underlying dysponesis. Treatment of the latter requires systematic desensitization training via biobehavioral feedback methods. Dysponetic responses are probably learned, but there may be a genetic susceptibility.

According to Whatmore, depressives are particularly prone toward excessive bracing and misdirected representing errors. Bracing causes the limbic system to deplete high energy phosphate reserves. The resulting fatigue feeds into negative, perseverative thought preoccupations which are conducive to depression. The negative thoughts lead to further bracing and more fatigue.

Both acute depressives and schizophrenics tend to be persistently hyperponetic, that is to have hyperactive neuronal pathways as measured electromyographically (Whatmore, 1966). A sustained reduction in hyperponesis tends to precede clinical improvement in schizophrenics. Also, in remission schizophrenics tend to have much more labile electromyographics than matched nonspychiatric controls. Relapses in schizophrenics are preceded by electromyographs with increased lability and higher baseline recordings. Depressives often show a temporary reduction in hyperponesis with clinical improvement, but quickly return to a hyperponetic state even if improvement is sustained. This hyperponesis continues during remissions and becomes even greater before a clinical relapse. Degree of hyperponesis is positively related to severity of clinical depression. Whatmore (1966) hypothesizes that depression results from neuronal fatigue. Both fatigue and disorganization (random neural discharge) are responses to prolonged hyperponesis. Additional stress from any source, including sleep deprivation, may precipitate neuronal fatigue or disorganization. Why some nervous systems respond to stress with fatigue and others with disorganization is unknown. Admixtures of these responses account for schizo-affective disorders, according to Whatmore. Commonly observed depression among recovering schizophrenics may likewise be accounted for on this basis.

Whatmore (1966) draws an analogy between the function of the nervous system in depressives and schizophrenics and the response of variously designed high gain amplifiers to strong signal-input. As in fatigue (or depression), some amplifiers continue to reproduce accurately until their tubes wear out, while others, as in disorganization (or schizophrenia), begin to oscillate before excessive wear occurs.

Whatmore's studies have involved quite small though well matched patient samples. His longitudinal and cross-diagnostic approach is exemplary. Unfortunately, the investigator is aware of the hypotheses and diagnostic categories of subjects, yet scores recordings. Independent replication with more adequate methodological safeguards and larger samples are clearly needed before the dysponesis hypothesis can be adequately evaluated.

Several related electromyographic studies of depressives have produced varying results. Goldstein (1965) found no difference in muscle tension between depressives and controls during a resting state. But after 15 minutes of electromyographic recording at rest, a 16–16,000cps white noise was introduced binaurally by earphones. Depressives responded more strongly to the stimulus than psychiatric and nonpsychiatric controls in all muscles sampled, especially in the frontalis and right trapezius muscles. Goldstein conjectures that Whatmore's subjects may not have been fully adapted to laboratory conditions before recording began. This may account for conflicting findings on the muscular tension of resting depressives.

However, a carefully done study of 53 hospitalized male and female depressives by Rimon, Stenback, & Huhmar (1966) indicates that relations between residual muscular tension and depression are probably quite complex. Using Beck scale scores (1967) to assess severity of depression, subjects were divided into high and low depression groups. Rimon et al. found that (a) tension in the masseter (jaw muscle) was inversely related to severity of depression for both sexes; (b) tension in forearm and forehead was positively related to severity of depression in males only; (c) leg muscle tension is unrelated to depression; (d) quality of recovery was positively related to increased muscle tension; patients with poor recoveries showed decreased tension; and (e) age is positively related to muscular tension. These discrepancies from Whatmore's findings are particularly striking, since Rimon et al. reputedly replicated his EMG technique. The experimenter in Rimon et al.'s study was unaware of the patients' clinical status.

In addition to previously cited factors, some of the disparate findings on muscle tension in depressives may be due to varying proportions of hysterical depressives within samples (Shipman, Oken, Goldstein, Grinker, & Heath, 1964). Shipman et al. recorded depressives' muscle tension and autonomic responses over four experimental sessions. These sessions involved a stress interview, self-control induction, neutral conversation, and solitary rest, respectively. Personality trait and state functioning were assessed with an extensive range of tests, ratings, and interviews. State measures were negligibly related to psychophysiological response, except that patients who became most depressed during the first two sessions had the lowest bicep muscle tension. The investigators speculate on a possible linkage between bicep tension and assertiveness, with low pressure reflecting a lost will to fight. More importantly, patients with high overall muscle tension across sessions tended to be unanxious, emotionally stable, and to have an active fantasy life and a clear sense of personal boundaries. In contrast, patients with the lowest muscle and cardiovascular values at rest were rated as strongly hysteroid, that is, emotionally labile and impulsive.

It is clearly premature to attempt generalizations about empirical relations between muscle tension and depression.

Electroencephalography (EEG)

The resting cortical electrical activity of depressives and normals is not reliably different (Shagass, 1966). Previously reported differences were apparently artifacts of age disparities between depressives and controls. Findings are also inconsistent for alleged differences in the activated EEGs of depressives and controls. Activated EEGs are usually obtained by having subjects hyperventilate or by administering auditory or visual stimuli. Such stimulation blocks or suppresses the alpha activity of the resting state. Several studies (e.g. Zung, Wilson, & Dodson, 1964) suggest that depressives' photically elicited arousal responses are significantly more prolonged than normals' responses. According to Zung et al. (1964), this response pattern may reflect heightened activity of the caudal midbrain arousal mechanism and diminished activity of the reticular activating system which is involved in more refined discrimination between stimuli.

Evoked potentials have been used to measure the cortical excitability cycle. Shagass & Schwartz (1962) electrically stimulated the ulnar nerve at the wrist with paired stimuli separated by varied time intervals. The initial sensory evoked response amplitude of psychotic depressives was greater than in neurotic depressives, who did not differ from normals. Application of repeated stimuli to normals resulted in full response recovery within 20 milliseconds (msec), followed by reduced responsiveness until a second recovery peak at about 100 msec. In contrast, psychotic depressives averaged only about 50% of full response amplitude recovery during the first 20 msec. This deficiency is reversible; upon recovery, psychotic depressives recover as rapidly and fully as normals. Shagass (1966) cautious that many studies of evoked potentials may be confounded by failure to make covariance adjustments for initial response amplitude. Replication of his work with controls and adjustments failed to substantiate the earlier findings of increased amplitude of initial response in psychotic depressives as compared with normals but did support ($p < .001$) the slower recovery of amplitude during the 20 msec. after its initial stimulus (Shagass & Schwartz, 1966). Shagass cites these results as further support for altered cerebral excitability in depressives, which may implicate impaired function of the mesencephalic reticular formation. However, Shagass notes the nonspecificity of his findings; schizophrenics and patients with personality disorders also had deviant evoked potentials (1966, p. 101).

Visual evoked potentials in bipolars and unipolars. Reduction of subject heterogeneity by splitting depressives into unipolars and bipolars yields substantial group differences in visual average evoked potentials (AER) (Buchsbaum, Goodwin, Murphy, & Borge, 1971). Bipolars responded like 'augmenters' (regardless of whether they were manic or depressed) and unipolars like 'reducers.' In augmenters, the amplitude of response is positively related to increased stimulus intensity, whereas in reducers the variables are inversely related. Among college students, 'reducers' score high on the MMPI D Scale and score low on a scale of adventure and thrill seeking, whereas 'augmenters' score high on the latter scale. Bipolars who respond as augmenters are especially likely to improve clinically with lithium carbonate treatment; with clinical improvement, their AER augmentation regresses toward normal levels.

Just what AER differences reflect about neurophysiological processes or structures is uncertain. They may reflect the functioning of sensory pathways, although these in turn may be related to behavioral states causally, concomitantly, or consequentially.

Auditory evoked potentials in hypo- and hyper-recoverers. Satterfield (1969) studied auditory evoked cortical responses in a heterogeneous group of depressives. The depressives performed much more variably than the normal controls until categorized as low or hypo-recoverers (augmenters) and high or hyper-recoverers (reducers). Recovery measures generally refer to the averaged amplitude ratio of response 2 to response 1 during interstimulus intervals. If the ratio is one, the cell has fully recovered its excitability. In this particular study, the recovery rate for each patient was determined by using his average response amplitude to the slowest stimulus rate of one per eight seconds as a divisor for the average response amplitude of each of four faster stimulus rates (1:4", 1:2",

1:1"). The hyper-recoverers had shorter response latencies and lower response amplitudes for the slowest or base stimulus rate.

All hypo-recoverers had first-degree relatives with depressive disorders, whereas none of the hyper-recoverers had a positive family history. Before ECT both groups had an equal number of depressive symptoms; after ECT the hyper-recovery group had fewer than the hypo-recovery group.

Satterfield conjectures that there are two types of nervous system disorders in depression: one in which the excitatory systems are overactive, which should be reduced by tranquilizers; and one in which inhibitory systems are overactive, which should be reduced by energizers. However, interpretation is complicated by the paradoxical pattern of results. In normals, excitability is usually indexed by short latency, high amplitude responses, and fast recovery, whereas inhibition is indexed by long latencies, low amplitude responses, and slow recovery. The response patterns of hyper- and hypo-recoverers combine elements of excitability and inhibition. Satterfield uses a negative feedback model to explain his results. He contends that there is too much inhibitory feedback in the hyper-recovery group and too little in the hypo-recovery group. While the n's are very small in Satterfield's study and he has capitalized on chance in organizing his groups, his data are interesting, and their linkage to a reasonably well articulated negative feedback model (Pribram & Melges, 1969) holds promise.

Contingent negative variations in depressives. Preliminary reports on the contingent negative variation (CNV) response in depressives are conflicting but of potential interest. This so-called expectancy wave is an electronegative potential on the surface of the frontal cortex that links conditional or preparatory signals with imperative signals; ". . . it reflects the subjective feeling that one event may lead to another [Walter, 1971, p. 66]." The CNV is terminated by decisions or actions. There is agreement so far that CNV responses are very small in depressives and manics and that they increase with lithium administration in manics. However, Small & Small (1969) contend that the CNV is also negligible during clinical remission, whereas Walter (1971) contends that in manic-depressives, at least, it is essentially normal.

Sedation Threshold

Shagass (1966) devised the sedation threshold technique as another measure of cerebral responsiveness or excitability. This procedure entails intravenous injection of 0.5mg/kg/40 sec. of sodium amytal until sedation occurs. Sedation is indexed by slurred speech and an inflection of the increase in 15–30cps EEG activity. Initial findings indicated that sedation threshold effectively discriminated neurotic from psychotic depressives. The threshold for psychotic depressives is similar to normals, whereas the threshold for neurotic depressives is higher. These results have not been consistently corroborated by others (Stern et al., 1970, pp. 183–184).

However, Perez-Reyes (1969) has developed a related sedation threshold technique which may represent a significant advance. Susceptibility to sodium thiopental sedation is assessed by GSR inhibition and sleep threshold. Significantly different thresholds were obtained ($p < .001$ for all comparisons) between neurotic depressives, normals, and psychotic depressives in descending order of threshold level. Perez-Reyes hypothesizes that neurotic depressives as compared with normals have an increased net level of descending sympathetic GSR facilitation and an increase in the basal excitation of the ascending reticular activating system, whereas psychotic depressives have a decreased level in both regards. Schizophrenic and anxiety state controls have increased levels somewhat higher than neurotic depressives. Support for the hypothesis is provided by experiments in which normals were pretreated with either a CNS stimulant drug (methamphetamine) or a metabolic suppressant of the CNS (insulin-induced hypoglycemia). The stimulant elevated GSR and sleep sedation thresholds in normals to neurotic depressive levels, whereas the suppressant lowered thresholds to psychotic depressive levels. Further investigation will seek to clarify whether neurotic depressives have an increased central excitatory state, a decreased central inhibitory state, or a combination of the two, and whether psychotic depressives have a decreased central excitatory state, an increased central inhibitory state, or a combination thereof.

Manipulated Cerebral Electrical Polarity

Interesting explorations are underway on the behavioral effects of manipulating the polarity of cerebral electrical currents. Costain, Redfearn, & Lippold (1964), in a well designed double-blind crossover study, randomly assigned 24 hospitalized depressives to one of two groups. All patients were outfitted with an anode-electrode over the eyebrow and a cathode on one leg. A shunting device prevented the patient or observer from knowing whether current was being applied. During treatment a mild 250μ amp current was used. Subjects in one group received current eight hours a day, six days a week during the first two weeks, and none for the next two weeks, while subjects in the other group experienced the reversed procedure. Repeated ratings were made for activity, mood, and talkativeness by the subjects, nurses, and psychiatrists. Ratings by the latter two groups showed significantly greater improvement during active treatment over placebo treatment, but patients' own ratings did not discriminate between the two treatment phases. The investigators speculate that highest current densites occur in the reticular activating system which controls the excitability of the cerebral cortex. Shagass (1966) conjectures that, since neuronal excitability depends upon electrolyte distribution, the effects of transcranial polarization may be due to changes in ionic balance.

10
BIOLOGICAL ASPECTS OF DEPRESSION: 2

... I do not feel embarrassed anymore, since I have heard data based on few experiments, few subjects, poor sampling, few controls, and profound disagreements among the members of the same generation—from significance to no significance. I've heard conclusions with statistics running far ahead of the data and sometimes more interpretations than data. These two points remind me of another field, criticized by having even more interpretation based on one or two subjects. Maybe we should wrap the psychoanalytic and biochemical interpretations in one package, incubate, and recover an "idzyme," "ego inhibitor," and a "super-ego-ase"! (Grinker, 1969, p. 295).

BIOCHEMISTRY

Endocrine Metabolism

The endocrine glands secrete their hormones directly into the blood or lymph, which transports them to the organs whose functions the hormones regulate or control. In humans, hormone levels are determined from urinary and plasma assays, which has serious drawbacks. Since only total peripheral levels can be ascertained, critical changes that are localized within the central nervous system may not be accurately assessed. Furthermore, only selected derivatives or metabolites of hormones are studied. It is always possible that fluctuations in metabolites and their functionally related processes are due to unassayed derivatives. Obviously, much caution is needed in assuming causal relations between covarying physiological processes or between one of the former and either psychological processes or behavior, since both may be determined by as yet unknown factors. Nonetheless, some extremely interesting empirical relations have been found, as for example between the glucocorticoid hormonal derivatives of the adrenal cortex and certain depressive phenomena. Many other hormones have been investigated in depression, which suggests that current biochemical formulations are probably oversimplified (Mandell, 1969), but the results are too fragmentary and unreplicated to explicate within the scope of this volume.

17-OHCS. Adrenal steroids play a critical role in regulating amino acid enzymes. Output of the cortical steroid metabolite 17 hydroxycorticosteroid (17-OHCS) has been used repeatedly as an index of the so called pituitary-adrenal stress response. In infrahumans, the strength of the adrenal cortical reaction has a strong positive relation to the severity of the induced stress. Initial attempts to replicate this relation with humans led to conflicting results. Animal paradigms neglect the mediating effects of psychological defense mechanisms. As Sachar (1969) noted,

> This buffer system of psychological defenses, it became clear, could be extraordinarily effective in preserving emotional and endocrine homeostasis even in the face of what seemed to be very severe distresses [p. 220].

Sachar cites a convincing series of studies on depressives, schizophrenics, parents of leukemic children, women awaiting breast surgery, and combat pilots in support of his contention.

Studies done on cortisol production in depressives by Sachar, Bunney, and their respective associates use a sophisticated longitudinal case study approach which combines independent descriptive, psychodynamic, and endocrinological assessment. In general, the more adequate the defense in warding off grief, anguish, and turmoil, acknowledgment of conflict, and of loss, the lower the 17-OHCS excretion, regardless of the chronicity and severity of the personality disorder. The assumption that mania serves as a psychological defense against depression is supported by normal 17-OHCS levels in manic patients (Bunney, 1969). The overall relation between adrenocortical overactivity and severity or subtype of depression remains highly controversial (e.g., Shopsin & Gershon, 1971). Plasma-free fatty acid concentration reputedly shows better promise of a positive correlaton with severity of depression (Mueller, Davis, Bunney, Weil-Malherbe, & Cardon, 1970) than 17-OHCS level. Since pituitary-adrenal stress response is not specific to depression, this quite intricate and intriguing topic will not be elaborated here, except to indicate that elevated 17-OCHS levels may have practical utility for suicide prediction (Bunney, Fawcett, Davis, & Gifford, 1969). Evidence is accumulating from animal studies that plasma concentration of cortisol is positively related to concentrations beyond the blood brain barrier and that altered steroid metabolism affects neurotransmission (Henkin, Daly, & Ojemann, 1966).

Cyclic AMP. The glucocorticoids control the production of cyclic AMP (adenosine 3′, 5′ cyclic monophosphate). Cyclic AMP is a nucleotide involved in multiple metabolic processes. It may act as an important mediator of biogenic amine neurotransmitters and thus have a significant role in synaptic transmission

(McAffee, Schorderet, & Greengard, 1971). Studies of AMP urinary excretion (Paul, Cramer & Goodwin, 1971) suggest that manics secrete the most AMP, severe depressives the least, and controls and moderate depressives intermediate amounts. Lithium administration moves manic and depressive AMP toward the normal range. Cyclic AMP may trigger the rapid shift that frequently occurs from depression to mania (Paul, Cramer, & Bunney, 1971). Just before a manic episode total sleep and REM drop and brain catecholamine metabolism (as inferred from urinary norepinephrine excretion) rises sharply. It is hypothesized that the massive shift in mood, thought, and behavior reflect an abrupt shift in brain metabolism (Bunney, Goodwin, & Murphy, 1972). Paul et al.'s data is based on a small sample and can only be regarded as tentative. But as with most studies done at NIMH's Laboratory of Clinical Science, many possibly confounding factors such as diet, drugs, age, sex, and activity level are controlled or are examined for possible effects on the dependent variable. As with all metabolic studies of affective disorders to date, it is impossible to be certain that urinary metabolites reflect central as well as peripheral metabolic processes.

Biogenic Amines

Amines play a crucial role as neural transmitters. Their relation to affect was first noted by W. B. Cannon (1915), who found that rage and fear reactions were accompanied by a sharply increased secretion of epinephrine (adrenalin). Interest in a possible relation between amine metabolism and depression resulted from a serendipitous finding. In an experiment on chronic tuberculars (who are frequently depressed) which involved a new drug, iproniazid, many patients responded with a much brighter mood. Iproniazid inhibits the action of the monoamine oxidase enzyme (MAO). A prime function of MAO is to break down intracellular norepinephrine and thus reduce the amount of norepinephrine available for release in free form for neural transmission across synapses to receptor sites.

The catecholamine hypothesis. Equivocal evidence indicates (Mandell, 1970; Mandell & Spooner, 1968) that norepinephrine depletion or inactivation at central adrenergic receptor sites tends to be related to sedation and norepinephrine increase or potentiation to activation. The so-called "catecholamine hypothesis" of affective disorders states that

> ... depressions are associated with an absolute or relative deficiency of catecholamines, particularly norepinephrine, at functionally important adrenergic receptor sites in the brain. Elation conversely may be associated with an excess of such amines (Schildkraut, 1965, p. 509).

Three biogenic amines have attracted most attention: norepinephrine, a precursor of epinephrine; dopamine, a precursor of norepinephrine; and the indole amine serotonin. Epinephrine per se occurs in limited quantities in the brain and does not seem to be involved in neural transmission or modulation. Norepinephrine is produced by adrenergic neurons. Within the brain, adrenergic neurons are most concentrated in the limbic system, which is believed to play a critical role in affective regulation. Outside the CNS, or peripherally, adrenergic neurons occur mostly in the sympathetic nervous system. There is direct evidence that norepinephrine functions as a neural transmitter within the peripheral nervous system, but only inferred evidence that it does so within the CNS. As indicated before, functioning human brains are not directly accessible for assaying biochemical processes, although recently developed histochemical fluorescent methods permit a mapping of the regional distribution of some brain amines (Hillarp, Fuxe, & Dahlstrom, 1966). Therefore, peripheral measures such as urinary and plasma metabolite volume and concentration, most of which are jointly determined by CNS and peripheral metabolism, must be relied upon. However, the metabolite MHPG-sulphate may prove to be a specific derivative of free CNS norepinephrine (Gordon & Oliver, 1971).

Figure 3 from Schildkraut & Kety (1967) graphically depicts the key hypothesized processes in the CNS metabolism of norepinephrine. They describe the process as follows:

> It is thought that, at synapses, which are the junctions of two adjacent neurons, the chemical transmitter released from the presynaptic nerve endings causes changes in the postsynaptic neuronal membrane potential, which may thereby generate a nerve impulse. It has been suggested that norepinephrine, dopamine, and serotonin may each function directly as a transmitter substance in the central nervous system. None of the biogenic amines has yet been definitively established as a chemical neurotransmitter in the brain, however, and some investigators have suggested . . . that one or more of these amines may act instead as modulators or regulators of synaptic transmission mediated by some other chemical transmitter—for example, acetylcholine.
>
> Norepinephrine is synthesized from the amino acid tyrosine, through the intermediates 3,4-dihydroxyphenylalanine (dopa) and dopamine; it is stored within the nerve in intraneuronal granules. These granules have been observed by electron microscopy to occur at presynaptic nerve endings, and their contents may be released into the synaptic cleft in response to nerve impulses. Norepinephrine discharged from neuronal endings in physiologically active form, by either nerve impulses or the action of sympathomimetic drugs, is inactivated mainly by cellular re-uptake or by enzymatic conversion by catechol-O-methyltransferase to form normetanephrine. Norepinephrine released intracellularly, either spontaneously or by reserpine-like drugs, may be inactivated mainly by mitochondrial monoamine oxidase, forming deaminated catechol metabolites—for example, 3,4-dihyroxy-mandelic acid—before leaving the cell; monoamine oxidase may thus regulate tissue levels of norepinephrine (Figs. 1 and 2). . . . Secondary O-methylation or deamination reactions involved in the formation of 3-methoxy-4-hydroxymandelic acid (vanillylmandelic acid, or VMA), the major urinary metabolite or norepinephrine and epinephrine in man, presumably can occur in the liver or kidney as well as in the nervous system [pp. 21–22].

Indirect evidence for the heuristic utility of the catecholamine hypothesis stems from clinical and research observations on the effects of reserpine administration. Reserpine depletes intracellular norepinephrine and induces depressive-like states, including suicidal tendencies, in about 15% of humans. In animals, reserpine induces sedation. Several studies in animals and humans suggest that administration of amino acid precursors of catecholamines and

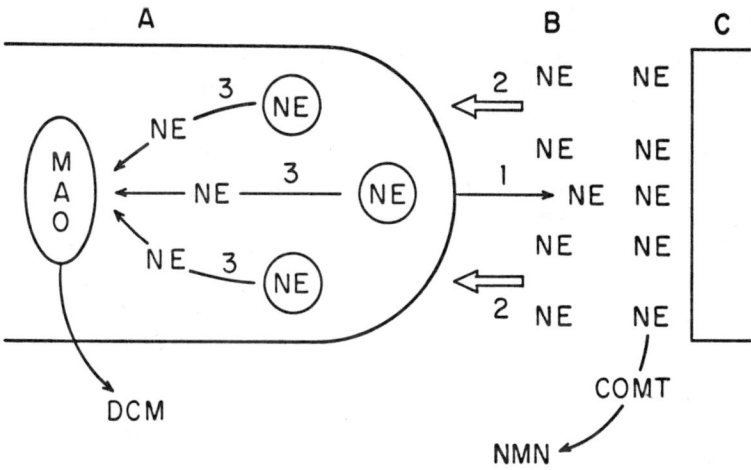

FIG. 3. Schematic representation of (A) a noradrenergic nerve ending, (B) synaptic cleft, and (C) receptor. NE=norepinephrine; NMN=normetanephrine; DCM=deaminated catechol metabolites; COMT=catechol O-methyltransferase; MAO=monoamine oxidase (within a mitochondrion); 1, disharge of norepinephrine into synaptic cleft and onto receptor; 2, reuptake of norepinephrine from synaptic cleft; 3, intracellular release of norepinephrine from storage granules into cytoplasm and onto mitochondrial monoamine oxidase. (*Schildkraut, J. J. and Kety, S. S. Biogenic amines and emotion. "Science," 1967, 156, 21-30.*)

serotonin to subjects previously given reserpine counteracts the latter effects. Similar results are obtained by administering MAO inhibitors prior to reserpine (Schildkraut & Kety, 1967).

In the clinical treatment of depressives, two classes of drugs, the MAO inhibitors and the tricyclics, have been used extensively. While the MAO inhibitors decrease the depletion of intracellular norepinephrine, the tricyclics are thought to reduce the reuptake of free norepinephrine from the synaptic cleft. These antidepressants seem to be especially effective with endogenous depressives. Schildkraut speculates that moods are regulated by internal and environmental events. Although endogenous depressives tend to be unresponsive to the latter, he observes that if they receive antidepressants within a benign milieu, lesser amounts are required for clinical improvement. Presumably, the drugs enhance the receptivity of depressives to their environment, which in turn has an interactive effect with the drugs on improving mood (Schildkraut, 1969).

Clinical studies of catecholamine excretion in affective disorders generally report an increase in mania, a decrease in depression, and an increase in depressives with clinical improvement. However, much may depend on the severity, acuteness, and responsiveness of the depressive sample. Much higher and more variable urinary norepinephrine excretion has been reported in acute psychotic depressives than in neurotic depressives (Bunney, Davis,

Weil-Malherbe, & Smith, 1967). Bunney et al. (1967) do not construe their findings as necessarily at variance with the hypothesis of a functional deficit of norepinephrine in depression. They suggest that the rapidity of amine breakdown in acute states may limit its functional availability at the synaptic junction, and Mendels (1971) speculates that sustained high levels of amine production may exhaust the metabolic process or alternatively lead to a "bottleneck" in the synthetic process.

Schildkraut (1972) readily acknowledges the many gaps and inconsistencies in supporting evidence for the catecholamine hypothesis. Indeed, he explicitly labels it a reductionist hypothesis. His present focus of investigation is the effects of acute and chronic administration of antidepressants on the biogenic-amines in rats. To bypass the blood-brain barrier, radioactive NE (NE-H^3) is injected intracisternally into the brain, where it mixes with endogeneous NE. The effects of acute and chronic administration of various antidepressants and their precursors prior to the injection of NE-H^3 are then examined. Acute imipramine administration diminishes NE reuptake, decreases turnover, and does not effect endogenous levels, whereas chronic administration decreases reuptake, restores turnover to normal levels, and decreases endogenous NE levels. Schildkraut concludes that chronic imipramine administration may restore normal functioning despite reduced levels of endogenous NE or diminished discharge of NE from presynaptic noradrenergic neurons. He further suggests that combining thyroid hormones with imipramine hastens and increases the effects over the administration of imipramine alone. While the empirical findings are quite interesting, they are susceptible to multiple interpretations (Lipton, Prange, Jr., & Wilson, 1972).

Lipton et al. indicate that many clinical and research findings are difficult to reconcile with an unelaborated catecholamine hypothesis. As a sampling of these complications, depression and mania often occur simultaneously, and depression can be fairly readily evoked during an interview with a depressive. Why do 80%-85% of humans who receive reserpine or other NE depleters such as 5HT not get depressed? Either peripheral events do not accurately reflect central events and there may not be the postulated central NE depletion, or many humans may be able to sustain massive central NE depletion without depression. Brains of suicides tend to show very limited NE depletion and only about a 30% serotonin depletion. As Lipton et al. note, great redundancy is characteristic of biological systems, so that selective interference with neural transmitters could probably be compensated. Why are depressions so much more frequent than manias and depressives particularly resistant to favorable experience?

Reserpine has almost immediate peripheral effects but a much slower impact on mood, if any. Even centrally, reserpine seems to reduce synaptic uptake of NE within mere hours. Lipton et al. hypothesize that the amine system is either working satisfactorily or is overworked in depressives. They contend that drug induced changes in the amine system probably occur rapidly, but that it is the slowly induced consequences of this change which eventually change the mood state.

Lipton et al. speculate that Schildkraut's findings on the effects of acute and chronic imiprimamine administration with thyroid can be explained as follows: stress preceding a depressive episode activates the central adrenergic system to such as extent that a loss of sensitivity occurs in the receptor-effector synaptic complex, effective utilization of amines decreases, and depression ensues. Administration of imipramine initially reduces turnover, synthesis, and uptake of NE. The lessened stress on the refractor receptor-effector complex enables it to regain its sensitivity. Chronic administration of imipramine diminishes its inhibitory effects on synthesis and, since thyroid sensitizes the adrenergic receptors, the whole system responds more sensitively. Sensitivity of the adrenergic system to amines seems to be more important than the absolute amount of endogenous NE. The time required for these processes to occur might account for the slow acting clinical results of antidepressant drugs, despite the prompt peripheral reaction.

Mandell, an extremely sophisticated and constructively skeptical investigator, has been even more reserved in his estimate of the catecholamine hypothesis. Findings to date indicate correlates between biochemical and behavioral states, not causal relations (Mandell & Spooner, 1968). Even at a physiological level Mandell and Spooner contend that "There is remarkably little evidence for the physiological role of even the most accepted of substances present in the brain" [p. 1443].

Schildkraut & Kety's (1967) wise and cautious conclusions about the catecholamine hypothesis still provide an exemplary summation of the present status of biological approaches to depression:

> It is not likely that changes in the metabolism of the biogenic amines alone will account for the complex phenomena of normal or pathological affect. Whereas the effects of these amines at particular sites in the brain may be of crucial importance in the regulation of affect, any comprehensive formulation of the physiology of affective state will have to include many other concomitant biochemical, physiological, and psychological factors. Although in this review of the relationship of biogenic amines to affective state relatively little has been said concerning the intricate set of environmental and psychological determinants of emotion, the importance of these factors must be stressed.
>
> The normally occurring alterations in affective state induced by environmental events is well known to all, from personal experience. The interactions between such environmental determinants of affect, various physiological factors, and the complexity of psychological determinants, including cognitive factors derived from the individual's remote and immediate past experiences, have received only limited study under adequately controlled conditions. It may be anticipated, however, that this will prove to be a particularly fruitful area for future research, for only within such a multifactorial framework may one expect to understand fully the relationship of the biogenic amines to emotional state [p. 28].

Neurochemistry and psychodynamics. Mandell examines some relations between neurochemical and psychodynamic approaches to affect (1970). He contends that psychodynamic theory is especially weak in regard to affective behavior; it has only paid 'lip-service' to constitutional factors. Mandell postulates that to a large extent affects are determined by individual constitutional variations in relatively autonomous neural systems which contain varying distributions of neural transmitters. He delineates several neurochemically determined human mood-character types. The neurochemical system underlying each mood type is activated by a specific drug family which induces relatively specific 'up' moods.

One organized neural system is the dopamine system, which is activated by amphetamines and produces hyperactive, optimistic states. Dopamine-containing neurones are closely associated with the extrapyramidal nervous system. Mandell (1970) postulates a

... pacer system in the brain having to do with active coping, initiative and the 'psychic energy' available for 'doing' that has as its substrate dopamine and is regulated by the dopanergic system in the brain [p. 4].

The dopaminergic system may be innately vulnerable in retarded (but not agitated) depressives. Stimulation of the dopaminergic system reduces retardation in depressives. The relation to psychodynamic theory is straightforward but ingenious. If the predepressive's self-esteem is largely regulated by meeting the high, rigid standards of parental introjects, and these standards entail activity and initiative, a neurochemically induced decrease in the availability of requisite energy should deflate self-esteem. If the victim is unaware of the source of his difficulty, he is apt to cognize rationalizations of his state, including self-denunciations of his worth and guilty recriminations. Such an outcome is enhanced given the likelihood that his overly rigid standards were derived from overly critical and self-punitive parents.

Mandell's second posited neural organization is the norepinephrine system, which when activated by imipramine produces a calm, placid state. Norepinephrine-containing neurones are associated with the diffuse projection system from the cortex to the spinal cord. This system is thought to regulate the general physiological level of activation. Whereas the dopamine system may regulate "active, motoric coping," the norepinephrine system "may regulate more subtle and tonic baseline states of calm, arousal, and anxiety" [p. 8]. Mandell takes issue somewhat with the prevailing catecholamine hypothesis, which contends that available norepinephrine in the central synapses has an antidepressant effect. Segal & Mandell (in press) have demonstrated a biphasic effect in rats such that small initial interventricular infusion of norepinephrine increases activity, but larger subsequent infusions decrease activity. Essentially, Mandell argues that the relation of available norepinephrine in synapses to depression is complicated by quantitative and temporal exposure factors (especially to the postsynaptic receptor) and by several long- and short-term biochemical processes that regulate norepinephrine dynamics within the synapse.

Paradoxically perhaps, Mandell concludes that neurochemistry has produced apparently significant but very conflicting results regarding mechanisms within neurochemical systems as well as their relative importance. Nonetheless, he urges "consideration of the *combination* of the rich material from psychoanalytic observation and the new discoveries of neuromolecular biology" [p. 9].

Electrolyte Balance

Neuronal excitability is partly regulated by a balance between the relatively greater concentration of extracellular, positively-charged sodium ions and intracellular, negatively-charged potassium ions. Ions are electrically charged atoms or electrolytes. Calcium and magensium ions are also important in neural excitation and transmission, but they have been studied less because estimation of their concentration and distribution is more difficult than for sodium and potassium (Coppen, 1967). Normally the intracellular concentration of sodium is 1/10 the extracellular concentration. The intracellular concentration is maintained by a metabolic process, the sodium pump. An increased ratio of intracellular sodium lowers the resting potential of the neuron, thus decreasing its activation threshhold. That is, a weaker than normal impulse generates an action potential or nerve impulse. A shift in electrolyte distribution would probably affect the brain by altering both neuronal excitability and the production of monoamines (Woodbury, Timiras, & Vernadakis, 1957), which are thought to modulate synaptic transmission (Coppen, 1967). Behavioral changes would almost inevitably accompany any sizable shift in electrolyte distribution. Early studies of water and electrolyte metabolism and distribution in patients with rapid mood fluctuation using so-called balance techniques indicated physiological-mood consistencies within but not between patients (Gibbons, 1963). Electrolyte studies of remitting and nonremitting severe depressives initially resulted in conflicting results, probably due to differences in methodology. The introduction of radioactive isotopes yielded a more sensitive distribution measure of exchangeable sodium and potassium by so-called isotope dilution methods. In summarizing a series of investigations using the isotope dilution method, Coppen (1967) reported that increased concentration of intracellular sodium was the most striking anomaly in depressives. The latter was 50% higher than normal during depression and returned to normal levels with clinical remission. Intracellular potassium concentration was low both in depression and in remission. Both intracellular changes, increased sodium and decreased potassium, would significantly reduce the neuronal action potential level. Coppen hypothesizes a deficient sodium transport mechanism across the cell membrane in depressives. Indirect studies indicated a very sizable deficiency in transfer during depression. The transfer reverts to normal with clinical remission. Whereas in depressives residual sodium is 50% greater than in normals, in manics it is 200% greater. When manics shift to a depressive phase, their residual sodium reduces to a 50% surplus and reverts to normal levels with clinical remission.

Whether the electrolyte anomalies of depressives have etiological significance is unclear. It is equally unclear whether these metabolic changes are secondary to alterations in endocrine function. Since steroid hormones significantly influence electrolytes, several of these have been investigated.

Lithium carbonate salts have as yet unclear effects on electrolyte metabolism. Their use in the treatment of mania by Cade was first reported in 1949. Numerous well controlled double-blind studies have confirmed lithium's beneficial effects in about 80% of manic episodes. Its antidepressant effects and prophylactic value are highly controversial issues (Fieve, 1972). Chronic administration of lithium may prevent manic episodes and seems to attenuate the severity of depressive episodes in bipolars. In unipolars, there is some evidence for an antidepressant effect in endogenous depression (Goodwin, Murphy, & Bunney, 1969). The specificity of the clinical effects of lithium on mania suggest the possibility of a direct linkage to the pathophysiology of the disorder (Greenspan, Goodwin, Bunney, & Durrell, 1968).

It was commonly assumed that lithium altered an unbalanced distribution of sodium or potassium ions, which in turn effected neural transmission. But Laragh (1969), in summarizing a recent NIH symposium on electrolyte metabolism, concluded, "I am convinced . . . that there is no evidence whatever that there is anything wrong with the total sodium and potassium space in these patients (depressives)" [p. 77].

While no unifying hypothesis or model is yet possible, a number of reasonably well validated findings on lithium effects (in rat brains especially) have been established. In rats lithium alters norepinephrine metabolism from O-mythylation to deamination and increases norepinephrine turnover, while probably decreasing serotonin turnover (Schildkraut, Schanberg, Breese, & Kopin, 1968). Studies of lithium's effects on nerve tissue preparations indicate that it may change membrane transport or permeability (Schou, 1957). Abnormal slow wave production with lithium intake reflects altered electrical conductivity. Fieve (1972) notes the interesting parallels and disparities in the sodium balance fluctuations in rats and humans on lithium intake. Both go through a sodium depletion and retention cycle within 5 days (and manic behavior diminishes), but rats develop a state of chronic sodium depletion, while humans do not.

In short, the biological rationale underlying the two most effective treatments for certain affective disorders, ECT and lithium, remains obscure.[37]

MISCELLANEOUS BIOLOGICAL ASPECTS

Sleep

Although disturbed sleep is common in many forms of psychopathology, its frequency and severity in depression seem acute. The sleep disturbance may be symptomatic of underlying pathophysiology, but the biological and psychological consequences of sleep loss may help to sustain depressive episodes. Everyone is familiar with the grouchy irritability resulting from prolonged sleep loss.

[37] For a very readable and informative account of the discovery of lithium and its subsequent investigation see Gattozzi (1970).

Early endogenous-reactive studies.   Early sleep research in depression focused on alleged differences between reactive and endogenous depressives. According to clinical lore, reactive depressives have initial insomnia (i.e., difficulty in falling asleep), whereas endogenous depressives have terminal insomnia (i.e., early morning awakening). Initial studies based on relatively subjective methods such as patient reports (Kiloh & Garside, 1963) or nurses' observations (Costello & Selby, 1965) obtained contradictory results. The former study supported traditional clinical lore, whereas the latter found no differences between groups. Interest in this problem has waned with recent advances in knowledge about sleep states and improved methods for their objective study.

Sleep stages.   Developments in sleep studies include the discovery of a positive relation between rapid eye movement (REM) and dreaming during sleep (Aserinsky & Kleitman, 1953) and between cyclic variations in electrical brain activity and sleep stages (Dement & Kleitman, 1957). These cyclic variations are chiefly identified by electroencephalographic (EEG) monitoring of electrical activity within the brain. The EEG waves of each sleep stage have a characteristic frequency and amplitude. Rapid eye movement occurs mostly during parts of stage 1, the lightest of the sleep stages. Normally this stage occupies about 20% of sleep time. High frequency, low-amplitude EEG waves accompany this phase. Most sleep time is spent in moderately deep stage 2, which is characterized by short bursts of fast wave activity (sleep spindles). The deep sleep of stages 3 and 4 is associated with slow, high-amplitude (delta) waves.

Although interdependent, REM and delta sleep appear to have different central nervous system control mechanisms (Jouvet, 1969). They respond selectively to specific drugs and lesions. REM or "paradoxical" sleep seems to involve activation of the autonomic nervous system and is strongly influenced by catecholamine metabolism, whereas delta sleep, a physiologically quiescent state, is strongly affected by serotonin metabolism. Phylogenetically, both states appear to be outgrowths of the neo or cerebral cortex (Iskander & Kaebling, 1970). Gross sleep disturbance results in depletion of catecholamines and serotonin (Jouvet, 1969) and a rebound or compensatory pressure to make up the lost sleep and available supplies of biogenic amines. Selective sleep deprivation of either REM or delta results in rebound pressure specific to the selective deprivation (Agnew, Webb, & Williams, 1967).

Sources of inconsistent findings.   There are many inconsistent findings on the sleep of depressives. These inconsistencies are probably due to factors such as the heterogeneity of patients' age, subtype, dynamics, severity, stage of disorder (acute, chronic, improving), and method of assessment. Some studies are conducted from the patient's regular bed by telemetric devices, others within unfamiliar experimental laboratories. Sometimes the patients are given several days' exposure to the experimental set-up, sometimes they are not. The effects of such variations in experimental procedure are now being systematically investigated. It is not surprising that Snyder's review of the REM literature on depressive sleep (1969) concluded that reports were still too contradictory to allow much confidence in their implications. The wide inter- and intra-individual variation in depressive sleep disturbance requires longitudinal rather than cross-sectional studies (Mendels & Hawkins, 1971a).

Consistent findings. The most consistent findings in studies of depressive sleep (Snyder, 1969) are sizable deficits in the total amount of sleep, especially stage 4, and a short initial REM latency (time interval between falling asleep and the onset of REM activity). Severity of depression (especially psychotic ideation) seems to be closely related to the magnitude of these deficits. Hospitalized psychotic depressives average only 3–4 hours of sleep per night and neurotics 5–6 hours. Also, the more severe the depression the more fragmented the sleep-time. Severe depressives have difficulty getting to sleep, then rapidly lapse into intense REM amidst light sleep, awaken fitfully because of a low arousal threshhold (Zung, Wilson, & Dodson, 1964), and frequently fluctuate among light sleep, REM, and wakefulness. With clinical improvement, sleep stage cycles and latencies approximate normality, except that stage 4 continues to be deficient (Hawkins, 1969).

Sleep in Bipolar and Unipolar Depressives

Depressed bipolar manic-depressives appear to have different sleep patterns from other psychotic depressives, according to Hartmann (1969a). He conducted longitudinal sleep studies on 10 manic-depressives for several years, following them through normal, depressed and manic clinical conditions. Using bipolars as their own controls, Hartmann reported least sleep when patients are manic (4–5 hours) and about the same amount when they are normal or depressed (about 6½ hours). Stage 4 sleep time does not vary significantly between clinical conditions. REM latency is lowest in the depressed condition, and REM time and percentage of sleep time are greatest during depression, all indicating considerable REM pressure. Least REM pressure occurs during mania by all three indices, which may account for the manic's diminished need for sleep. Reduction in REM time from about 90 minutes when depressed to 55 when manic is especially striking. Furthermore, he found no compensatory REM rebound after mania. Hartmann speculates that all depressives have REM pressure, but, unlike other depressives, bipolars do not have a general disturbance of the sleep-wake mechanism.

Unlike Synder (1969b), Hartmann (1969a) contends that REM pressure is intrinsically related to depression and not necessarily to sleep deprivation. He ventures the interesting notion that mania is a natural antidepressant, biochemically and psychologically. It affects sleep much like the monoamine oxidase inhibitor and tricyclic antidepressant compounds. Also, when phasic shifts occur in bipolars during sleep, it is always from depression to mania. He suggests a relation to normal dream phenomena wherein dreams progressively shift during the night toward greater activity, drama, and pleasantness, with strong elements of denial of unplesant reality and wish-fulfillment. Presumably bipolars are strongly disposed toward the use of these defenses, especially when their reality testing capacity is diminished by sleep. However, the only longitudinal study on a drug-free hypomanic yielded sleep disturbances closely akin to those in psychotic depressives (Mendels & Hawkins, 1971b) which supports Synder's (1969b) observations on drugged manics. And a briefly reported questionnaire survey of remitted bipolars has indicated a very high, hitherto rarely noted tendency toward a high prevalence of hypersomnia during their last episode (Detre, Himmelhoch, Swartzburg, Anderson, Byck, & Kupfer, 1972).

Theoretical Explanations

A widely accepted working hypothesis (Hartmann, 1969b) contends that depletion of the catecholamine neural transmitter norepinephrine at synaptic brain sites accounts for the signs of REM pressure in depressives. REM pressure is evident in the short latencies, short cycles between REM, and high intensity or frequency of eye movements during REM. Actual amount of REM time in depressives is subnormal until improvement, when it tends to increase to above average amounts and then levels off. Observations on the effects of reserpine support the depletion hypothesis. Reserpine depletes the available supply of CNS epinephrine, produces REM sleep pressure, and in some humans produces "...a depression usually indistinguishable from a spontaneous clinical depression" [p. 311]. Also during the late progestational phase of the premenstrual cycle, some women experience increased REM pressure, depression, and suicidal tendencies (Hartmann, 1969a). Other investigators contend that sleep research has focused on too narrow a range of amines and has thus probably underestimated the role of other metabolic transformations such as transmethylation (Mandell, Spooner, & Brunet, 1969). Mendels & Hawkins (1970) posit an unstable state of central nervous system hyperexcitability in depressives as the most tenable unifying hypothesis at this time:

> The overall changes in sleep of the depressed patients studied by us are compatible with the hypothesis that there is an increased activity of central nervous system arousal mechanisms in depression. Such a hypothesis would explain the difficulty depressed patients have in falling asleep, their tendency to sleep in the 'lightest' stages, the frequent awakenings, the increased responsiveness to external stimuli, the frequent changes from one stage to another, and the admixture of wave forms. It would also explain why they sleep so poorly in the last third of the night by which time they have had several hours of sleep and the central sleep mechanisms are no longer operating at such pressure. In this way, it is possible to envisage a precarious balance between central arousal and sleep control mechanisms with the arousal center dominating until sufficient pressure has been built up to overcome them, and to achieve sleep [pp. 44-45].

Snyder (1969b) points out that the sleep disturbances of psychotic depressives are "...predictable results of the normal dynamics of sleep mechanisms" [p. 189]. He observes that sleep disturbances in psychotic depressives are similar to those of the normal aged, but exaggerated. He speculates that the increased cortical excitability caused by REM reduction in disturbed sleep may be an adaptive energizer up to a limited point. Beyond that point a vicious cycle may occur in which increased cortical excitability further disrupts sleep, which leads to emotional and cognitive disturbance, despair, and depression. Synder describes the increased vulnerability to disruption of sleep in the aged as their Achilles heel.

Few comparisons have been made between the sleep patterns of depressives and other psychopathological groups. Snyder reports (1969a) that, unlike depressives, schizophrenics show few signs of sleep disorder until just before the onset of the disorder, and they do not compensate for the REM deficit acquired during the acute psychotic phase when they are improving. It increasingly appears that sleep disturbance is not unique to depression, although as yet unidentified aspects may yet prove to be so (Mendels & Hawkins, 1971a).

Circadian Rhythms

An analogy between the 24-hour cyclic nature of some affective disorders and physiological processes has been noted. "Circadian" physiological rhythms occur in approximately 24-hour cycles, which probably reflects the impact of the earth's 24-hour rotations on the evolutionary process. Some circadian rhythms are largely regulated by external factors such as light and temperature, whereas others are largely regulated by internal biological clocks (Siegel, Gerathewohl, & Mohler, 1969). The latter are linked, oscillating subsystems. According to Richter's (1965) shock-phase hypothesis, the higher the evolutionary form, the more biological organs and centers function out-of-phase, which is optimally conducive to homeostatic balance. However, shock or trauma may thow the oscillating subsystems into phase, which is maladaptive.

At least 11 cases of patients with 48-hour manic-depressive cycles have been reported (Bunney & Hartmann, 1965; Bunney, Hartmann, & Mason, 1965). Bunney & Hartmann (1965) describe the behavioral and biochemical correlates of a case whose "cycles persisted with clock-like regularity over a two-year period" (p. 619) (other cyclic cases continue for decades). Shifts from depression to mania occurred regularly at about 3:30 a.m. on alternate days and from mania to depression at about 5:45 a.m. In this, as in most reported cases, the switch follows sleep, leading to the speculation that sleep-related neurophysiological changes may be a significant factor in the switch. Both descriptively and dynamically, the patient seemed typically manic-depressive. When manic, there was denial of illness and loss of memory for the intervening depressed phase; when depressed, the patient was intensely aware of the cyclic nature of her disturbance, guilty, and hopeless. During the restless transitional hours between a shift from depression to mania she expressed conflicting attitudes: she welcomed the impending alleviation of her misery, but was concerned over the prospective loss of meaningful interpersonal contact. On manic days, with high denial of illness, 17-OHCS levels were low, whereas they were high for depressed days.

As indicated previously, exogenous factors strongly influence some circadian rhythms. An effort was made to determine whether the periodicity of a cycling

48-hour manic-depressive could be altered by changing environmental factors (Jenner, Goodwin, Sheridan, Tauber, & Lobban, 1968). In a heroic study, Jenner spent 11 days in an artificial environment with a 48-hour cycling manic-depressive of 11 years' duration. The laboratory was a suspended chamber, sound-proofed, air-conditioned, and heat controlled. An experimental time-table was used in which 11 real days were arranged to equal 12 22-hour experimental days. A regular schedule of eating, sleeping, activity, and data collection (temperature, pulse, respiration, urine, and behavior ratings) was established. The subject promptly switched to a 22-hour cycle until the 11th experimental day, when he received a traumatic letter from his wife; just as under nonexperimental conditions, this prolonged his manic stage. With the termination of the experiment, the patient quickly reverted to his pre-experimental 48-hour, real-time cycle. "The results were an unequivocal demonstration of complete and immediate entrainment of mood to environmental factors...." [Jenner et al., 1968, p. 218]. Whereas mood rhythms were entrained by the environmental manipulation, the 24-hour circadian rhythms of calcium and magnesium metabolism were unaffected. The data are fascinating, but their implications are unclear.

Other work with circadian rhythms has already yielded clinical applications. Richter (1965), for example, noted that removal of parathyroid glands in monkeys shifted their ingestion of calcium lactate to a 40-day cycle. A patient with a 40-day affective cycle, 20 days depressed-20 days normal, was found to have signs of parathyroid deficiency resulting from inhalation of ammonia fumes. Treatment with calcium lactate and dehydrotachysterol terminated the cycling.

Mendels (1971) has noted that some depressives show disturbed cortisol blood level rhythms. They peak several hours earlier than normals and awaken sooner.

In sum, the relation of circadian rhythms to affective disturbances is an intriguing and promising frontier of investigation whose implications are obscure at present.

Hopelessness, Helplessness, and Organic Disease

Most writers would agree that a significant proportion of depressive reactions are preceded by a despair about a significant real, threatened, or symbolic loss. A similar combination of stressors and reactions reportedly precedes many physical ailments (Engel & Ader, 1967). A speculative hypothesis is that emotional distress results in high cortisol production (e.g. Bunney, 1969, Sachar, 1969), which interferes with the production of interferon, a protein substance produced by the interaction between viruses and animal cells. Interferon increases the resistance of animal cells to viruses.

The problems in determining validly who has had an emotional distress and responded with giving up are formidable. Nonetheless, the convergence of postdictive, predictive, and animal model studies is impressive. As an example of this work, Schmale & Iker (1966) interviewed 51 females admitted to a gynecological service for suspected cancer of the cervix. Tissue smears had shown so-called class III cells, possibly indicative of cancer. Patients were admitted for cone biopsies, which permit more definitive diagnosis. Schmale and Iker attempted to predict what the biopsy would show, depending upon whether or not the patient had responded to a significant event with hopelessness during the six months prior to the tissue smear. Eleven of 18 women predicted to have cancer were positive, and 25 of 33 predicted not to have it were negative ($p <$ .02). It is, of course, conceivable that actually having cancer depletes the individual in multiple ways that enhance the probability of responding to stresses with helplessness or hopelessness. However, this study is embedded within a matrix of theory, experiment, and clinical observation that fully warrants intensive exploration.

Psychiatric and medical patients differ chiefly in regard to how long feelings of stress and despair have preceded the onset of overt disturbance. A heterogeneous group of acute hospitalized psychiatric patients typically reported much longer periods of distress preceding the onset of illness. Again, it is unclear why some individuals respond to similar situations without disturbance and others with a physical and/or a personality disorder. It can only be speculated that genetic-constitutional, developmental, and contemporary environmental factors almost always operate separately and interactively. Engel's (1962) group is quite cognizant of the complexity of issues involved, but their relevant investigations are beyond the scope of this volume.

Separation and Dominance in Nonhuman Primates

Spitz's clinical observations (1945, 1946) on the effects of early infant-mother separation have spawned considerable research and theoretical speculation. Spitz noted that a substantial proportion of infants separated from their mothers between 6 and 12 months of age went through an initial phase of protest followed by withdrawal and developmental arrest, or so-called anaclitic depression. Restoration of the mother within 3–5 months resulted in full recovery. If the mother did not return within this time span, "hospitalism" or progressive mental and physical deterioration frequently ensued with a high mortality rate. Bowlby (1969) described a similar sequence of "protest" and "despair" in 2 to 3 year old hospitalized children separated from their mothers. These findings have led to a series of studies on the effects of separating subhuman primates from their parents and/or peers (Kaufman & Rosenblum, 1967; McKinney, Suomi, & Harlow, 1971; 1972).

Engel (1962) hypothesizes two innate response systems to mounting distress: an initial active mobilization for flight or fight, which, if unsuccessful, yields to passive conservation-withdrawal designed to avert exhaustion. The two primary unpleasurable affects, anxiety and depression, respectively, are associated with the two systems. In species linked by social bonds, separation tends to be highly stressful. The adaptive or survival value of this distress resides in its fostering of group cohesiveness. If the group's viability depends upon its cohesiveness for foodgathering, protection, and reproduction, members must be strongly motivated to maintain their group attachment.

Whether these distress reactions to social separation are adaptive for individual as well as group preservation is somewhat controversial. Kaufman & Rosenblum (1967) point out that the initial protest phase of screeching and searching is probably designed to summon and seek assistance. However, prolongation of such activity would betray the separated infant's location to predators and physically exhaust him. Nonreinforcement would also tend to extinguish the response. In the conservation-withdrawal state, infant subhuman primates huddle into a ball with their heads between their legs. This posture reduces their visibility, exposure to the elements, and heat loss. Also, this posture may have communicative value: the cooing, depressed facies, and huddled position are expressively similar to physically "sick" behavior. In some monkey species, when the separated infant manifests depressive conservation-withdrawal behavior, males will protect the infant from assault, and lower status female friends of the mother will sometimes mother the infant. Offspring of dominant mothers in the primate status hierarchy tend to fare better during separation. Whether this is due to better genetic endowment, less intense preseparation mothering, a broader hierarchy of adaptive behaviors, or some combination of factors, is unclear. Social relations among primates are so pervasively regulated by the dominance hierarchy that the depression-elation mood dimension may be intrinsically related to it. Price (1967) speculates that upward movement in the hierarchy is related to elation and downward movement to depression. The adaptive aspect of depression is the inhibition of aggression that might result in retaliatory behavior.

Averill (1968) argues against the concept of physiological conservation during grief or separation. As he indicates, very little data are available on physiological concomitants of grief, and the extensive physiological literature on depression suggests if anything that it is a catabolic state of high activation. He likens the grief state to passive avoidance, in which overt activity is inhibited while physiological activation is intense. Overt activity is inhibited because it would only result in more intense frustration and disappointment.

Monkey separation studies may provide a useful animal model for aspects of human depression (McKinney & Bunney, 1969; McKinney et al., 1971, 1972). Whereas assessment of the primary depressive symptoms of low mood, decreased self-esteem, hopelessness, and helplessness in humans depends largely on self-reports, the assessment of depression in subhumans must rely primarily on objectively specifiable secondary signs such as retardation, loss of weight and libido, and sleeplessness. The secondary accompaniments of depression are less invariantly present than the primary symptoms, and they overlap extensively with other personality disturbances. Nonetheless, given the ethical and practical constraints on experimentally manipulating or breeding humans so as to induce depression or depressive susceptibility, and the virtual inaccessibility of the human brain for the direct testing of biochemical and neurophysiological hypotheses about the etiology and pathophysiology of depression, it becomes apparent that subhuman primate analogs of depression may help to sharpen present conceptualizations of this disorder. If the traditional view of depression as a primary mood disorder is essentially correct, and if mood shifts are a relatively primitive method for regulating personality functioning, as Jacobson (1957) contends, then, as McKinney & Bunney (1969) indicate,

> It might, indeed, be true that we share with higher animals disorders of mood more than disorders involving the higher thought processes, and that these disturbances could profitably lend themselves to comparative study [p. 247].

Much of the work of McKinney et al. (1971, 1972) derives from the earlier observations on the effects of infant-maternal separation by Spitz and Bowlby. Rhesus monkeys are reared with their mothers or peers and then separated at various ages and for varying lengths of times. When separated, infant monkeys go through protest (vocalization and locomotion) and despair (self-clasping and huddling) phases similar to those described by Bowlby. But when reunited, they do not experience Bowlby's so-called detachment phase; rather there is a sharp increase in ventral clinging and contact over preseparation base rates. Monkeys do not adapt to multiple separations; reactions to the 20th separation were much like those toward the first. Furthermore, a severe developmental arrest results. In most of the infant separation studies, the separations began periodically at three months of age and continued until nine months of age. At nine months of age the social developmental maturity of the experimental monkeys resembles that of normal three month olds. In a normal developmental progression from three to nine months, clinging and self-orality decline, while locomotion, exploration, and play increase greatly. These developmental changes did not occur in the experimental infants subjected to repeated separations. In contrast, when three year old monkeys are separated from their peers no untoward effects are apparent. During separation they increase their locomotion and exploration, decrease their passivity, and evidence no despair.

Much more devastating and seemingly irreversible changes are caused by isolating infant monkeys in vertical confinement chambers. They can move about the chamber and see and hear most environmental events, but the apparatus which was intuitively designed to produce a sense of despair is extremely successful. Monkeys in such environments eat and drink normally but otherwise huddle continuously in a corner. When returned to their home cages there is virtually no locomotion or environmental exploration, and self-clasping, rocking, and huddling are greatly increased over prevertical chamber confinement levels. These depressive behaviors seem to continue indefinitely despite socialization opportunities with peers. The effects of vertical chamber confinement are more severe and pervasive than any other experimental technique used, including total social isolation.

Exploratory efforts toward rehabilitating these experimentally depressed monkeys with antidepressant drugs and play experience with animals at their developmental rather than chronological level show promise. This series of

TABLE 9

Characteristics of Depression and Change in Hierarchical Status

Feature of depressive illness	Feature of fall in dominance hierarchy
1. Loss of appetite	Less access to food
2. Loss of libido	Less acess to sex outlets
3. Avoids company	Must avoid animals who previously avoided him
4. Ideas of unworthiness and inferiority	More submissive behavior
5. Selective forgetting of favorable memories	Must forget or forgo well established habits of dominance
6. Average duration six months	Recovery from injury or illness allows resumption of former dominance
7. Commoner in later life	Commoner when powers waning, and more difficult to adjust
8. Commoner in females	Female status varies within harem (often monthly) and between harems
9. Associated with separation and bereavement	May follow loss of allies
10. Increase of anxiety and irritability	Increase of all "dominance hierarchy" behavior

Source: Price (1968).

investigations at Wisconsin may well prove to be among the most fruitful animal studies of depression underway.

Price speculates (1967; 1968) that depressive behavior may have evolved because of its species-adaptive facilitation of peace within dominance hierarchies:

> The behavior associated with the hierarchy has various affective tones. Aggression and irritability characterize behavior to subordinates, who are constantly reminded of their position by acts of minor threat and provocation, such as the direct gaze. The subordinate responds with anxiety and withdrawal; he grins or looks away from the direct gaze, gets out of the way when a superior approaches, or presents his hindquarters in a gesture of submission. Thus firm habits of response are built up to each individual in the group. The whole bearing of the animal depends on his position in the hierarchy; at the top there is a relaxed confidence, whereas the animals at the bottom are typically 'hen-pecked' and might be said to pass their lives in a state of neurotic depression [1968, p. 47].

Depression associated with downward mobility for whatever reason would tend to preclude disruptive intragroup aggression. In Table 9, Price has summarized intriguing parallels between features of depressive illness and decline in hierarchical status.

11
CONCLUSIONS

No findings *specific* to depression have been firmly validated as yet. Furthermore, such specificity may never be achieved. It is still possible that bipolar manic-depressives, for example, will prove to have a highly specific genetic anomaly which transmits a highly specific and potent biochemical anomaly. And this anomaly may operate in a highly predictable fashion, either regardless of other biological and/or environmental factors or as a reliable function of such specific, characterizable moderating parameters, but it seems unlikely.

Subject heterogeneity which contributes to error variance rather than predictive validity must be reduced. The bipolar-unipolar, obsessive-hysteroid, and factor-analytically derived subtypes look promising, especially if additional dimensions such as severity of disorder and premorbid psychosexual maturation are assessed as well. In an excellent paper on depressive heterogeneity, Blumenthal (1971) notes how the problem of reducing heterogeneity is compounded by the probability that etiology, symptomatology, and treatment response may each be heterogeneously determined. It is highly unlikely that nature has arranged matters so that each of several specific etiologies manifests itself in a relatively independent and specific symptomatology, which in turn responds in relatively specific fashion to relatively specific treatments. Clinical depression is probably a final common pathway for many sources of distress (within and between individuals) with great overlapping of expression and responsiveness to treatment, regardless of source. As examples, Blumenthal cites two endocrinological disorders, Cushing's syndrome (which involves abnormal adrenal steroid metabolism), and hypothyroidism, each of which produces a wide spectrum of overlapping psychiatric disorders. It is well authenticated that some treatments are effective for some symptoms regardless of their etiology, whereas other treatments are effective for certain etiologies regardless of the manifest symptoms. Cushing's syndrome and hypothyroidism are prime examples.

A major source of variability in etiological studies of depression may be rooted in what Blumenthal (1971) terms a causal sequence of etiologic agents. For example, there may well be a genetic predisposition to respond depressively to certain classes of psychological events (e.g. loss) whose stress sequentially imbalances hormone, electrolyte, and neural transmitter levels. Furthermore, it may be possible to enter this etiologic chain at any point; still further, the relations between etiologic agents may be interactive rather than simply sequential. As Blumenthal rightfully argues, only a multidimensional, multivariate approach could effectively validate such an etiological model. Even in the relatively simple sequential model of etiologic agents, the closer one samples toward the beginning of the chain for relations with depression, the less replicable results will be; many subjects will have become depressed due to etiological agents closer to the final common pathway. She recommends path analysis (Hand, 1969) as a promising method for testing such models.

This writer is somewhat more pessimistic with regard to our present knowledge about depressive disorders than others. For example, Blumenthal (1971) writes, "... there is already a large and rapidly growing body of knowledge relating to specific psychobiological aspects of this illness" [p. 524]. Dramatic breakthroughs seem less likely than a gradual clarification of how basic bio-psycho-social mood determinants interactively relate to depression. The rate of progress will depend greatly on the adequacy of training to match the task.

APPENDIX

Classification of Depressions in the Diagnostic and Statistical Manual of the American Psychiatric Association (2nd ed., 1968)

Depressive disorders are listed under three major headings of the Manual: 1) Psychoses Not Attributed to Physical Conditions Listed Previously; 2) Neuroses; and 3) Personality Disorders and Certain Other Nonpsychotic Mental Disorders, as follows.

III. Psychoses not Attributed to Physical Conditions Listed Previously (295-298)

This major category is for patients whose psychosis is not caused by physical conditions listed previously. Nevertheless, some of these patients may show additional signs of an organic condition. If these organic signs are prominent the patient should receive the appropriate additional diagnosis.

296 *Major affective disorders* (Affective psychoses)

This group of psychoses is characterized by a single disorder of mood, either extreme depression or elation, that dominates the mental life of the patient and is responsible for whatever loss of contact he has with his environment. The onset of the mood does not seem to be related directly to a precipitating life experience and therefore is distinguishable from *Psychotic depressive reaction* and *Depressive neurosis*.

296.0 *Involutional melancholia*

This is a disorder occurring in the involutional period and characterized by worry, anxiety, agitation, and severe insomnia. Feelings of guilt and somatic preoccupations are frequently present and may be of delusional proportions. This disorder is distinguishable from *Manic-depressive illness* (q.v.) by the absence of previous episodes; it is distinguished from *Schizophrenia* (q.v.) in that impaired reality testing is due to a disorder of mood; and it is distinguished from *Psychotic depressive reaction* (q.v.) in that the depression is not due to some life experience. Opinion is divided as to whether this psychosis can be distinguished from the other affective disorders. It is, therefore, recommended that involutional patients not be given this diagnosis unless all other affective disorders have been ruled out.

Manic-depressive illnesses
(Manic-depressive psychoses)

These disorders are marked by severe mood swings and a tendency to remission and recurrence. Patients may be given this diagnosis in the absence of a previous history of affective psychosis if there is no obvious precipitating event. This disorder is divided into three major subtypes: manic type, depressed type, and circular type.

296.1 *Manic-depressive illness, manic type* (Manic-depressive psychosis, manic type)

This disorder consists exclusively of manic episodes. These episodes are characterized by excessive elation, irritability, talkativeness, flight of ideas, and accelerated speech and motor activity. Brief periods of depression sometimes occur, but they are never true depressive episodes.

296.2 *Manic-depressive illness, depressed type* (Manic-depressive psychosis, depressed type)

This disorder consists exclusively of depressive episodes. These episodes are characterized by severely depressed mood and by mental and motor retardation progressing occasionally to stupor. Uneasiness, apprehension, perplexity and agitation may also be present. When illusions, hallucinations, and delusions (usually of guilt or of hypochondriacal or paranoid ideas) occur, they are attributable to the dominant mood disorder. Because it is a primary mood disorder, this psychosis differs from the *Psychotic depressive reaction*, which is more easily attributable to precipitating stress. Cases incompletely labelled as 'psychotic depression' should be classified here rather than under *Psychotic depressive reaction.*

296.3   *Manic-depressive illness, circular type*
(Manic-depressive psychosis, circular type)

This disorder is distinguished by at least one attack of both a depressive episode *and* a manic episode. This phenomenon makes clear why manic and depressed types are combined into a single category. The current episode should be specified and coded as one of the following: (a) 296.33* *Manic-depressive illness, circular type, manic**; (b) 296.34* *Manic-depressive illness, circular type, depressed.**

296.8   *Other major affective disorder* (Affective psychosis, other)

Major affective disorders for which a more specific diagnosis has not been made are included here. It is also for "mixed" manic-depressive illness, in which manic and depressive symptoms appear almost simultaneously. It does not include *Psychotic depressive reaction* (q.v.) or *Depressive neurosis* (q.v.).

296.9   *Unspecified major affective disorder*
Affective disorder not otherwise specified
Manic-depressive illness not otherwise specified

IV. Neuroses (300)

Anxiety is the chief characteristic of the neuroses. It may be felt and expressed directly, or it may be controlled unconsciously and automatically by conversion, displacement and various other psychological mechanisms. Generally, these mechanisms produce symptoms experienced as subjective distress from which the patient desires relief.

The neuroses, as contrasted to the psychoses, manifest neither gross distortion or misinterpretation of external reality, nor gross personality disorganization. A possible exception to this is hysterical neurosis, which some believe may occasionally be accompanied by hallucinations and other symptoms encountered in psychoses.

Traditionally, neurotic patients, however severely handicapped by their symptoms, are not classified as psychotic because they are aware that their mental functioning is disturbed.

300.4   *Depressive neurosis*

This disorder is manifested by an excessive reaction of depression due to an internal conflict or to an identifiable event such as the loss of a love object or cherished possession. It is to be distinguished from *Involutional melancholia* (q.v.) and *Manic-depressive illness* (q.v.). *Reactive depressions* or *Depressive reactions* are to be classified here.

---

*Indicates categories added to international classification of diseases, eight for use in the U.S. only.

V. Personality Disorders and Certain Other Nonpsychotic Mental Disorders (301–304)

301 *Personality disorders*

This group of disorders is characterized by deeply ingrained maladaptive patterns of behavior that are perceptibly different in quality from psychotic and neurotic symptoms. Generally, these are lifelong patterns, often recognizable by the time of adolescence or earlier. Sometimes the pattern is determined primarily by malfunctioning of the brain, but such cases should be classified under one of the non-psychotic organic brain syndromes rather than here.

301.1 *Cyclothymic personality* (Affective personality)

This behavior pattern is manifested by recurring and alternating periods of depression and elation. Periods of elation may be marked by ambition, warmth, enthusiasm, optimism, and high energy. Periods of depression may be marked by worry, pessimism, low energy, and a sense of futility. These mood variations are not readily attributable to external circumstances. If possible, the diagnosis should specify whether the mood is characteristically depressed, hypomanic, or alternating. (American Psychiatric Association, 1968)

Note that at times no qualifier follows the disorder proper; at others, "illness" or "reaction" is added. While the Manual fails to explain this variation, "illness" probably reflects a consensual leaning toward a probably organic etiology, and "reaction" toward a psychoenvironmental etiology. As Zubin (1967) noted, the APA Manual's diagnostic system is derived by committee consensus, and as his Tables 1 and 2 indicated, application of the system has been markedly unreliable.

REFERENCES

Ableson, R., & Lesser, G. The measurement of persuasibility in children. In C. Hovland & I. Janis (Eds.), *Personality and persuasion*. New Haven: Yale University Press, 1959.

Abraham, K. (1911) Notes on the psycho-analytical investigation and treatment of manic-depressive insanity and allied conditions. In *Selected papers of Karl Abraham*. London: Hogarth Press, 1949.

Abraham, K. (1916) The first pregenital stage of the libido. In *Selected papers of Karl Abraham*. London: Hogarth Press, 1949.

Abraham, K. (1924) A short study of the development of the libido, viewed in the light of mental disorders: Part I, manic-depressive states and the pregenital levels of the libido. In *Selected papers of Karl Abraham*. London: Hogarth Press, 1949.

Abrahams, M. J., & Whitlock, F. A. Childhood experience and depression. *British Journal of Psychiatry*, 1969, **115**, 883–888.

Abramowitz, S. I. Locus of control and self-reported depression among college students. *Psychological Reports*, 1969, **25**, 149–150.

Ackner, B., & Pampiglione, G. An evaluation of the sedation threshhold test. *Journal of Psychosomatic Research*, 1959, **2**, 272 –281.

Adams, J. S. Inequity in social exchange. In L. Berkowitz (Ed.), *Advances in experimental social psychology*. Vol. 2. New York: Academic Press, 1965.

Adler, A. *The practice and theory of individual psychology*. Paterson, N. J.: Littlefield, Adams, 1959.

Adler, K. Depression in the light of individual psychology. *Journal of Individual Psychology*, 1961, **17**, 56–76.

Adorno, T. W., Frenkel-Brunswick, E., Levinson, D. J., & Sanford, R. N. *The authoritarian personality*. New York: Harper, 1950.

Agnew, H. W., Webb, W. B., & Williams, R. L. Comparison of stage four and 1-REM sleep deprivation. *Perceptual and Motor Skills*, 1967, **24**, 851–858.

Amdur, M. J., & Harrow, M. Conscience and depressive disorders. *British Journal of Psychiatry*, 1972, **120**, 259–264.

American Psychiatric Association. *Diagnostic and statistical manual of mental disorders*. (2nd edition) Washington, D.C.: American Psychiatric Association, 1968.

American Psychological Association, Validity: Technical recommendations for psychological tests and diagnostic techniques. *Psychological Bulletin*, 1954, **51** (supplement), 13 –28.

Anderson, W. McC., & Dawson, J. The clinical manifestation of depressive illness with abnormal acetyl methyl carbinol metabolism. *Journal of Mental Science*, 1962, **108**, 80–87.

Angst, J. *Zur Ätiologie und Nosologie endogener depressiver Psychosen*. Berlin: Springer, 1966.

Angst, J., & Perris, C. Nosology of endogenous depression, a comparison of the findings of two studies. *Archiv für Psychiatrie und Nervenkrankheiten*, 1968, **210**, 373–386.

Anthony, E. J., Bene, P., & Bene, E. Anthony Family Relations Test. *Journal of Mental Science*, 1957, **103**, 541–555.

Arieti, S. Manic-depressive psychosis. In S. Arieti (Ed.), *American handbook of psychiatry*. New York: Basic Books, 1959.

Arlow, J. A., & Brenner, C. *Psychoanalytic concepts and the structural theory*. New York: International Universities Press, 1964.

Asch, S. E. Studies of independence and conformity: A minority of one against a unanimous majority. *Psychological Monographs*, 1956, 70, (9, Whole No. 416).

Ascher, E. A criticism of the concept of neurotic depression. *American Journal of Psychiatry*, 1952, 108, 901–908.

Aserinsky, E., & Kleitman, N. Regularly occurring periods of eye motility, and concomitant phenomena during sleep. *Science*, 1953, 118, 273–274.

Astrup, C. *Pavlovian psychiatry: A new synthesis*. Springfield, Ill.: C. C. Thomas, 1965.

Atkinson, J. W., & Reitman, W. R. Performance as a function of motive strength and expectancy of goal attainment. *Journal of Abnormal and Social Psychology*, 1956, 53, 361–366.

Averill, J. R. Grief: Its nature and significance. *Psychological Bulletin*, 1968, 70, 721–749.

Azrin, N. H., Hutchinson, R. R., & Hake, D. F. Extinction-induced aggression. *Journal of the Experimental Analysis of Behavior*, 1966, 9, 191–204.

Babigian, H. M., Gardner, E. A., Miles, H. C., & Romano, J. Diagnostic consistency in a follow-up study of 1215 patients. *American Journal of Psychiatry*, 1965, 121, 895–901.

Baker, M., Dorzab, J., Winokur, G., & Cadoret, R. J. Depressive disease: Evidence favoring polygenic inheritance based on an analysis of ancestral cases. *Archives of General Psychiatry*, 1972, 27, 320–327.

Baker, R. R. The effects of psychotropic drugs on psychological testing. *Psychological Bulletin*, 1968, 69, 377–388.

Ban, T. A. Conditioning and psychiatry. Chicago: Aldine, 1964.

Ban, T. A., Choi, S. M., Lehmann, H. E., & Adamo, E. Conditional reflex studies in depression. *Canadian Psychiatric Association Journal*, 1966, 11 (special supplement), 98–105.

Bandura, A. *Principles of behavior modification*. New York: Holt, Rinehart & Winston, 1969.

Beck, A. T. A systematic investigation of depression. *Comprehensive Psychiatry*, 1961, 2, 163–170.

Beck, A. T. *Depression: Clinical, experimental, and theoretical aspects*. New York: Harper & Row, 1967.

Beck, A. T. Cognitive therapy: Nature and relation to behavior therapy. *Behavior Therapy*, 1970. 1, 184–200. (a)

Beck, A. T. The core problem in depression: The cognitive triad. *Science and Psychonalysis*, 1970, 17, 47–55. (b)

Beck, A. T. Role of fantasies in psychotherapy and psychopathology. *Journal of Nervous and Mental Disease*, 1970, 150, 3–17. (c)

Beck, A. T. Sexuality and depression. *Medical Aspects of Human Sexuality*, 1968, 2, 44–51.

Beck, A. T. Measuring depression: The Depression Inventory. In T. A. Williams, M. M. Katz, & J. A. Shield (Eds.), *Proceedings of the NIMH workshop and recent advances in the psychology of depressive illnesses*. (1969) Washington, D. C.: U.S. Government Printing Office, In press.

Beck, A. T., & Hurvich, M. S. Psychological correlates of depression. *Psychosomatic Medicine*, 1959, 21, 50–55.

Beck, A. T., & Ward, C. H. Dreams of depressed patients: Characteristic themes in manifest content. *Archives of General Psychiatry*, 1961, 5, 462–467.

Beck, A. T., Ward, C. H., Mendelson, M., Mock, J., & Erbaugh, J. An inventory for measuring depression. *Archives of General Psychiatry*, 1961, 4, 561–571.

Beck, J. C., & Worthen, K. Precipitating stress, crisis theory, and hospitalization in schizophrenia and depression. *Archives of General Psychiatry*, 1972, 26, 123–129.

Becker, E. Toward a comprehensive theory of depression: A cross disciplinary appraisal of objects, games and meaning. *Journal of Nervous and Mental Disease*, 1962, 135, 26–33.

Becker, J. Achievement related characteristics of manic-depressives. *Journal of Abnormal and Social Psychology*, 1960, 60, 334–339.

Becker, J., & Altrocchi, J. Peer conformity and achievement in female manic-depressives. *Journal of Abnormal Psychology*, 1968, 73, 585–589.

Becker, J., & Nichols, C. H. Communality of manic-depressives and "mild" cyclothymic characteristics. *Journal of Abnormal and Social Psychology*, 1964, 69, 531–538.

Becker, J., Spielberger, C. D., & Parker, J. B. On the relationship between manic-depressive psychosis and inner-directed character. *Journal of Social Psychology*, 1962, 57, 149–153.

Becker, J., Spielberger, C. D., & Parker, J. B. Value achievement and authoritarian attitudes in psychiatric patients. *Journal of Clinical Psychology*, 1963, 19, 57–61.

Beigel, A., & Murphy, D. L. Unipolar and bipolar affective illness. *Archives of General Psychiatry*, 1971, 24, 215–220.

Berkowitz, L. The concept of aggressive drive: Some additional considerations. In L. Berkowitz (Ed.), *Advances in experimental social psychology*. New York: Academic Press, 1965.

Bibring, E. The so-called English school of psychoanalysis. *Psychoanalytic Quarterly*, 1947, 16, 69–93.

Bibring, E. The mechanism of depression. In P. Greenacre (Ed.), *Affective disorders*. New York: International Universities Press, 1953.

Birtchnell, J. Depression in relation to early and recent parent death. *British Journal of Psychiatry*, 1970, 116, 299–306.

Blumenthal, M. D. Heterogeneity and research on depressive disorders. *Archives of General Psychiatry*, 1971, 24, 524–531.

Bockoven, J. S. *Moral treatment in American psychiatry*. New York: Spring Publishing Co., 1963.

Bodin, A. M., & Geer, J. H. Association responses of depressed and non-depressed patients to words of three hostility levels. *Journal of Personality*, 1965, 33, 392–409.

Bonime, W. The psychodynamics of neurotic depression. In S. Arieti (Ed.), *American handbook of psychiatry*. Vol. 3. New York: Basic Books, 1966.

Borge, G. F., Buchsbaum, M., Goodwin, F. K., Murphy, D. L., & Silverman, J. Neuropsychological correlates of affective disorders. *Archives of General Psychiatry*, 1971, 24, 501–505.

Botwinick, J., & Thompson, J. W. Depressive affect, speed of response, and age. *Journal of Consulting Psychology*, 1967, 31, 106.

Bowlby, J. *Attachment*. New York: Basic Books, 1969.

Brehm, J. W. *A theory of psychological reactance*. New York: Academic Press, 1966.

Brenner, C. *An elementary textbook of psychoanalysis*. New York: International Universities Press, 1955.

Brill, H. The role of classification in hospital psychiatry. In M. M. Katz, J. O. Cole, & W. E. Barton (Eds.), *The role and methodology of Classification in psychiatry and psychopathology*. Washington, D. C.: U.S. Public Helath Service Publication No. 1584. U.S. Government Printing Office, 1965.

Bromet, E., Harrow, M., & Tucker, G. J. Factors related to short-term prognosis in schizophrenia and depression. *Archives of General Psychiatry* 1971, 25, 148–154.

Bronowski, J. *The identity of man*. New York: American Museum of Science Books, 1966.

Brown, J. S., & Farber, I. R. Emotions conceptualized as intervening variables: With suggestions toward a theory of frustration. *Psychological Bulletin*, 1951, 48, 465–495.

Buchsbaum, M., Goodwin, F. K., Murphy, D. L., & Borge, G. F. AER in affective disorders. *American Journal of Psychiatry*, 1971, 128, 19–24.

Bull, N., & Strongin, E. I. The complex of frustration. *Journal of Nervous and Mental Diseases*, 1956, 123, 531–535.

Bunney, W. E., Jr. Psychoendocrine parameters and psychopathology. In A. J. Mandell & M. P. Mandell (Eds.), *Psychochemical research in man: Methods, strategy, and theory*. New York: Academic Press, 1969.

Bunney, W. E., Jr., Davis, J. M., Weil-Malherbe, H., & Smith, E. R. B. Biochemical changes in psychotic depression. *Archives of General Psychiatry*, 1967, 16, 448–460.

Bunney, W. E., Jr., Fawcett, J. A., Davis, J. M., & Gifford, S. Further evaluation of urinary 17-Hydroxycorticosteroids in suicidal patients. *Archives of General Psychiatry*, 1969, **21**, 138-150.

Bunney, W. E., Jr., Goodwin, F. K., & Murphy, D. L. The "Switch Process" in manic-depressive illness. *Archives of General Psychiatry*, 1972, **27**, 312-317.

Bunney, W. E., Jr., & Hartmann, E. L. Study of a patient with 48-hour manic-depressive cycles: I. An analysis of behavioral factors. *Archives of General Psychiatry*, 1965, **12**, 611-619.

Bunney, W. E., Jr., Hartmann, E. L., & Mason, J. W. Study of a patient with 48-hour manic-depressive cycles: II. Strong positive correlation between endocrine factors and manic defense patterns. *Archives of General Psychiatry*, 1965, **12**, 619-625.

Burke, L., Deykin, E. Y., Jacobson, S., & Haley, S. The depressed woman returns. *Archives of General Psychiatry*, 1967, **16**, 548-553.

Burnham, D. I., Gladstone, A. I., & Gibson, R. W. *Schizophrenia and the need-fear dilemma*. New York: International Universities Press, 1969.

Burns, S. J., & Offord, D. R. Achievement correlates of depressive illness: A study of school records and social mobility. *Journal of Nervous and Mental Disease*, 1972, **154**, 344-351.

Byrne, D. The repression-sensitization scale: Rationale, reliability, and validity. *Journal of Personality*, 1961, **29**, 334-349.

Cade, J. F. J. Lithium salts in the treatment of psychotic excitement. *Medical Journal of Australia*, 1949, **36**, 349-352.

Caine, T. M. The expression of hostility and guilt in melancholic and paranoid women. *Journal of Consulting Psychology*, 1960, **24**, 18-22.

Campbell, D. T., & Fiske, D. W. Convergent and discriminant validity. *Psychological Bulletin*, 1959, **56**, 81-105.

Cannon, W. B. *Bodily change in pain, hunger, fear and rage*. New York: Appleton, 1915.

Caplan, G. *Principles of preventive psychiatry*. London: Tavistock Publications, 1964.

Carney, M. W. P., Roth, M., & Garside, R. F. The diagnosis of depressive syndromes and the prediction of ECT response. *British Journal of Psychiatry*, 1965, **111**, 659-674.

Carney, M. W. P., & Sheffield, B. F. Depression and the Newcastle Scales: Their relationship to Hamilton's Scale. *British Journal of Psychiatry*, 1972, **121**, 35-40.

Chapman, L. J., Chapman, J. P., & Miller, G. A. A theory of verbal behavior in schizophrenia. In B. A. Maher (Ed.), *Progress in experimental personality research*. Volume 1. New York: Academic Press, 1964.

Chodoff, P. The core problem in depression: Interpersonal aspects. *Science and Psychoanalysis*, 1970, **17**, 56-61.

Clayton, P. J., Halikas, J. A., & Maurice, W. L. The depression of widowhood. *British Journal of Psychiatry*, 1972, **120**, 71-78.

Clyde, D. J. Self-ratings. In L. Uhr & J. G. Miller (Eds.), *Drugs and behavior*. New York: Wiley, 1960.

Clyde, D. J. *Clyde mood scale manual*. Coral Gables, Fla.: University of Miami, Biometrics Laboratory, 1963.

Cohen, M. B., Baker, G., Cohen, R. A., Fromm-Reichmann, F., & Weigert, E. B. An intensive study of twelve cases of manic-depressive psychosis. *Psychiatry*, 1954, **17**, 103-137.

Cohen, S. M., Allen, M. G., Pollin, W., & Hrubec, Z. Relationship of schizo-affective psychosis to manic-depressive psychosis and schizophrenia. *Archives of General Psychiatry*, 1972, **26**, 539-545.

Cohen, Y. A. The sociological relevance of schizophrenia and depression. In Y. A. Cohen (Ed.), *Social structure and personality*. New York: Holt, Rinehart & Winston, 1961.

Colbert, J., & Harrow, M. Depression and organicity. *Psychiatric Quarterly*, 1966, **40**, 96-103.

Colbert, J., & Harrow, M. Psychomotor retardation in depressive syndromes. *Journal of Nervous and Mental Disease*, 1968, **145**, 405-418.

Comrey, A. L. A factor analysis of items on the MMPI Depression Scale. *Educational and Psychological Measurement*, 1957, 17, 578-585.

Cooper, J. The Leyton Obsessional Inventory. *Psychological Medicine*, 1970, 1, 48-64.

Cooper, J. E., Kendell, R. E., Gurland, B. J., Sharpe, L., Copeland, J. R. M., & Simon, R. *Psychiatric diagnosis in London and New York*. London: Oxford University Press, 1971. Maudsley Monograph No. 20.

Coopersmith, S. *The antecedents of self-esteem*. San Francisco: Freeman, 1967.

Coppen, A. The Marke-Nyman temperament scale: An English translation. *British Journal of Medical Psychology*, 1966, 39, 55-59.

Coppen, A. The biochemistry of affective disorders. *British Journal of Psychiatry*, 1967, 113, 1237-1264.

Coppen, A., Cowie, V., & Slater, E. Familial aspects of "neuroticism" and "extraversion." *British Journal of Psychiatry*, 1965, 111, 70-83.

Coppen, A., & Metcalfe, M. Effect of a depressive illness on MMPI scores. *British Journal of Psychiatry*, 1965, 111, 236-239.

Costain, R., Redfearn, J. W. T., & Lippold, O. C. J. A controlled trial of the therapeutic effects of polarization of the brain in depressive illness. *British Journal of Psychiatry*, 1964, 110, 786-799.

Costello, C. G., & Belton, G. P. Depression: Treatment. In C. G. Costello (Ed.), *Symptoms of psychopathology; a handbook*. New York: Wiley, 1970.

Costello, C. G., & Comrey, A. L. Scales for measuring depression and anxiety. *Journal of Psychology*, 1967, 66, 303-313.

Costello, C. G., & Selby, M. M. The relationships between sleep patterns and reactive and endogenous depressions. *British Journal of Psychiatry*, 1965, 111, 497-501.

Crutchfield, R. S. Conformity and character. *American Psychologist*, 1955, 10, 191-198.

Cytryn, L., & McKnew, D. H., Jr. Proposed classification of childhood depression. *American Journal of Psychiatry*, 1972, 129, 149-155.

Davis, D. R. Recovery from depression. *British Journal of Medical Psychology*, 1952, 25, 104-113.

Davis, D. R. The psychological mechanisms of depression. In E. B. Davies (Ed.), *Depression*. Cambridge: Cambridge University Press, 1964.

Davis, D. R. Depression as adaptation to crisis. *British Journal of Medical Psychology*, 1970, 43, 109-116.

Davis, D. R., Lamberti, J., & Ajans, Z. A. Crying and depression. *British Journal of Psychiatry*, 1969, 115, 597-598.

DeCharms, R. A self-scored projective measure of achievement and affiliation motivation. *Journal of Consulting Psychology*, 1958, 22, 172.

DeCharms, R., Morrison, H. W., Reitman, W. R., & McClelland, D. C. Behavioral correlates of directly and indirectly measured achievement motivation. In D. C. McClelland (Ed.), *Studies in motivation*. New York: Appleton-Century-Crofts, 1955.

Dement, W., & Kleitman, H. Cyclic variations in EEG during sleep and their relation to eye movements, body motility, and dreaming. *Electroencephalography and Clinical Neurophysiology*, 1957, 9, 673-690.

Dempsey, P. The dimensionality of the MMPI clinical scales among normal subjects. *Journal of Consulting Psychology*, 1963, 27, 492-497.

Dempsey, P. A unidimensional depression scale for the MMPI. *Journal of Consulting Psychology*, 1964, 28, 364-371.

Detre, T., Himmelhoch, J., Swartzburg, M., Anderson, C. M., Byck, R., & Kupfer, D. J. Hypersomnia and manic-depressive disease. *American Journal of Psychiatry*, 1972, 128, 1301-1305.

Deykin, E. Y., Jacobson, S., Klerman, G. L., & Solomon, M. The empty nest: Psychosocial aspects of conflict between depressed women and their grown children. *American Journal of Psychiatry*, 1966, 122, 1422-1426.

DiMascio, A., Meyer, R. E., & Stifler, L. Effects of imipramine on individuals varying in level of depression. *American Journal of Psychiatry*, 1968, **124** (supplement), 55–58.

Dorzab, J., Baker, M., Cadoret, R. J., & Winokur, G. Depressive disease: Familial psychiatric illness. *American Journal of Psychiatry*, 1971, **127**, 1128–1134.

Dunner, D. L., Gershon, E. S., & Goodwin, F. K. Heritable factors in the severity of affective illness. Paper presented at the May 1970 Annual Meeting of the American Psychiatric Association.

Eaton, J. W., & Weil, R. J. *Culture and mental disorders*. Glencoe, Ill.: Free Press, 1955.

Edwards, A. L. *The social desirability variable in personality assessment and research*. New York: Dryden, 1957.

Edwards, A. L. Correlation of "A unidimensional depression scale for the MMPI" with the SD scale. *Journal of Consulting Psychology*, 1965, **29**, 271–273.

Ellenberger, H. F. A clinical introduction to psychiatric phenomenology and existential analysis. In R. May, E. Angel, & H. F. Ellenberger (Eds.), *Existence: A new dimension in psychiatry and psychology*. New York: Basic Books, 1958.

Ellis, A. *Reason and emotion in psychotherapy*. New York: Lyle Stuart, 1962.

Engel, G. L. Is grief a disease? *Psychosomatic Medicine*, 1961. **23**, 18–22.

Engel, G. L. *Psychological development in health and disease*. Philadelphia: W. B. Saunders, 1962.

Engel, G. L. Attachment behaviour, object relations and the dynamic-economic points of view: Critical review of Bowlby's "Attachment and Loss." *International Journal of Psychoanalysis*, 1971, **52**, 183–196.

Engel, G. L., & Ader, R. Psychological factors in organic disease. *Mental Health Program Reports*, 1967, **1**, 1–25.

English, O. S. Observation of trends in manic-depressive psychosis. *Psychiatry*, 1949, **12**, 125–134.

Erikson, E. H. *Childhood and society*. New York: Norton, 1950.

Everitt, B. S. Cluster analysis: A brief discussion of some of the problems. *British Journal of Psychiatry*, 1972, **120**, 143–145.

Everitt, B. S., Gourlay, A. J., & Kendell, R. E. An attempt at validation of traditional syndromes by cluster analysis. *British Journal of Psychiatry*, 1971, **119**, 399–412.

Excerpta Medica Foundation. *Depression-1970: Symposium highlights*. Excerpta Medica Foundation, 1971.

Eysenck, H. J. Schizothymia-cyclothymia as a dimension of personality: I. Historical review. *Journal of Personality*, 1952, **19**, 123–152. (a)

Eysenck, H. J. Schizothymia-cyclothymia as a dimension of personality: II. Experimental. *Journal of Personality*, 1952, **20**, 345–384. (b)

Eysenck, H. J. Principles and methods of personality description, classification and diagnosis. *British Journal of Psychology*, 1964, **55**, 284–294.

Eysenck, H. J. The classification of depressive illness. *British Journal of Psychiatry*, 1970, **117**, 241–271.

Eysenck, H. J., Granger, G. W., & Brenglemann, J. C. *Perceptual processes and mental illness*. London: Maudsley Monographs, No. 2. Chapman & Hall, 1957.

Eysenck, H. J., & Rachman, S. *The cause and cures of neurosis*. London: Routledge & Kegan Paul, 1965.

Farberow, N. L., & Schneidman, E. S. *The cry for help*. New York: McGraw-Hill, 1961.

Fast, I. Some relationships of infantile self-boundary development to depression. *International Journal of Psychoanalysis*, 1967, **48**, 259–266.

Federn, P. Some variations in ego feeling. *International Journal of Psychoanalysis*, 1926, **7**, 434–444.

Fenichel, O. *The psychoanalytic theory of neurosis*. New York: Norton, 1945.

Ferster, C. B. Classification of behavioral pathology. In L. Krasner & L. P. Ullman (Eds.), *Research in behavior modification*. New York: Holt, Rinehart & Winston, 1965.

Festinger, L. *A theory of cognitive dissonance* New York: Row Peterson, 1957.

Fieve, R. R. Lithium studies and manic-depressive illness. In J. Zubin & F. A. Freyhan (Eds.), *Disorders of mood*. Baltimore: Johns Hopkins Press, 1972, 135–146.

Finley, C. B., & Wilson, D. C. The relation of the family to manic-depressive psychosis. *Diseases of the Nervous System*, 1951, **12**, 39–43.

Fleiss, J. L., Lawlor, W. G., Platman, S. R., & Fieve, R. R. On the issue of inverted factor analysis for generating typologies. *Journal of Abnormal Psychology*, 1971, **77**, 127–132.

Fontana, A. E. Familial etiology of schizophrenia: Is a scientific methodology possible. *Psychological Bulletin*, 1966, **66**, 214–227.

Ford, L. H., Jr. A forced-choice, acquiescence-free, social desirability (defensiveness) scale. *Journal of Consulting Psychology*, 1964, **28**, 475.

Ford, L. H., Jr., & Herson, M. Need approval, defensive denial, and direction of aggression in a failure-frustration situation. *Journal of Personality and Social Psychology*, 1967, **6**, 228–233.

Foulds, G. A. *Personality and personal illness*. London: Tavistock Publications, 1965.

Fremming, K. The expectation of mental infirmity in a sample of the Danish population. *Occasional Papers on Eugenics*, No. 7. London: Cassell & Co., 1951.

Freud, S. (1914) On Narcissism: An introduction. In J. Strachey (Ed.), *The standard edition*. Vol. 14. London: Hogarth Press, 1957.

Freud, S. (1917) Mourning and melancholia. In J. Strachey (Ed.), *The standard edition*. Vol. 14. London: Hogarth Press, 1957.

Freud, S. (1921) Group psychology and the analysis of the ego. In J. Strachey (Ed.) *The standard edition*. Vol. 19. London: Hogarth Press, 1957.

Freud, S. (1923) The ego and the id. In J. Strachey (Ed.), *The standard edition*. Vol. 19. London: Hogarth Press, 1957.

Friedman, A. S. Minimal effects of severe depression on cognitive functioning. *Journal of Abnormal and Social Psychology*, 1964, **69**, 237–243.

Friedman, A. S. Hostility factors and clinical improvement in depressed patients. *Archives of General Psychiatry*, 1970, **23**, 524–537.

Friedman, A. S., Cowitz, B., Cohen, H. W., & Granick, S. Syndromes and themes of depression. *Archives of General Psychiatry*, 1963, **9**, 504–510.

Fromm-Reichmann, F. Discussion of paper by Dr. English. *Psychiatry*, 1949, **12**, 133–134.

Garmany, G. Depressive states; their etiology and treatment. *British Medical Journal*, 1938, **ii**, 341–344.

Garmezy, N. Process and reactive schizophrenia: Some conceptions and issues. In M. M. Katz, J. O. Cole, & W. E. Barton (Eds.), *The role and methodology of classification in psychiatry and psychopathology*. Washington, D. C.: U.S. Public Health Service Publication No. 1584. U. S. Government Printing Office, 1965.

Gattozzi, A. A. *Lithium in the treatment of mood disorders*. National Clearinghouse for Mental Health Information, Publication No. 5033. Washington, D.C.: U.S. Government Printing Office, 1970.

Gershon, E. S., Cromer, M., & Klerman, G. L. Hostility and depression. *Psychiatry*, 1968, **31**, 224–235.

Gershon, E. S., Dunner, D. L., & Goodwin, F. K. Toward a biology of affective disorders: Genetic contributions. *Archives of General Psychiatry*, 1971, **25**, 1–15.

Gibbons, J. L. Electrolytes and depressive illnesses. *Postgraduate Medical Journal*, 1963, **39**, 19–25.

Gibson, R. W. The family background and early life experience of the manic-depressive patient. *Psychiatry*, 1958, **21**, 71–90.

Gillespie, R. D. The clinical differentiation of types of depression. *Guy's Hospital Reports*, 1929, **79**, 306–344.

Goldstein, I. B. The relationship of muscle tension and autonomic activity to psychiatric disorders. *Psychosomatic Medicine*, 1965, **27**, 39–52.

Goodwin, F. K., Murphy, D. L., & Bunney, W. E., Jr. Lithium in depression and mania: A double-blind behavioral and biochemical study. *Archives of General Psychiatry*, 1969, 21, 486–496.

Gordon, E. K., & Oliver, J. 3-Methoxy-4-Hydroxyphenylethylene oycol in human cerebrospinal fluid. *Clinica Chimica Acta*, 1971, 35, 145–150.

Gottschalk, L. A., Gleser, G. C., & Springer, K. J. Three hostility scales applicable to verbal samples. *Archives of General Psychiatry*, 1963, 9, 254–280.

Granville-Grossman, K. L. The early environment in affective disorder. In A. Coppen & A. Walk (Eds.), *Recent developments in affective disorders. British Journal of Psychiatry*, Special Publication No. 2, 1968.

Greenblatt, M., Grosser, G. H., & Wechsler, H. Differential response of hospitalized depressed patients to somatic therapy. *American Journal of Psychiatry*, 1964, 120, 935–944.

Greenson, R. R. On mood and introjects. *Bulletin of the Menninger Clinic*, 1954, 18, 1–11.

Greenspan, K., Goodwin, F. K., Bunney, W. E., Jr., & Durrell, J. Lithium ion retention and distribution. *Archives of General Psychiatry*, 1968, 19, 664–674.

Grinker, R. R., Sr. Reception of communications by patients in depressive states. *Archives of General Psychiatry*, 1964, 10, 576–580.

Grinker, R. R. The phenomena of depression. In T. A. Williams *et al.* (Eds.), *Recent advances in the psychobiology of the depressive illnesses*. Chevy Chase, Maryland: U. S. Department of Health, Education, and Welfare, 1969, 295–299.

Grinker, R. R., Miller, J. B., Sabshin, M., Nunn, R., & Nunnally, J. C. *The phenomena of depressions*. New York: Harper & Row, 1961.

Grinker, R. R., & Spiegel, J. P. *Men under stress*. Philadelphia: Blakiston, 1945.

Groesbeck, B. L. Toward description of personality in terms of configurations of motives. In J. W. Atkinson (Ed.), *Motives in fantasy, action, and society*. Princeton, N. J.: Van Nostrand, 1958.

Grosser, G. H. Social and cultural considerations in the treatment of depression. In J. O. Cole & J. R. Wittenborn (Eds.), *Pharmacotherapy of depression*. Springfield, Ill.: C. C. Thomas, 1966.

Gruenberg, E. M. Epidemiology and medical care statistics. In M. M. Katz, J. O. Cole, & W. E. Barton (Eds.), *The role and methodology of classification in psychiatry and psychopathology*. Washington, D. C.: U. S. Public Health Service Publication No. 1584. U. S. Government Printing Office, 1965.

Gurland, B. J., Fleiss, J. L., Sharpe, L., Simon, R., Barrett, J. E., Jr., Copeland, J. R. M., Cooper, J. E., & Kendell, R. E. The mislabeling of depressed patients in New York State hospitals. In J. Zubin & F. A. Freyhan (Eds.) *Disorders of mood*. Baltimore: Johns Hopkins Press, 1972, 17–29.

Hagnell, O. *A prospective study of the incidence of mental disorder*. London: Lund Humphreys, 1966.

Hamburg, D. A. *Emotions in the perspective of human evolution*. In P. H. Knapp (Ed.), *Expression of emotions in man*. New York: International Universities Press, 1963.

Hamilton, D. M., & Mann, W. W. The hospital treatment of involutional psychoses. In P. H. Hoch & J. Zubin (Eds.), *Depression*. New York: Grune & Stratton, 1954.

Hamilton, D. M., Development of a rating scale for primary depressive illness. *Journal of Clinical and Social Psychology*, 1967, 6, 278–296.

Hamilton, D. M., & White, J. Clinical syndromes in depressive states. *Journal of Mental Science*, 1959, 105, 985–998.

Hand, K. C. Principles in path analysis. In E. F. Borgatta & G. W. Bohrnsteat (Eds.), *Sociological methodology*. San Francisco: Jossey-Bass, 1969.

Hanna, B. L. Genetic studies of family units. In J. O. Neil, M. W. Shaw, & W. J. Schull (Eds.), *Genetics and the epidemiology of chronic diseases*. Washington, D. C.: U. S. Department of Health, Education, and Welfare, 1965.

Hargreaves, W. A. Longitudinal measurement of depressive symptoms. In T. A. Williams et al. (Eds.) *Recent advances in the psychobiology of the depressive illnesses*. Chevy Chase, Maryland: U. S. Department of Health, Education & Welfare, 1969, 303-309.

Harrow, M., & Amdur, M. J. Guilt and depressive disorders. *Archives of General Psychiatry*, 1971, 25, 240-246.

Harrow, M., Colbert, J., Detre, T., & Bakeman, R. Symptomatology and subjective experiences in current depressive states. *Archives of General Psychiatry*, 1966, 14, 203-213.

Hartman, T. F. Dynamic transmission, elective generalization, and semantic conditioning. In W. F. Prokasy (Ed.), *Classical conditioning*. New York: Appleton-Century-Crofts, 1965.

Hartmann, E. L., Antidepressants and sleep: Clinical and theoretical implications. In A. Kales (Ed.), *Sleep physiology and pathology: A symposium*. Philadelphia: Lippincott, 1969. (a)

Hartmann, E. L., Mania, depression and sleep. In A. Kales (Ed.), *Sleep physiology and pathology: A symposium*. Philadelphia: Lippincott, 1969. (b)

Harvey, O. J., Hunt, D. E., & Schroder, H. M. *Conceptual systems and personality organization*. New York: John Wiley & Sons, 1961.

Hathaway, S. R., & McKinley, J. C. A multiphasic personality schedule (Minnesota: III. The measurement of symptomatic depression). *Journal of Psychology*, 1942, 14, 73-84.

Hawkins, D. R. Sleep research and depression. In T. A. Williams et al. (Eds.), *Recent advances in the psychobiology of the depressive illnesses*. Chevy Chase, Maryland: U. S. Department of Health, Education, and Welfare, 1969, 141-147.

Hempel, C. G. Introduction to problems of taxonomy. In J. Zubin (Ed.), *Field studies in the mental disorders*. New York: Grune & Stratton, 1961.

Henkin, R. I., Daly, R. L., & Ojemann, G. A. On the action of steroid hormones on the central nervous system in man. *Journal of Clinical Investigations*, 1966, 45, 1021-1022.

Heston, L. L. The genetics of schizophrenic and schizoid disease. *Science*, 1969, 167, 249-256.

Hildreth, H. M. A battery of feeling and attitude scales for clinical use. *Journal of Clinical Psychology*, 1946, 2, 214-221.

Hillarp, N. A., Fuxe, K., & Dahlstrom, A. Central monoamine neurones. In U. S. Von Euler, S. Rosell, & B. Urnas (Eds.), *Mechanisms of release of biogenic amines*. New York: Pergamon Press, 1966.

Hollander, E. P., & Willis, R. H. Some current issues in the psychology of conformity and nonconformity. *Psychological Bulletin*, 1967, 68, 62-76.

Hollingshead, A. B., & Redlich, F. C. *Social class and mental illness: A community study*. New York: John Wiley, 1958.

Hollister, L. E., Overall, J. E., Johnson, M. H., Shelton, J., Kimbell, I., & Brunse, A. Amitryptiline alone and combined with perphenazine in newly admitted depressed patients. *Journal of Nervous and Mental Disease*, 1966, 142, 460-469.

Holmes, T. H., & Rahe, R. H. The social readjustment rating scale. *Journal of Psychosomatic Research*, 1967, 11, 213-218.

Holzman, P. S. *Psychoanalysis and psychopathology*. New York: McGraw-Hill, 1971.

Hopkinson, G. A genetic study of affective illness in patients over 50. *British Journal of Psychiatry*, 1964, 110, 244-254.

Hopkinson, G., & Ley, P. A genetic study of affective disorder. *British Journal of Psychiatry*, 1969, 115, 917-922.

Hudgens, R. W., Morrison, J. R., & Barchha, R. G. Life events and onset of primary affective disorders. *Archives of General Psychiatry*, 1967, 16, 134-145.

Hunt, S. M., Jr., Singer, K., & Cobb, S. Components of depression. *Archives of General Psychiatry*, 1967, 16, 441-448.

Huston, P. E. Neglected approach to cause and treatment of psychotic depression. *Archives of General Psychiatry*, 1971, 24, 505-509.

Iskander, T. N., & Kaebling, R. Catecholamines, a dream sleep model, and depression. *American Journal of Psychiatry*, 1970, **127**, 43–51.

Jacobson, E. The effect of disappointment on ego and super-ego formation in normal and depressive development. *Psychoanalytic Review*, 1946, **33**, 129–148.

Jacobson, E. Contribution to the metapsychology of cyclothymic depression. In P. Greenacre (Ed.), *Affective disorders*. New York: International Universities Press, 1953.

Jacobson, E. Contribution to the metapsychology of psychotic identifications. *Journal of the American Psychoanalytic Association*, 1954, **2**, 339–362.

Jacobson, E. Manic-depressive partners. In V. M. Eisenstein (Ed.) *Neurotic interaction in marriage*. New York: Basic Books, 1956.

Jacobson, E. On normal and pathological moods. *The Psychoanalytic Study of the Child*, 1957, **12**, 73–114.

Jacobson, E. Problems in the differentiation between schizophrenic and melancholic states of depression. In R. M. Loewenstein, *et al.* (Eds.), *Psychoanalysis: A general psychology*. New York: International Universities Press, 1966.

Jacobson, E. *Depression: Comparative studies of normal, neurotic, and psychotic conditions*. New York: International Universities Press, 1971.

Jacobson, S., & Klerman, G. L. Interpersonal dynamics of hospitalized depressed patients' home visits. *Journal of Marriage and the Family*, 1966, **28**, 94–102.

Janowsky, D. S., Leff, M. J., & Epstein, R. S. Playing the manic game: Interpersonal maneuvers of the acutely manic patient. *Archives of General Psychiatry*, 1970, **22**, 252–261.

Jenner, F. A., Goodwin, J. C., Sheridan, M., Tauber, I. J., & Lobban, M. D. The effect of an altered time regime on biological rhythms in 48-hour periodic psychosis. *British Journal of Psychiatry*, 1968, **114**, 215–225.

Jouvet, M. Biogenic amines and the states of sleep. *Science*, 1969, **163**, 32–41.

Kallman, F. J. Genetic principles in manic-depressive psychosis. In. P. H. Hoch & J. Zubin (Eds.), *Depression*. New York: Grune & Stratton, 1954.

Katkin, E. S., Sasmor, D. E., & Tan, R. Conformity and achievement related characteristics of depressed patients. *Journal of Abnormal Psychology*, 1966, **71**, 407–413.

Katz, M. M. Classification and measurement of the psychopathology of depression. In T. A. Williams et al. (Eds.), *Recent advances in the psychobiology of the depressive illnesses*. Chevy Chase, Maryland: U. S. Department of the Health, Education and Welfare, 1969, 367–373.

Katz, M. M., Cole, J. O., & Barton, W. E. (Eds.) *The role and methodology of classification in psychiatry and psychopathology*. Washington, D. C: U. S. Public Health Service Publication No. 1584. U. S. Government Printing Office, 1965.

Kaufman, C. I., & Rosenblum, L. A. Depression in infant monkeys separated from their mothers. *Science*, 1967, **155**, 1030–1031.

Kay, D. W. K., Garside, R. F., Beamish, P., & Roy, J. R. Endogenous and neurotic syndromes of depression: A factor analytic study of 104 cases. Clinical features. *British Journal of Psychiatry*, 1969, **115**, 377–389.

Keith, H., Brodie, H., & Leff, M. J. Bipolar depression: A comparative study of patient characteristics. *American Journal of Psychiatry*, 1971, **127**, 1086–1091.

Kellerman, H., & Plutchik, R. Emotion trait interrelations and the measurement of personality. *Psychological Reports*, 1968, **23**, 1107–1114.

Kelly, D., & Walter, C. J. S. A clinical and physiological relationship between anxiety and depression. *British Journal of Psychiatry*, 1969, **115**, 401–406.

Kelly, G. A. *The psychology of personal constructs*. Vol. 1. New York: Norton, 1955.

Kendell, R. E. *The classification of depressive illnesses*. London: Oxford University Press, 1968.

Kendell, R. E. Relationship between aggression and depression. *Archives of General Psychiatry*, 1970, **22**, 308–319.

Kendell, R. E., & Discipio, W. J. Obsessional symptoms and obsessional personality traits in patients with depressive illnesses. *Psychological Medicine*, 1970, 1, 65–73.

Kendell, R. E., & Gourlay, J. The clinical distinction between psychotic and neurotic depressions. *British Journal of Psychiatry*, 1970, 117, 257–260. (a)

Kendell, R. E., & Gourlay, J. The clinical distinction between the affective psychoses and schizophrenia. *British Journal of Psychiatry*, 1970, 117, 261–266. (b)

Kety, S. S. Problems in psychiatric nosology from the viewpoint of the biological sciences. In M. M. Katz, J. O. Cole, & W. E. Barton (Eds.), *The role and methodology of classification in psychiatry and psychopathology*. Washington, D. C.: U. S. Public Health Service Publication No. 1584. U. S. Government Printing Office, 1965.

Kiloh, L. G., Andrews, G., Neilson, M., & Bianchi, G. N. The relationship of the syndromes called endogenous and neurotic depression. *British Journal of Psychiatry*, 1972, 121, 183–196.

Kiloh, L. G., & Garside, R. F. The independence of neurotic depression and endogenous depression. *British Journal of Psychiatry*, 1963, 109, 451–463.

King, H. E. Psychomotility: A dimension of behaviour disorder. In J. Zubin & C. Shagass (Eds.), *Neurobiological aspects of psychopathology*. New York: Grune & Stratton, 1969, 99–128.

Klein, M. (1934) Mourning and its relation to manic-depressive states. In *Contributions to psychoanalysis*, 1921–1945. London: Hogarth Press, 1948.

Klein, M. (1940) Mourning, its relation to manic-depressive states. In *Contributions to psychoanalysis*, 1921–1945. London: Hogarth Press, 1948.

Klein, M. (1945) Oedipus complex in the light of early anxieties. In *Contributions to psychoanalysis* 1921–1945. London: Hogarth Press, 1948.

Klerman, G. L. Modes of action of antidepressant drugs. In J. O. Cole & J. R. Wittenborn (Eds.), *Pharmacotherapy of depression*. Springfield, Ill.: C. C. Thomas, 1966.

Klerman, G. L. Clinical phenomenology of depression: Implications for research strategy in the psychobiology of the affective disorders. In T. A. Williams et al. (Eds.), *Recent advances in the psychobiology of the depressive illnesses*. Chevy Chase, Maryland; U. S. Department of Health, Education, and Welfare, 1969, 331–343.

Klerman, G. L. Clinical research in depression. *Archives of General Psychiatry*, 1971, 24, 305–319.

Klerman, G. L., & Cole, J. O. Clinical pharmacology of the imipramine and related antidepressant compounds. *Pharmacology Review,* 1965, 17, 101–141.

Klerman, G. L., & Gershon, E. S. Imipramine effects upon hostility in depression. *Journal of Nervous and Mental Disease*, 1970, 150, 127–132.

Koch, S. Epilogue. In S. Koch (Ed.), *Psychology: A study of a science*. Vol. 3. New York: McGraw-Hill, 1959.

Koran, L. M., & Maxim, P. E. Field dependence in manic-depressive patients. *Journal of Nervous and Mental Disease*, 1972, 155, 205–209.

Kraepelin, E. (1913) Manic-depressive insanity and paranoia. In R. M. Barclay (Trans.), *Lehrbuch der Psychiatrie*. (8th ed.) Edinburgh: Livingstone, 1921.

Kraines, S. H. *Mental depressions and their treatment*. New York: Macmillan, 1957.

Kramer, M. Discussion of the concepts of incidence and prevalence as related to epidemiologic studies of mental disorders. *American Journal of Public Health*, 1957, 47, 826–840.

Kramer, M. Classification of mental disorders for epidemiologic and medical care purposes: Current status, problems, and needs. In M. M. Katz, J. O. Cole, & W. E. Barton (Eds.), *The role and methodology of classification in psychiatry and psychopathology*. Washington, D. C.: U. S. Public Health Service Publication No. 1584. U. S. Government Printing Office, 1965.

Kramer, M. Cross-national study of diagnosis of the mental disorders: Origin of the problem. *American Journal of Psychiatry*, 1969, **125**, (supplement no. 10), 1–12.

Lamont, J. N. *Resistance to influence in depressives.* Unpublished doctoral dissertation, University of Washington, 1969.

Langer, T. S., & Michael, S. T. *The midtown Manhattan study: Life stress and mental health.* Vol. 2. New York: McGraw-Hill, 1963.

Laragh, J. H. Discussion of panel on electrolyte metabolism. In T. A. Williams et al. (Eds.), *Recent advances in the psychobiology of the depressive illnesses.* Chevy Chase, Maryland: U. S. Department of Health, Education, and Welfare, 1969, 77–81.

Laxer, R. M. Relation of real self-rating to mood and blame and their interaction in depression. *Journal of Consulting Psychology*, 1964, **28**, 538–546. (a)

Laxer, R. M. Self-concept changes of depressive patients in general hospital treatment. *Journal of Consulting Psychology*, 1964, **28**, 214–219. (b)

Lazare, A., & Klerman, G. L. Hysteria and depression: The frequency and significance of hysterical personality features in hospitalized depressed women. *American Journal of Psychiatry*, 1968, **124** (supplement), 48–57.

Lazarus, A. A. Learning theory and the treatment of depression. *Behavioral Research and Therapy*, 1968, **6**, 83–89.

Lazarus, R. S. Emotions and adaptation: Conceptual and empirical relations. In W. J. Arnold (Ed.), *Nebraska symposium on motivation.* Lincoln, Nebr.: University of Nebraska Press, 1968.

Leff, M. J., Roatch, J. F., & Bunney, W. E., Jr. Environmental factors preceding the onset of severe depressions. *Psychiatry*, 1970, **33**, 293–311.

Lehmann, H. E. Discussant's remarks. In M. M. Katz, J. O. Cole, & W. E. Barton (Eds.), *The role and methodology of classification in psychiatry and psychopathology.* Washington, D. C.: U. S. Public Health Service Publication No. 1584. U. S. Government Printing Office, 1965.

Lehmann, H. E. Depression: Categories, mechanisms and phenomena. In J. O. Cole & J. R. Wittenborn (Eds.), *Pharmacotherapy of depression.* Springfield, Ill.: C. C. Thomas, 1966.

Lehmann, H. E. Clinical perspectives on antidepressant therapy. *American Journal of Psychiatry*, 1968, **124** (supplement), 12–21.

Lehmann, H. E. Epidemiology of depressive disorders. In R. R. Fieve (Ed.), *Depression in the 70's: Modern theory and research.* Princeton, N. J.: Excerpta Medica, 1971, 21–31.

Leonhard, K. *Aufteilung der endogenen Psychosen.* Berlin: Akademie-Verlag, 1959.

Leonhard, K., Korff, I., & Schulz, H. Die Temperamente in den Familien der monopolaren und bipolaren phasichen Psychosen. *Psychiatria et Neurologia*, 1962, **143**, 416–434.

Levinson, D. J., & Huffman, P. E. Traditional family ideology and its relation to personality. *Journal of Personality*, 1955, **23**, 251–273.

Lewinsohn, P. M. *Clinical and theoretical aspects of depression.* Paper presented at 1972 Georgia Symposium in Experimental Clinical Psychology. Available from the author in mimeo, University of Oregon.

Lewinsohn, P. M., & Atwood, G. E. Depression: A clinical-research approach. *Psychotherapy: Theory, research and practice*, 1969, **6**, 166–171.

Lewinsohn, P. M., & Flippo, J. Effects of success and failure upon self-esteem in depressed and non-depressed individuals. Unpublished manuscript available from the senior author, University of Oregon, 1969.

Lewinsohn, P. M., & Libet, J. Pleasant events, activity schedules, and depressions. *Journal of Abnormal Psychology*, 1972, **79**, 291–296.

Lewinsohn, P. M., Lobitz, W. C., & Wilson, S. "Sensitivity" of depressed individuals to aversive stimuli. Unpublished mimeo available from the senior author, Psychology Department, University of Oregon, 1972.

Lewinsohn, P. M., & Shaffer, M. Use of home observations as an integral part of the treatment of depression: Preliminary report and case studies. *Journal of Consulting and Clinical Psychology*, 1971, **37**, 87–95.

Lewis, A. J. Melancholia: A historical review. *Journal of Mental Science*, 1934, 80, 1–42.

Lewis, A. J. Melancholia: A prognostic study and case material. *Journal of Mental Science*, 1936, 82, 488–558.

Lewis, A. J. States of depression: Their clinical and etiological differentiation. *British Medical Journal* 1938, ii, 875–878.

Lewis, A. J. General review of depressive conditions. In E. B. Davies (Ed.), *Depression*. Cambridge: Cambridge University Press, 1964.

Lewis, A. J. 'Endogenous' and 'exogenous': A useful dichotomy? *Psychological Medicine*, 1971, 1, 191–196.

Lewis, D. A., & Piotrowski, Z. A. Clinical diagnosis of manic-depressive psychosis. In P. H. Hoch & J. Zubin (Eds.), *Depression*. New York: Grune & Stratton, 1954.

Liberman, R. P., & Raskin, D. E. Depression: A behavioral formulation. *Archives of General Psychiatry*, 1971, 24, 515–523.

Libet, J., & Lewinsohn, P. M. Concept of social skill with special relevance to behavior of depressed persons. *Journal of Consulting and Clinical Psychology*, in press.

Lichtenberg, P. Time perspective and the initiation of cooperation. *Journal of Social Psychology*, 1956, 43, 247–260.

Lichtenberg, P. A definition and analysis of depression. *Archives of Neurology and Psychiatry*, 1957, 77, 519–527.

Lidz, M. D., Fleck, S., & Cornelison, A. R. *Schizophrenia and the family*. New York: International Universities Press, 1965.

Lidz, T., & Rubenstein, R. Psychology of gastrointestinal disorders. In S. Arieti (Ed.), *American handbook of psychiatry*, Vol. I. New York: Basic Books, 1959.

Lindemann, E. Symptomatology and management of acute grief. *American Journal of Psychiatry*, 1944, 101, 141–148.

Lindzey, G. Some remarks concerning incest, the incest taboo, and psychoanalytic theory. *American Psychologist*, 1967, 22, 1051–1059.

Lipton, M. A., Prange, A. J., Jr., & Wilson, D. C. Sources of contribution to the understanding of the etiology of mood disorders. In J. Zubin & F. A. Freyhan (Eds.) *Disorders of mood*. Baltimore: Johns Hopkins Press, 1972, 117–135.

Loeb, A., Feshbach, S., Beck, A. T., & Wolf, A. Some effects of reward upon the social perception and motivation of psychiatric patients varying in depression. *Journal of Abnormal and Social Psychology*, 1964, 68, 609–616.

Loeb, A., Beck, A. T., & Diggory, J. Differential effects of success and failure on depressed and nondepressed patients. *Journal of Nervous and Mental Disease*, 1971, 152, 106–114.

Loew, D. Sindrom, Diagnose und Speichelsekretion bei depressiven Patienten. *Psychopharmacologia* (Berlin), 1965, 7, 339–348.

Lorr, M. Classification of behavior disorders. *Annual Review of Psychology*, 1961, 12, 195–216.

Lorr, M. The depressive syndromes and the endogenous vs. reactive dichotomy: An integration. Paper delivered at the American Psychological Association Meetings, 1969. Available from the author at Catholic University.

Lorr, M., Sonn, T. M., & Katz, M. M. Toward a definition of depression. *Archives of General Psychiatry*, 1967, 17, 183–185.

Lubin, A. W. Discussant's remarks. In M. M. Katz, J. O. Cole, & W. E. Barton (Eds.), *The role and methodology of classification in psychiatry and psychopathology*. Washington, D.C.: U.S. Public Health Service Publication No. 1584, U.S. Government Printing Office, 1965.

Lubin, B. Adjective checklists for measurement of depression. *Archives of General Psychiatry*, 1965, 12, 57–63.

Lubin, B. Fourteen brief depression adjective checklists. *Archives of General Psychiatry*, 1966, 15, 205–208.

Lubin, B., Dupre, V. A., & Lubin, A. W. Comparability and sensitivity of set 2 (lists E. F, and G) of the Depression Adjective Check Lists. *Psychological Reports*, 1967, 20, 756–758.

Lunneborg, C. E. *Program MLRC: Multiple linear regression with linear contrasts.* University of Washington Bureau of Testing, 1967.

Maddison, D. The relevance of conjugal bereavement for preventive psychiatry. *British Journal of Medical Psychology*, 1968, 41, 223–333.

Mandell, A. J. Neurochemical considerations relevant to human affective states. *Science and Psychoanalysis*, 1970, 17, 1–12.

Mandell, A. J., & Spooner, C. E. Psychochemical research studies in man. *Science*, 1968, 162, 1442–1453.

Mandell, A. J., Spooner, C. E., & Brunet, D. Whither the sleep transmitter. *Biological Psychiatry*, 1969, 1, 13–30.

Mapother, E. Opening paper of discussion on manic-depressive psychosis. *British Medical Journal*, 1926, ii, 872–876.

Marris, P. *Widows and their families.* London: Routledge & Kegan Paul, 1958.

Masserman, J. H. Preface: An historical review of the psychodynamic theories of affect. *Science and Psychoanalysis*, 1970, 17, vii–xvii.

Maxwell, A. E. Difficulties in a dimensional description of symptomatology. *British Journal of Psychiatry*, 1972, 121, 19–26.

Mayer-Gross, W. Mental Health survey in a rural area. *Eugenics Review*, 1948, 140, 50–58.

McAfee, D. A., Schorderet, M., & Greengard, P. Adenosine 3', 5' - monophosphate in nervous tissue: Increase associated with synaptic transmission. *Science*, 1971, 171, 1156–1159.

McClelland, D. C. Some social consequences of achievement motivation. In M. R. Jones (Ed.), *Nebraska symposium on motivation: 1955.* Lincoln, Nebr.: University of Nebraska Press, 1955.

McClelland, D. C. *The achieving society.* Princeton: D. Van Nostrand, 1961.

McClelland, D. C., Atkinson, J. W., Clark, R. H., & Lowell, E. L. *The achievement motive.* New York: Appleton-Century-Crofts, 1953.

McConaghy, N., Joffe, J. D., & Murphy, B. The independence of neurotic and endogenous depression. *British Journal of Psychiatry*, 1967, 113, 479–484.

McGuire, W. J. Personality and susceptibility to social influence. In E. F. Borgatta & W. W. Lambert (Eds.), *Handbook of personality theory and research.* Chicago: Rand McNally, 1968.

McKinney, W. T., & Bunney, W. E., Jr. Animal model of depression. I. Review of evidence: Implications for research. *Archives of General Psychiatry*, 1969, 21, 240–248.

McKinney, W. T., Suomi, S. J., & Harlow, H. F. Depression in primates. *American Journal of Psychiatry*, 1971, 127, 1313–1320.

McKinney, W. T., Suomi, S. J., & Harlow, H. F. Repetitive peer separations of Juvenile-age Rhesus monkeys. *Archives of General Psychiatry*, 1972, 27, 200–203.

Mednick, S. A. Breakdown in individuals at high risk for schizophrenia: Possible predispositional perinatal factors. *Mental Hygiene*, 1970, 54, 50–63.

Mednick, S. A., & McNeil, T. F. Current methodology in research on the etiology of schizophrenia: Serious difficulties which suggest the use of the High-Risk group method. *Psychological Bulletin*, 1968, 70, 681–694.

Meehl, P. E. Some ruminations on the validation of clinical procedures. *Canadian Journal of Psychology*, 1959, 13, 102–128.

Meehl, P. E. Schizotaxia, schizotypy, schizophrenia. *American Psychologist*, 1962, 17, 827–838.

Melges, F. T., & Bowlby, J. Types of hopelessness in psychopathological process. *Archives of General Psychiatry*, 1969, 20, 690–699.

Mendels, J. Depression: The distinction between syndrome and symptom. *British Journal of Psychiatry*, 1968, 114, 1549–1554.

Mendels, J. *Concepts of depression.* New York: Wiley & Sons, 1971.

Mendels, J., & Cochrane, C. The nosology of depression: The endogenous-reactive concept. *American Journal of Psychiatry*, 1968, **124** (May supplement), 1–11.

Mendels, J., & Hawkins, D. R. Electroencephalographic sleep studies in depression. *Science and Psychoanalysis*, 1970, **17**, 29–47.

Mendels, J., & Hawkins, D. R. Sleep and depression. IV. Longitudinal studies. *Journal of Nervous and Mental Disease*, 1971, **153**, 251–272. (a)

Mendels, J., & Hawkins, D. R. Longitudianal sleep study in hypomania. *Archives of General Psychiatry*, 1971, **25**, 274–277. (b)

Mendels, J., & Hawkins, D. R. Sleep and depression: Further considerations. *Archives of General Psychiatry*, in press.

Mendelson, M. *Psychoanalytic concepts of depression.* Springfield, Ill.: C. C. Thomas, 1960.

Mendlewicz, J., Fieve, R. R., Rainer, J. D., & Fleiss, J. L. Manic-depressive illness: A comparative study of patients with and without a family history. *British Journal of Psychiatry*, 1972, **120**, 523–530.

Menninger, K. The psychiatric diagnosis. *Bulletin of the Menninger Clinic*, 1959, **23**, 226–239.

Metcalfe, M. The personality of depressive patients. In A. Coppen & A. Walk (Eds.), *Recent developments in affective disorders. British Journal of Psychiatry* Special Publication No. 2, 1968.

Metcalfe, M., & Goldman, E. Validation of an inventory for measuring depression. *British Journal of Psychiatry*, 1965, **111**, 240–242.

Meyer, A. A discussion on the classification of the melancholics. *Journal of Nervous and Mental Disease*, 1905, **32**, 114–117.

Millenson, J. R. *Principles of behavioral analysis.* New York: Macmillan, 1967.

Miller, G. A., Galantes, E., & Pribram, K. H. *Plans and the structure of behavior.* New York: Henry Holt, 1960.

Miller, J. B. Dreams during varying stages of depression. *Archives of General Psychiatry*, 1969, **20**, 560–565.

Miranda, M. Situational factors effecting resistance to influence in depressives. Unpublished doctoral dissertation, University of Washington, 1971.

Moran, P. A. P. The establishment of a psychiatric syndrome. *British Journal of Psychiatry*, 1966, **112**, 1165–1171.

Mowrer, O. H. *Learning theory and behavior.* New York: John Wiley, 1960.

Mowrer, O. H. *The crisis in psychiatry and religion.* New York: Van Nostrand, 1961.

Mueller, P. S., Davis, J. M., Bunney, W. E., Jr., Weil-Malherbe, H., & Cardon, P. V., Jr. Plasma free fatty acids concentration in depressive illness. *Archives of General Psychiatry*, 1970, **22**, 216–222.

Muncie, W. *Psychobiology and psychiatry.* St. Louis: Mosby, 1939.

Munro, A. Some familial and social factors in depressive illness. *British Journal of Psychiatry*, 1966, **112**, 429–441.

Noble, P., & Lader, M. Depressive illness, pulse rate and forearm blood flow. *British Journal of Psychiatry*, 1971, **119**, 261–266.

Nowlis, V. The concept of mood. In S. M. Farber & R. H. L. Wilson (Eds.), *Conflict and creativity*: Part 2. New York: McGraw-Hill, 1963.

Nowlis, V. Research with the mood adjective checklist. In S. S. Tomkins & C. E. Izard (Eds.), *Affect, cognition and personality.* New York: Springer Publishing Company, 1965.

Nowlis, V. Mood: Behavior and experience. In M. B. Arnold (Ed.), *Feelings and emotions.* New York: Academic Press, 1970.

O'Connor, J. P., Stefic, E. C., & Gresock, C. J. Some patterns of depression. *Journal of Clinical Psychology*, 1957, **13**, 122–125.

Ogden, C. K., & Richards, I. A. *The meaning of meaning.* London: Routledge & Kegan Paul, 1930.

Opler, M. K. *Culture and social psychiatry*. New York: Atherton Press, 1967.

Overall, J. E. Associations between marital history and the nature of manifest psychopathology. *Journal of Abnormal Psychology*, 1971, 78, 213–221.

Overall, J. E., Hollister, L. E., Johnson, M. H., & Pennington, V. Nosology of depression: Differential response to drug. *Journal of the American Medical Association*, 1966, 195, 946–948.

Pao, P. On manic-depressive psychosis: A study of the transition of states. *Journal of the American Psychonalytic Association*, 1968, 16, 809–833.

Parker, J. B., Spielberger, C. D., Wallace, D. K., & Becker, J. Factors in Manic-depressive reactions. *Diseases of the Nervous System*, 1959, 20, 1–7.

Parkes, C. M. Recent bereavement as a cause of mental illness. *British Journal of Psychiatry*, 1964, 110, 198–204.

Parkes, C. M. Bereavement and mental illness. *British Journal of Medical Psychology*, 1965, 38, 1–27.

Parkes, C. M. The first year of bereavement. *Psychiatry*, 1970, 33, 448–468.

Paul, M. I., Cramer, H., & Bunney, W. E., Jr. Urinary adenosine 3', 5' - monophosphate in the switch process from depression to mania. *Science*, 1971, 171, 300–303.

Paul, M. I., Cramer, H., & Goodwin, F. K. Urinary cyclic AMP excretion in depression and mania. *Archives of General Psychiatry*, 1971, 24, 327–334.

Pavlov, I. P. *Conditioned reflexes and psychiatry*. New York: International Universities Press, 1941.

Pavlov, I. P. *Psychopathology and psychiatry*. Moscow: Foreign Languages Publishing House, 1960.

Paykel, E. S. Correlates of a depressive typology. *Archives of General Psychiatry*, 1972, 27, 203–210.

Paykel, E. S., Myers, J. K., Dienelt, M. N., Klerman, G. L., Lindenthal, J. J., & Pepper, M. P. Life events and depression. *Archives of General Psychiatry*, 1969, 21, 753–760.

Paykel, E. S., Weissman, M. M., Prusoff, B. A., & Tonks, C. M. Dimensions of social adjustment in depressed women. *Journal of Nervous and Mental Disease*, 1971, 152, 158–172.

Payne, R. W., & Hewlett, J. H. G. Thought disorder in psychotic patients. In H. J. Eysenck (Ed.), *Experiments in personality*. Vol. II. New York: Humanities Press, 1960.

Perez-Reyes, M. Differences in sedative susceptibility between types of depression: Clinical and neurophysiological significance. In T. A. Williams et al. (Eds.) *Recent advances in the psychophysiology of the depressive illnesses*. Chevy Chase, Maryland: U. S. Department of Health, Education and Welfare, 1969, 119–130.

Perris, C. A study of bipolar (manic-depressive) and unipolar recurrent depressive psychoses. *Acta Psychiatrica Scandinavica*, 1966, 42 (supplement no. 194), 1–189.

Perris, C. Genetic transmission of depressive psychoses. *Acta Psychiatrica Scandinavica*, 1968, 42 (supplement no. 203), 45–52.

Perris, C. The separation of bipolar (manic-depressive) from unipolar recurrent depressive psychoses. *Behavioral Neuropsychiatry*, 1969, 1, 17–25.

Perris, C. Abnormality on paternal and maternal sides: Observations in bipolar (manic-depressive) and unipolar depressive psychoses. *British Journal of Psychiatry*, 1971, 118, 207–210.

Pichot, P., & Lempérière, T. Analyse factorielle d'un questionnaire d'auto-evaluation des symptomes dépressifs. *Revue Psychologique Appliqué*, 1964, 14, 15–29.

Pilowski, I., Levine, S., & Boulton, D. M. The classification of depression by numerical taxonomy. *British Journal of Psychiatry*, 1969, 115, 937–945.

Platman, S. R., Plutchik, R., Fieve, R. R., & Lawlor, W. G. Emotion profiles associated with mania and depression. *Archives of General Psychiatry*, 1969, 20, 210–214.

Pokorny, A. D. Suicide rates in various psychiatric disorders. *Journal of Nervous and Mental Disease*, 1964, 139, 499–506.

Pollin, W., & Stabenau, J. R. Biological, psychological and historical differences in a series of monozygotic twins discordant for schizophrenia. In D. Rosenthal & S. S. Kety (Eds.), *Transmission of schizophrenia*. New York: Pergamon Press, 1968.

Pollitt, J. Depression and the functional shift. *Comprehensive Psychiatry*, 1960, **1**, 381–390.

Pollitt, J. Suggestions for a physiological classification of depression. *British Journal of Psychiatry*, 1965, **111**, 489–497.

Pollitt, J. The relationship between genetic and precipitating factors in depressive illness. *British Journal of Psychiatry*, 1972. **121**, 67–70.

Poznanski, E., & Zrull, J. P. Childhood depression: Clinical characteristics of overtly depressed children. *Archives of General Psychiatry*, 1970, **23**, 8–15.

Pribram, K. H., & Melges, F. T. Psychophysiological basis of emotion. *Handbook of Clinical Neurology*, 1969, **4**, 316–342.

Price, J. S. The dominance hierarchy and the evolution of mental illness. *Lancet*, 1967, **2**, 243–246.

Price, J. S. The genetics of depressive behaviour. In A. Coppen & A. Walk (Eds.), *Recent developments in affective disorders*. *British Journal of Psychiatry*, Special Publication No. 2, 1968.

Prusoff, B. A., Klerman, G. L., & Paykel, E. S. Concordance between clinical assessments and patients' self-report in depression. *Archives of General Psychiatry*, 1972, **26**, 546–552.

Race, R. R., & Sanger, R. X_g and sex chromosome abnormalities. *British Medical Bulletin*, 1969, **25**, 99–103.

Rado, S. The problem of melancholia. *International Journal of Psychoanalysis*, 1928, **9**, 420–438.

Rado, S. Psychosomatics of depression from the etiologic point of view. *Psychosomatic Medicine*, 1951, **13**, 51–55.

Rao, C. R. Discrimination among groups and assigning new individuals. In M. M. Katz, J. O. Cole, & W. E. Barton (Eds.), *The role and methodology of classification in psychiatry and psychopathology*. Washington, D. C.: U. S. Public Health Service Publication No. 1584. U. S. Government Printing Office, 1965.

Rapaport, D. (1959) Edward Bibring's theory of depression. In M. M. Gill (Ed.), *The collected papers of David Rapaport*. New York: Basic Books, 1967.

Rapaport, D., Gill, M., & Schafer, R. *Diagnostic psychological testing*. Chicago: Year Book Publishers, 1945.

Raskin, A., Schulterbrandt, J. C., Reating, N., & McKeon, J. J. Differential response to chlorpromazine, imipramine, and placebo: A study of hospitalized depressed patients. *Archives of General Psychiatry*, 1970, **23**, 164–174.

Rawnsley, K. Epidemiology of affective disorders. In A. Coppen & A. Walk (Eds.), *Recent developments in affective disorders*. *British Journal of Psychiatry*, Special Publication No. 2, 1968, 27–36.

Rees, L. Constitutional factors and abnormal behavior. In H. J Eysenck (Ed.), *Handbook of abnormal psychology*. New York: Basic Books, 1960.

Reich, T., Clayton, P. J., & Winokur, G. Family history studies: V. The genetics of mania. *American Journal of Psychiatry*, 1969, **125**, 1358–1368.

Renwick, J. H., & Schulze, J. An analysis of some data on the linkage between X_g and colorblindness in man. *American Journal of Human Genetics*, 1964, **16**, 410–418.

Reusch, J. *Therapeutic communication*. New York: W. W. Norton, 1962.

Richter, C. P. *Biological clocks in medicine and psychiatry*. Springfield, Ill.: C. C. Thomas, 1965.

Rie, H. E. Depression in childhood: A survey of some pertinent contributions. *Journal of the American Academy of Child Psychiatry*, 1966, **5**, 653–685.

Riesman, D. *The lonely crowd*. New Haven: Yale University Press, 1950.

Rimon, R., Stenback, A., & Huhmar, E. Electromyographic findings in depressive patients. *Journal of Psychosomatic Research*, 1966, 10, 159–170.

Robins, E., & Guze, S. B. Classification of affective disorders: The primary-secondary, the endogenous-reactive, and the neurotic-psychotic concepts. In T. A. Williams et al. (Eds.), *Recent advances in the psychobiology of the depressive illnesses.* Chevy Chase, Maryland: U. S. Department of Health, Education, and Welfare, 1969, 283–295.

Robins, E., Munoz, R. A., Martin, S., & Gentry, K. A. Primary and secondary affective disorders. In J. Zubin & F. A. Freyhan (Eds.), *Disorders of mood.* Baltimore: Johns Hopkins Press, 1972, 33–46.

Robins, E., Murphy, G. E., Wilkinson, R. H., Gassner, S., & Kayes, J. Some clinical considerations in the prevention of suicide based on a study of 134 successful suicides. *American Journal of Public Health*, 1959, 49, 888–899.

Roff, M., & Ricks, D. F. (Eds.) *Life history research in psychopathology.* Minneapolis: University of Minnesota Press, 1970.

Rogers, C. R. *Client-centered therapy.* Boston: Houghton-Mifflin, 1951.

Rosenfeld, H. An investigation into the psycho-analytic theory of depression. *International Journal of Psychoanalysis*, 1959, 40, 105–130.

Rosenthal, D. The heredity-environment issue in schizophrenia: Summary of the conference and present status of our knowledge. In D. Rosenthal & S. S. Kety (Eds.), *The transmission of schizophrenia.* New York: Pergamon Press, 1968.

Rosenthal, D. *Genetics of Psychopathology.* New York: McGraw-Hill, 1971.

Rosenthal, S. H., & Gudeman, J. E. The self-pitying constellation in depression. *British Journal of Psychiatry,* 1967, 113, 485–489.

Rosenthal, S. H., & Klerman, G. L. Endogenous features in depressed women. *Canadian Psychiatric Association Journal*, 1966, 11 (supplement), 511–516.

Rosenzweig, S. The effects of failure and success on evaluation of self and others. Unpublished doctoral dissertation, Indiana University, 1959.

Rosenzweig, S., Fleming, E. C., & Clarke, H. J. Revised scoring manual for the Rosenzweig Picture-Frustration study. *Journal of Psychology*, 1947, 24, 165–208.

Roth, M., Gurney, C., Garside, R. F., & Kerr, T. A. Studies in the classification of affective disorders: The relationship between anxiety states and depressive illnesses – I. *British Journal of Psychiatry*, 1972, 121, 147–161.

Sachar, E. J. Psychological homeostasis and endocrine function. In A. J. Mandell & M. P. Mandell (Eds.), *Psychochemical research in man: Methods, strategy, and theory.* New York: Academic Press, 1969.

Safirstein, S. L., & Kaufman, M. R. The higher they climb, the lower they fall: A contribution to the psychodynamics of depression. *Canadian Psychiatric Association Journal*, 1966, 11 (supplement), 229–235.

Salzman, L. Depression: A clinical review. *Science and Psychoanalysis*, 1970, 17, 109–117.

Sandifer, M. G. Jr., Psychiatric diagnoses: Cross-national research findings. *Proceedings of the Royal Society of Medicine*, 1972, 65, 497–500.

Sandler, J., & Joffe, W. G. Notes on childhood depression. *International Journal of Psychoanalysis*, 1965, 46, 88–96.

Satterfield, J. H. Auditory evoked cortical response studies in depressed patients and normal control subjects. In T. A. Williams et al. (Eds.), *Recent advances in the psychobiology of the depressive illnesses.* Chevy Chase, Maryland: U. S. Department of Health, Education, and Welfare, 1969, 87–99.

Schachter, S. *The psychology of affiliation.* Stanford: Stanford University Press, 1959.

Schachter, S. The interaction of cognitive and physiological determinants of emotional state. In L. Berkowitz (Ed.), *Advances in experimental social psychology.* Vol. I. New York: Academic Press, 1964.

Schapira, K., Roth, M., Kerr, T. A., Gurney, C. The prognosis of affective disorders: The differentiation of anxiety states from depressive illnesses. *British Journal of Psychiatry*, 1972, 121, 175–181.

Schildkraut, J. J. The catecholamine hypothesis of affective disorders: A review of supporting evidence. *American Journal of Psychiatry*, 1965, 122, 509–522.

Schildkraut, J. J. Biogenic amine metabolism in depressive illnesses: Basic and clinical studies. In T. A. Williams et al. (Eds.), *Recent advances in the psychobiology of the depressive illnesses*. Chevy Chase, Maryland: U. S. Department of Health, Education and Welfare, 1969, 11–24.

Schildkraut, J. J. Neuropharmacological studies of mood disorders. In J. Zubin & F. A. Freyhan (Eds.), *Disorders of mood*, Baltimore: Johns Hopkins Press, 1972, 65–85.

Schildkraut, J. J., & Kety, S. S. Biogenic amines and emotion. *Science*, 1967, 156, 21–30.

Schildkraut, J. J., Schanberg, S. M., Breese, G. R., & Kopin, I. J. Effects of psychoactive drugs on the metabolism of intracisternally administered serotonin in rat brain. *Pharmacology*, 1968, 18, 1971–1978.

Schmale, A. H., Jr., & Iker, H. The psychological setting of uterine cervical cancer. *Annals of New York Academy of Science*, 1966, 125, 807–813.

Schou, M. Biology and pharmacology of the lithium ion. *Pharmacological Review*, 1957, 9, 17–58.

Schwab, J. J., Bialow, M. R., Holzer, C. E., Brown, J. M., & Stevenson, B. E. Sociocultural aspects of depression in medical inpatients: I Frequency and social variables. *Archives of General Psychiatry*, 1967, 17, 533–538. (a)

Schwab, J. J., Bialow, M. R., Brown, J. M., Holzer, C. E., & Stevenson, B. E. Sociocultural aspects of depression in medical inpatients: II. Symptomatology and class. *Archives of General Psychiatry*, 1967, 17, 539–543. (b)

Segal, D. S., & Mandell, A. J. Behavioral activation of rats during intraventricular infusion of norepinephrine. *Science*, in press.

Seligman, M. E. P. Depression and learned helplessness. (1971) unpublished. Available from the author, Department of Psychology, University of Pennsylvania.

Shagass, C. Electrophysiology of depression. In J. O. Cole & J. R. Wittenborn (Eds.), *Pharmacotherapy of depression*. Springfield, Ill.: C. C. Thomas, 1966.

Shagass, C., & Jones, A. L. A neurophysiological test for psychiatric diagnosis: Results in 750 patients. *American Journal of Psychiatry*, 1958, 114, 1002–1009.

Shagass, C., & Schwartz, M. Cerebral cortical reactivity in psychotic depressions. *Archives of General Psychiatry*, 1962, 6, 235–242.

Shagass, C., & Schwartz, M. Somatosensory cerebral evoked responses in psychotic depression. *British Journal of Psychiatry*, 1966, 112, 799–809.

Shields, J. Summary of the genetic evidence. In D. Rosenthal & S. S. Kety (Eds.) *The transmission of schizophrenia*. London: Pergamon Press, 1968, 95–129.

Shipman, W. C., Oken, D., Goldstein, I. B., Grinker, R. R., Sr., & Heath, H. A. Study in psychophysiology of muscle tension. *Archives of General Psychiatry*, 1964, 11, 330–346.

Shopsin, B., & Gershon, E. S. Plasma cortisol response to dexamethasone suppression in depressed and control patients. *Archives of General Psychiatry*, 1971, 24, 320–326.

Siegel, P. V., Gerathewohl, S. J., & Mohler, S. R. Time zone effects. *Science*, 1969, 164, 1249–1255.

Silverman, C. *The epidemiology of depression*. Baltimore: Johns Hopkins Press, 1968.

Skinner, B. F. *Science and human behavior*. New York: Macmillan, 1953.

Slater, E. Expectation of abnormality on paternal and maternal sides: A computational model. *Journal of Medical Genetics*, 1966, 3, 159–161.

Slater, E., Maxwell, J., & Price, J. S. Distribution of ancestral secondary cases in bipolar affective disorders. *British Journal of Psychiatry*, 1971, 118, 215–218.

Small, J. C., & Small, I. F. Expectancy waves in affective psychoses. In T. A. Williams et al. (Eds.), *Recent advances in the psychobiology of the depressive illnesses*. Chevy Chase, Maryland: U. S. Department of Health, Education, and Welfare, 1969, 109–119.

Smith, J. H. The metaphor of the manic-depressive. *Psychiatry*, 1960, 23, 375–383.

Smith, J. H. Identificatory styles in depression and grief. *International Journal of Psychoanalysis*, 1971, 52, 259–266.

Snaith, R. P., McGuire, R. J., & Fox, K. Aspects of personality and depression. *Psychological Medicine*, 1971, 1, 239–246.

Snyder, F. Sleep disturbance in relation to acute psychosis. In A. Kales (Ed.), *Sleep physiology and pathology: A symposium*. Philadelphia: Lippincott, 1969. (a)

Snyder, F. NIH studies of EEG sleep in affective illness. In T. A. Williams et al. (Eds.), *Recent advances in the psychobiology of the depressive illnesses*. Chevy Chase, Maryland: U. S. Department of Health, Education, and Welfare, 1969, 171–193. (b)

Sorensen, A., & Stromgren, E. Frequency of depressive states within geographically delimited population groups. *Acta Psychiatrica Scandinavica*, 1961, 37 (supplement).

Spiegel, J. P. The resolution of role conflict within the family. *Psychiatry*, 1957, 20, 1–16.

Spielberger, C. D. Theory and research on anxiety. In C. D. Spielberger (Ed.), *Anxiety and behavior*. New York: Academic Press, 1966.

Spielberger, C. D. Anxiety as an emotional state. In C. D. Spielberger (Ed.), *Current trends in theory and research*. Vol. 1. New York: Academic Press, 1972, 23–49.

Spielberger, C. D., Gorsuch, R. I., & Lushene, R. E. *The state-trait anxiety inventory* (STAI): *Test Manual for Form A*. Palo Alto: Consulting Psychology Press, 1969.

Spitz, R. A. *Hospitalism: An inquiry into the genesis of psychiatric conditions in early childhood*. New York: International Universities Press, 1945.

Spitz, R. A. Anaclitic depression. *Psychoanalytic Study of the Child*, 1946, 2, 313–341.

Stainbrook, E. A cross-cultural evaluation of depressive reactions. In P. H. Hoch & J. Zubin (Eds.), *Depression*. New York: Grune & Stratton, 1954.

Stenstedt, A. A study in manic-depressive psychosis: Clinical, social and genetic investigations. *Acta Psychiatrica et Neurologia Scandinavica*, 1952, 79 (supplement).

Stern, J. A., McClure, J. N., Jr., & Costello, C. G. Depression: Assessment and etiology. In C. G. Costello (Ed.), *Symptoms of psychopathology; a handbook*. New York: John Wiley, 1970.

Stewart, M. A., Winokur, G., Stern, J. A., Guze, S. B., Pfeiffer, E., & Hornung, F. Adaptation and conditioning of the galvanic skin response in psychiatric patients. *Journal of Mental Science*, 1959, 105, 1102–1111.

Stotland, E. *The psychology of hope*. San Francisco: Jossey-Bass, 1969.

Stricker, L. J., Messick, M., & Jackson, D. N. Conformity, anticonformity and independence: Their dimensionality and generality. *Journal of Personality and Social Psychology*, 1970, 16, 494–508.

Strongin, E. I., & Hinsie, L. E. A method for differentiating manic-depressive depressions from other depressions by means of parotid secretions. *Psychiatric Quarterly*, 1939, 13, 697–704.

Sullivan, H. S. *The interpersonal theory of psychiatry*. New York: Norton, 1953.

Szasz, T. S. The problem of psychiatric nosology. A contribution to a situational analysis of psychiatric operations. *American Journal of Psychiatry*, 1957, 114, 405–413.

Taylor, L., & Chave, S. *Mental Health and environment*. London: Longmans, Limited, 1964.

Teasdale, J. D., & Beaumont, J. G. The effect of mood on performance on the Modified New Word Learning Test (Walton-Black). *British Journal of Social and Clinical Psychology*, 1971, 10, 342–345.

Teja, J. S., Narang, R. L., & Aggarwal, A. K. Depression across cultures. *British Journal of Psychiatry*, 1971, 119, 253–260.

Temoche, A., Pugh, T. H., & MacMahon, B. Suicide rates among current and former mental institution patients. *Journal of Nervous and Mental Disease*, 1964, 136, 124–130.

Thompson, C. *Psychoanalysis, evolution and development*. New York: Thomas Nelson, 1950.

Thomson, K. C., & Hendrie, H. C. Environmental stress in primary depressive illness. *Archives of General Psychiatry*, 1972, 26, 130–132.

Thuline, H. C., Hodgkin, W. E., Fraser, G. R., & Motulsky, A. G. Genetics of proton and deutan color-vision anomalies: An instructive family. *American Journal of Human Genetics*, 1969, 21, 581–592.

Tippett, J. S., & Silber, E. Autonomy of self-esteem: An experimental approach. *Archives of General Psychiatry*, 1966, 14, 372–385.

Tolman, E. C. *Purposive behavior in animals and men*. Berkeley: University of California Press, 1951.

Tomkins, S. S. Affect, imagery, consciousness. Vol. I. *The positive affects*. New York: Springer, 1962.

Tonks, C. M., Paykel, E. S., & Klerman, G. L. Clinical depressions among Negroes. *American Journal of Psychiatry*, 1970, 127, 329–335.

Torgerson, W. S. Multidimensional representation of similarity structures. In M. M. Katz, J. O. Cole, & W. E. Barton (Eds.), *The role and methodology of classification in psychiatry and psychopathology*. Washington, D. C.: U. S. Public Health Service Publication No. 1584. U. S. Government Printing Office, 1965.

Wallace, J. E. Depressive affect and its relation to independence, conformity and anticonformity. Unpublished doctoral dissertation, University of Washington, 1969.

Walter, W. A. Physiological correlates of personality. *Biological Psychiatry*, 1971, 3, 59–69.

Wechsler, H., Grosser, G. H., & Busfield, B. L., Jr. The depression rating scale. *Archives of General Psychiatry*, 1963, 9, 334–343.

Weinshel, E. M. Some psychoanalytic considerations on moods. *International Journal of Psychoanalysis*, 1970, 51, 313–320.

Weiss, E. Clinical aspects of depression. *Psychoanalytic Quarterly*, 1944, 13, 445–461.

Weissman, M. M., Klerman, G. L., & Paykel, E. S. Clinical evaluation of hostility in depression. *American Journal of Psychiatry*, 1971, 128, 261–266.

Weissman, M. M., Paykel, E. S., & Klerman, G. L. The depressed woman as a mother. Submitted for publication. Available in mimeo from senior author. Department of Psychiatry, Yale University.

Weissman, M. M., Paykel, E. S., Siegel, R., & Klerman, G. L. The social role performance of depressed women: Comparisons with a normal group. *American Journal of Orthopsychiatry*, 1971, 41, 390–405.

Weitzman, B. Behavior therapy and psychotherapy. *Psychological Review*, 1967, 74, 300–318.

Wessman, A. E., & Ricks, D. F. *Mood and personality*. New York: Holt, Rinehart & Winston, 1966.

Wessman, A. E., Ricks, D. F., & Tyl, M. M. Characteristics and concomitants of mood fluctuation in college women. *Journal of Abnormal and Social Psychology*, 1960, 60, 117–126.

Whatmore, G. B. Some neurophysiologic differences between schizophrenia and depression. *American Journal of Psychiatry*, 1966, 123, 712–716.

Whatmore, G. B., & Kohli, D. R. Dysponesis: A neurophysiologic factor in functional disorders. *Behavioral Science*, 1968, 13, 102–124.

Whybrow, P. C., & Mendels, J. Toward a biology of depression: Some suggestions from neurophysiology. *American Journal of Psychiatry*, 1969, 125, 1491–1500.

Williams, J. E. Mode of failure, interference tendencies, and achievement imagery. *Journal of Abnormal and Social Psychology*, 1955, 51, 573–580.

Willis, R. H. Conformity, independence, and anticonformity. *Human Relations*, 1965, 18, 373–388.

Wilson, D. C. Families of manic-depressives. *Diseases of the Nervous System*, 1951, 12, 362–369.

Winokur, G. Genetic findings and methodological considerations in manic-depressive disease. *British Journal of Psychiatry*, 1970, 117, 267–274.

Winokur, G., Cadoret, R. J., Dorzab, J., & Baker, M. Depressive disease: A genetic study. *Archives of General Psychiatry*, 1971, 24, 135–142.

Winokur, G., Clayton, P. J., & Reich, T. *Manic-depressive illness*. St. Louis: C. V. Mosby, 1969.

Winokur, G., & Tanna, V. L. Possible role of X-linked dominant factor in manic-depressive disease. *Diseases of the Nervous System*, 1969, 30, 89–94.

Wittenborn, J. R. Depression. In B. J. Wolman (Ed.), *Handbook of clinical psychology*. New York: McGraw-Hill, 1965.

Wittkower, E. D., & Rin, H. Transcultural psychiatry. *Archives of General Psychiatry*, 1965, 13, 387–395.

Wolff, K. *The biological, social and psychological aspects of aging*. Springfield, Ill.: C. C. Thomas, 1959.

Wolpe, J. Neurotic depression: Experimental analog, clinical syndromes and treatment. *American Journal of Psychotherapy*, 1971, 25, 362–368.

Wolpe, J., & Lazarus, A. A. *Behavior therapy techniques*. Oxford: Pergamon Press, 1966.

Woodbury, D. M., Timiras, P. S., & Vernadakis, A. Influence of adrenocortical steroids on brain function and metabolism. In H. Hoagland (Ed.), *Hormones, brain function and behavior*. New York: Academic Press, 1957.

Woodruff, R. A., Jr., Robins, L. N., Winokur, G., & Reich, T. Manic-depressive illness and social achievement. *Acta Psychiatrica Scandinavica*, in press.

Woodruff, R. A., Jr., Robins, L. N., Winokur, G., & Walbran, B. Educational and occupational achievement in primary affective disorder. *American Journal of Psychiatry*, 1968, 124 (supplement), 57–64.

World Health Organization. *International classification of disease: Eighth revision*. New York: World Health Organization, 1968.

Zerbin-Rüdin, E. Endogene Psychosen. In P. E. Becker (Ed.), *Humangenetik: ein kurzes Handbuch in fünf Banden*. Vol. 2. Stuttgart: Gerg Thieme Verlag, 1967.

Zetzel, E. R. The depressive position. In P. Greenacre (Ed.), *Affective disorders*. New York: International Universities Press, 1953.

Zetzel, E. R. Depression and the capacity to bear it. In M. Schur (Ed.), *Drives, affects, behavior*. Vol. 2. New York: International Universities Press, 1965.

Zigler, E., & Phillips, L. Psychiatric diagnosis and symptomatology. *Journal of Abnormal and Social Psychology*, 1961, 63, 69–77.

Zigler, E., & Phillips, L. Social competence and the process-reactive distinction in psychopathology. *Journal of Abnormal and Social Psychology*, 1962, 65, 215–222.

Zubin, J. Classification of the behavior disorders. *Annual Review of Psychology*, 1967, 18, 373–407.

Zubin, J., & Fleiss, J. Current biometric approaches to depression. In R. R. Fieve (Ed.), *Depression in the 1970's: Modern theory and research*. The Hague: Excerpta Medica, International Congress Series No. 239, 1971, 7–21.

Zung, W. W. K. A self-rating depression scale. *Archives of General Psychiatry*, 1965, 12, 63–70.

Zung, W. W. K., Richards, C. B., & Short, M. J. Self-rating depression scale in an outpatient clinic. *Archives of General Psychiatry*, 1965, 13, 508–516.

Zung, W. W. K., Wilson, W. P., & Dodson, W. E. Effect of depression disorders on sleep EEG responses. *Archives of General Psychiatry*, 1964, 10, 439–445.

AUTHOR INDEX

SUBJECT INDEX

A

Abstraction, selective, 105
Abulia, 116
Acetyl methyl carbinol, fasting
    blood level of, 48
Achievement orientation, 139–143
Action potential, neuronal, 185
Adjective Check List (Nowlis), 26
Adopted depressives, studies
    involving, 161
Adrenocortical activity, 178
AER (*see* Average evoked potential)
Affect:
    hierarchical order of behavior, 2
Affective personality, 202
Affective regulation, 4
Affiliation orientation, 142
Age, incidence of depression by,
    48, 64, 128, 162–163
Age adjustment, in studies, 61
Aggression, 79–80, 86, 93
    behavioral theories, 117
    dual instinct theory of, 149
    expression of, 126
    See also Self-aggression
Aging effects on metabolic processes, 54
Agitated depression, 82, 107
Alcoholism, 124
Ambivalence, 85, 96

Amines, 179–185
Anaclitic depression, 93, 192
Anal developmental state, 77, 91
Anal eroticism, 77
Antidepressant drugs, 38, 44, 49–50,
    150, 181, 194
Anxiety, 31–34, 83–84, 103, 119, 201
Anxious depression, 49–50
APA system of classification, 23, 199–202
Assortative mating, 160
Atonement, melancholic, 80–81
Auditory evoked potential, 174–175
Authoritarian pressure, 140, 143
Average evoked potential (AER), 174–175
Avoidance, passive, 111
Avoidance behavior, 106, 118

B

Battery of Feeling and Attitude Scales, 26
Beck Depression Inventory, 24–25
Behavioral disorder, 9
Behavioral theories, 3, 116–119
Bereavement, 131–132
    See also Grief
Biochemical aspects of depression,
    177–186
Biogenic amines (*see* Amines)
Biological clock, 190